The Supply Chain Revolution

The Supply Chain Revolution

Unlocking the Sustainable Profit Chain

Art Koch

BEP

BUSINESS EXPERT PRESS

Leader in applied, concise business books

The Supply Chain Revolution: Unlocking the Sustainable Profit Chain

Copyright © Business Expert Press, LLC, 2024

Cover design by Tim Forrest, Eddie Tapp, and Sharon Holmes

Interior design by Exeter Premedia Services Private Ltd., Chennai, India

First published in 2024 by
Business Expert Press, LLC
222 East 46th Street, New York, NY 10017
www.businessexpertpress.com

ISBN-13: 978-1-63742-608-1 (paperback)
ISBN-13: 978-1-63742-609-8 (e-book)

Business Expert Press Supply and Operations Management Collection

First edition: 2024

10 9 8 7 6 5 4 3 2 1

To my wife, Sara. Your love, support, and encouragement have been essential to completing this book. Thank you for always believing in me and encouraging me along the way.

I am grateful to my past and current clients for the opportunity to serve you and your teams and learn from you. Your insights and challenges have helped shape my thinking about supply chain management. Most importantly, the latitude to experiment and find the correct solution to your challenges is the foundation of these methodologies.

To anyone reading, I hope that you will find this book to be a valuable resource for your work in supply chain management and business process improvement. I believe the principles and practices outlined in this book can help you create a more sustainable and profitable supply chain and improve your work-life balance.

Description

Does your company suffer from inventory obesity? Is the balance between your supply and demand a constant struggle?

In *The Supply Chain Revolution*, Art Koch unveils a masterful system for any organization to build better supply chain fundamentals and overcome the evils of inventory. This is the ultimate playbook for CEOs, COOs, and CFOs to revolutionize supply chains and convert them from cost centers to profit and value drivers.

Turn your supply chain into a powerful weapon for sustainable profitability by unlocking the power of inventory velocity with innovative strategies for process optimization, team engagement, and corporate valuation. **It's not just good management—it's a proven competitive advantage.**

Keywords

supply chain management; SCM; inventory management; enterprise resource planning; ERP; materials requirements planning; MRP; inventory pull processes; push and pull manufacturing; postponement strategy; lean manufacturing; inventory control; optimization; demand and supply planning; inventory innovation; replenishment- and exception-based planning; purchasing; procurement; supplier partnerships; production inventory control; inventory velocity; transformation agendas; supply chain sustainability; visual daily management; supply chain profit generation; supply chain as competitive differentiator; Art Koch's profit chain; entropy busters; the inventory doctor

Contents

Disclaimer

Every business situation is unique. I advise you to seek professional advice regarding all technical matters, including purchasing, sourcing, supply chain and inventory management, and other information. This book contains opinions, ideas, experiences, and exercises. The purchaser or reader of these materials assumes all responsibility for using this information. Art Koch and the Publisher assume no responsibility or liability whatsoever for any decisions made, actions taken, or outcomes by the purchaser or reader of these materials.

Acknowledgments

I am deeply grateful to my mother, whose unwavering belief in the value of hard work and dedication has been a guiding light throughout my journey. Her encouragement to continually seek knowledge and hone my skills has been instrumental in shaping my path.

I extend heartfelt appreciation to my initial mentors in the business world, Dave and Barb Taylor from Lucas Industries. Their confidence in my capabilities led to my inclusion in their esteemed leadership team and imparted crucial lessons in cash management and operational efficiency.

I wish to express sincere thanks to my former managers, Carl Steinbicker and Bob Ratay. Their consistent support and willingness to provide a canvas for my unconventional ideas have been pivotal in my professional growth.

This book owes its existence to the exceptional guidance and years of wisdom shared by my mentor, coach, and dear friend, Phil Symchych. His consistent ability to view challenges from unconventional perspectives has been an invaluable asset I will forever cherish.

A special acknowledgment goes to Deborah Brown for her remarkable patience and resilience. Her dedicated efforts in meticulously reading and refining the initial raw draft of this book are deeply appreciated and will always be held in high regard.

A special nod goes to Sharon Holmes, Graphic Designer. Her creative wizardry allows the reader to visualize key concepts.

Another special thanks goes to Stephen Frink for his remarkable patience while teaching the craft of underwater photography. Here's to never graduating.

Throughout my journey, I've had the privilege of collaborating with brilliant leaders in business transformation. Their proactive approach to driving organizational excellence and aiding clients in reaching their true potential has been inspiring. I thank Joel Stanwood; Chris Dupre; Sean Caetano; Kimo Oberloh; Bruce Haraty; David Menachof, PhD; Steve Melnyk, PhD; and Danny Davis.

Thank you to all those who have played a role in shaping my insights and experiences in the realm of supply chain management. Your contributions have been invaluable, and I am truly fortunate for the support and wisdom you have shared.

Introduction

Before my first dive, I viewed the ocean as nothing more than a vast reflective desert surface of waves. However, my view changed when I went into the water and experienced a significant emotional event. Under that reflective surface, beneath the waves, lay a vast richness of beautiful coral reefs, shimmering fish, and ever-changing sand flats. All had their unique beauty, not unlike the beauty of tropical rain forests, botanical gardens, and great savannas.

As a supply chain professional, I once looked across a sea of inventory at warehouses and manufacturing sites as nothing more than a faceless sea of boxes, crates, and pallets reflected under incandescent lights.

Over the decades, as I dove deeper into supply chain and my proficiencies grew, I developed insights that challenged the status quo. I saw endless opportunities for establishing inventory pull processes, challenging legacy policies, and planning parameters to increase inventory velocity, customer loyalty, and profitability.

The relaxation and disconnection of scuba diving and taking time away from the fast pace of manufacturing operations continue to be my meditation zone that brings clarity to my supply chain solutions and methodologies.

—Art Koch
Miami, Florida
October 31, 2023

CHAPTER 1

How to Navigate This Book

This book focuses on the fundamentals of process integrity, people development and team engagement, and commitment by CEO and leadership to create a supply chain revolution. Without these, you will never successfully implement and realize the full potential of any important strategic initiative, let alone one as complex and fundamental to your company as the supply chain and its related systems and technology.

In each chapter, I will share key concepts and case studies, which I call dive master briefings (client examples and success stories), to illustrate the concept further. Also, in each chapter, you'll see a dive log (Art's commentary) summarizing key points and learnings.

Also, at the end of each chapter, I will wrap up with a buddy check: questions from Coach Art to summarize learnings and essential points for you to focus upon in your business improvement.

The buddy check process requires further clarification. Before diving, all divers should complete a "Buddy Check" list. Divers do this to ensure that the air is on, the air tank is full, you know how to remove your dive buddy's weights, and you know the location of their secondary air supply. The checklist's design is to ensure neither of you runs out of air or enters a decompression dive, which could cause severe injury or death. With these critical checks completed, it is time for the fun to begin.

Being a good dive buddy is essential to enjoying the underwater ecosystem.

These best practices translate well to businesses; it's an excellent methodology to ensure peers learn key concepts and improve their skills.

Additionally, if you're competitive like me, having a buddy system helps create an environment of internally friendly competition and ensures you understand the subject matter to teach and educate others.

At the end of each chapter, Art's deep dive highlights essential points, specific ideas, and thoughts on the chapter content.

Reading Chapters 1 and 2 first is essential as you read and navigate this book. They establish critical knowledge regarding laying the first bricks of the supply chain foundation, erecting the structural walls, and creating sustainability.

It's best to read Chapters 3 through 20 in sequence since they build upon each other. However, readers can choose between chapters that best fit their objectives and needs.

Each chapter starts with a short dive analogy to help visualize your experience related to a core business process that will assist you as a supply chain management professional.

As a supply chain professional, you need a substantial body of knowledge and educational foundation that universities do an excellent job of teaching. However, I've discovered that universities, textbooks, and certification agencies cannot bridge the gap between theory, real-world application, and the expected results of customer loyalty, corporate culture, and profit.

To resolve this dilemma, I've created Art Koch's profit chain model—the three Fs of supply chain management—Figure 1.1, which I introduce in greater detail in Chapter 3.

- People and process foundation.
- Structural framework.
- Financial focal point.

The bottom section of the model is the functional foundation taught in universities. The top section is the pinnacle of sustainability, the results or output of the processes. This section is the output of all the efforts to build and establish the foundation and structural framework. It comes together to drive the enterprise into a perpetual profit-generating machine—Art Koch's profit chain. The supply chain becomes a competitive differentiator by achieving customer loyalty, corporate culture, and profits.

- **Loyal customers**—The ultimate partnership. Loyalty says everything.
- **Positive constructive corporate culture**—The ability to attract and retain the best and the brightest talent. Your organization is the one company where people want to work.

Art Koch's Profit Chain® Model
The Three Fs of Supply Chain Management

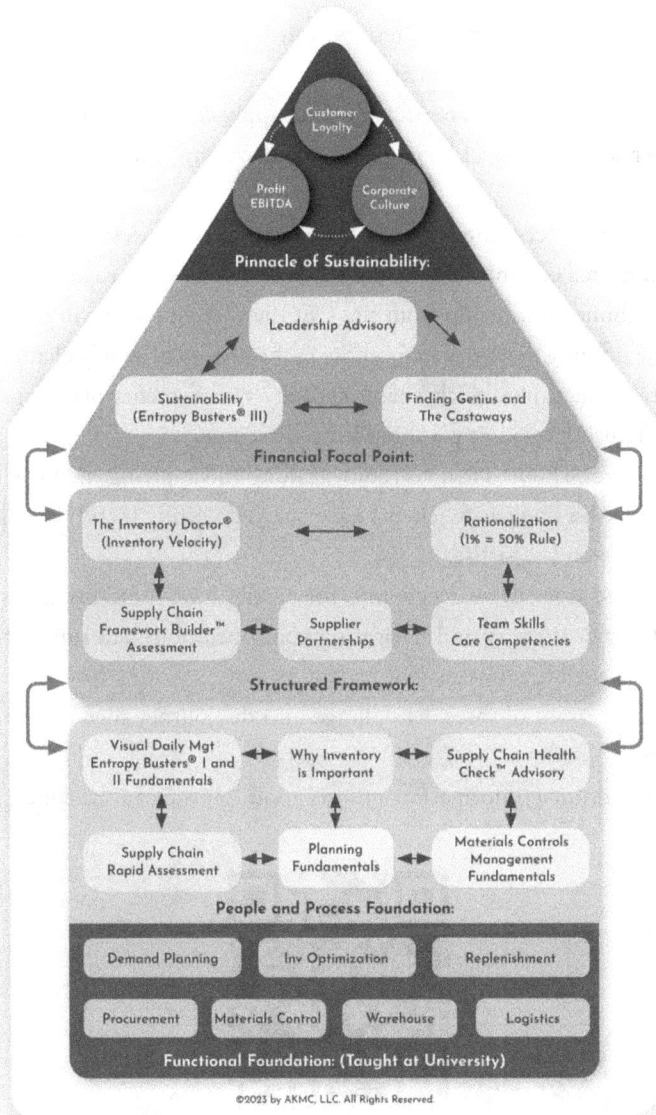

Figure 1.1 Art Koch's profit chain model

- **Profit/Shareholder value/EBITDA**—Not only are you achieving excellent returns but your company is the benchmark for industry peer groups. Additionally, an

excellent credit rating results in a lower cost of capital and
increases the chances of achieving the next level of growth.

These are the actions and results created in the middle of the model,
where this book mostly focuses.

Significant changes are occurring in supply chain management, such
as cyber security, artificial intelligence, and systems innovation, to name
a few.

What if process integrity, team engagement and development, and
organizational commitment by the CEO are not all synchronized? In that
case, without sponsorship from the CEO new technology will too often
become nothing more than a footnote in the history of supply chain management, much like block chain, capacity requirements planning, and
manufacturing resource planning II have become.

My sincere hope is that you enjoy reading and applying what you have
learned in this book as much as I have enjoyed writing it and sharing my
experiences and expertise.

Join me as we delve deeply into the possibilities, solutions, and strategies for transforming and navigating your operations and supply chain
into a sustainable profit chain.

On the count of three, let's plunge into the journey together. Ready?
One, two, three!

For additional information and free tools, please scan the code.

PART 1

People and Process Foundation

CHAPTER 2

Building Professionalism in Supply Chain Management

Learning to scuba dive and mastering the complexities of supply chain management (SCM) share a non-negotiable requirement: an unwavering commitment to foundational principles. Fail to grasp the basics of scuba diving, and you risk severe injury or even loss of life. In the world of SCM, the stakes are no less severe: A neglect of fundamentals could result in crippling operational setbacks and financial devastation—potentially sinking your business.

My first dive class was called open water certification, and it was for entry-level diving up to 60 feet deep. It consisted of four weeks of classwork and diving knowledge reviews, followed by dives into a pool for confined water training and skills practice. Before you realized it, you were ready for the open water checkout dives. If all goes well, the instructor signs off on your certification card.

Then, bam, all of a sudden, you're an open water diver, free to dive without an instructor up to 60 feet deep.

I was never more terrified! You mean I can go by myself? How can I be trusted not to kill myself?

During my first dive certification course, coincidentally, I was hired to lead the supply chain integration of relocating a 400,000 sq. ft. manufacturing facility and consolidating two outside warehouses into one location. The marching orders given to me were to meet or beat the budget with no impact on the customer. If you have never done this before, it's very intense. It is like holding your breath and changing a scuba air tank in 60 feet deep water in a swift current.

The same stress is valid for SCM.

You learn about a variety of subjects in university education. Still, the benefit of your knowledge stops there if you don't continue to learn new skills after you graduate. If you're not increasing your abilities, the business will suffer, and your career will stall.

It's common for people to get their open water certifications and never to proceed from there because they don't have the confidence to dive on their own without the tether and comfort of an instructor at arm's length. Therefore, they never have the opportunity to explore the entire underwater ecosystem and all its natural beauty.

As a diver, I worked on my core skills by logging more and more dives, combining what I had learned with taking additional specialty classes and then progressing to certification as a rescue diver. As a supply chain professional, I'm always learning and absorbing new ideas, information, and insights to strengthen my core skills so I may help my clients and teach others.

Understanding Supply Chain Professionalism to Achieve Excellence

When reading any contemporary business magazine or journal, many articles discuss operations or quality excellence and tout that both are your path to economic success. I'll never argue against the importance of either methodology.

However, in most organizations, SCM controls upward of 50 to 65 percent of the cost of goods sold, which includes raw material costs, logistical costs, and the cost of warehousing and staffing and managing the process. Even today, with the significant impact from the COVID-19 pandemic, SCM is often relegated to a mere footnote despite its significant operational and economic impact.

> *Art's Gold: Supply chain management impacts 50 to 65 percent of your total cost of goods sold.*

In my 30-plus years in SCM, I have experienced many leaders lacking an understanding of what SCM is and how to utilize it as a competitive advantage or a market differentiator.

In this chapter, we will examine the following crucial questions:

- How is the discipline of SCM treated as a profession in your organization?

- Does the SCM function have the necessary face time representation on the top floor, executive positions, and board meetings?
- How is the financial payback of developing SCM professionals for skills and processes at all levels of management understood?
- Is it clear to management why professionalism and training are necessary to bridge the gap between university textbooks and real-world applications?

Scuba Instructors Are Professionals; Are Your Supply Chain Leaders Treated Like Professionals?

Let me ask you a simple question. Would you consider taking a diving course from a nonprofessional, putting your life on the line, and then jumping into the open ocean?

I certainly would not!

I want to learn from an individual educated and trained by an organizational body with rigorous standards, who is focused on my safety, received consistent training standards, and has established a long-term development path in their certification body of knowledge. For years, many organizations have made this exact mistake with their SCM organizations. They staffed SCM with nonprofessionals without understanding the potential contribution to the organization of professionals and to financial performance, or they treated SCM managers and team members as second-class citizens, never allowing them to spread their wings to flex their true impact on the organization's operations and financial performance.

Is it possible your organization is guilty of this short-sightedness?

With SCM responsible for greater than 50 percent of cost of goods sold (COGS), you need the "best of the best" to lead this function.

SCM is a profession not unlike that of certified public accountants (CPA) and professional engineers (Peng). The top universities in the world offer a BSc, MBA, and PhD in SCM. Your SCM team deserves the same level of professional individuals found in these other disciplines.

Additionally, we, as supply chain professionals, must demand more professionalism from our peers and demonstrate more professionalism in all our interactions.

Four Reasons Why Organizations Are Not Inclined to Hire and Retain Top Supply Chain Talent

- A high demand from Apple, Amazon, and other desirable— and profitable—enterprises for supply chain professionals makes the competition for top talent intense and expensive. Many executives in smaller organizations believe they don't have the cachet to attract and retain top talent, so they don't try.
- Many hiring managers cannot do the proper cost-benefit analysis to conclude that supply chain professionals' higher-earning structure will translate into a higher value-added proposition or financial results. That's *because leadership does not understand* that SCM affects 50 to 65 percent of cost of goods sold and that SCM personnel have a direct impact on business performance and profit.
- Like many heavy professions, SCM can be tedious and requires relentless hard work. It takes a dedicated team and support from senior leaders to create disruptive and transformative change. A "one-person show" can't achieve the breakthrough results that, on the surface, appear easy to accomplish. The ability to achieve sustainable results requires a synergistic team environment with active and visible support from the top.
- Additionally, executive leadership must commit to providing SCM with the resources necessary to achieve the corporate vision.

SCM is essential to an organization's long-term success. A Deloitte survey of 400 worldwide executives in operations and retail found that of companies with world-class supply chains, 79 percent have higher earnings before interest, taxes, depreciation, and amortization (EBITDA) and 69 percent have higher revenue growth than industry peer groups.[1] Results such as these have caused executives to rethink their supply chain strategy. During the COVID-19 pandemic, 67 to 84 percent of North American executives have made plans to transform their supply chain organizations to become more professional and effective.

> *Companies with world-class supply chains have 79 percent higher EBITDA and 69 percent higher revenue growth than industry peers.*
> —Deloitte, Supply Chain Leadership 2014

Six Key Steps to Becoming a Professional Supply Chain Organization

I've identified six key steps, Figure 2.1, to turn the supply chain team into industry-leading professionals:

Six Key Steps to Becoming a Professional Supply Chain Organization

Figure 2.1 Six key steps to becoming a professional supply chain organization

- Promote from within the organization. Likely, you have already employed a few highly skilled SCM professionals who haven't been able to demonstrate their abilities or are properly supported.
- When you must hire from the outside, make sure applicants are SCM professionals who have graduated from a well-respected university and continued educating themselves.
- Is there a conscious effort to invest in the training and education of SCM for vocational team members? American Production and Inventory Control Society certifications are recognized globally as the standard for SCM body of knowledge. Classes are conducted in-house, at a local high school, community college, or online at www.apics.org.
- Are you recruiting new graduates from universities recognized for SCM Figure 2.2?[2]

Best Undergraduate Supply Chain Management / Logistics Programs - 2023

BEST COLLEGES US News RANKINGS

#1	Michigan State University	E. Lansing, MI	Supply Chain Management / Logistics
#2	Arizona State University	Tempe, AZ	Supply Chain Management / Logistics
#3	University of Tennessee	Knoxville, TN	Supply Chain Management / Logistics
#4	Pennsylvania State University	University Park, PA	Supply Chain Management / Logistics
#4	Massachusetts Institute of Technology	University Park, PA	Supply Chain Management / Logistics
#6	Ohio State University	Columbus, OH	Supply Chain Management / Logistics
#7	University of Michigan	Ann Arbor, MI	Supply Chain Management / Logistics
#8	University of Texas - Austin	Austin, TX	Supply Chain Management / Logistics
#9	University of Pennsylvania	Philadelphia, PA	Supply Chain Management / Logistics
#10	Georgio Institute of Technology	Atlanta, GA	Supply Chain Management / Logistics
#10	University of Arkansas	Cambridge, MA	Supply Chain Management / Logistics
#12	Purdue University - West Lafayette	West Lafayette, IN	Supply Chain Management / Logistics

Figure 2.2 Best Undergraduate Supply Chain Management/Logistics Programs—2023

- Does your organization have a leadership development program? Is there a leadership track for SCM team members? The top talent pool consists of ambitious individuals. Organizations must have a path for their growth and success.
- To whom does the top supply chain person report? Is it the president or CEO? SCM should report to the president or CEO for the optimal organizational structure. If they report to finance or operations, then SCM is *not* taken seriously. SCM must be part of the senior leadership team to have credibility among their peers.

Today, it's even more critical to employ professionals with big data and AI experience and better analytics. SCM must consist of the best and brightest team members. As Jim Collins wrote in *Good to Great*, we need the right people on the bus, in the right seats, and then eventually move to the front of the bus as leaders in the organization.

Dive Master Briefing (Client Example)

Early in my consulting career, I received a request to assist a general manager (GM) of a $300 million division of a $4 billion multinational consumer products company. The GM needed inventory reduction and raw material cost containment. I'm not saying this to impress anyone but rather to highlight that no matter the organization's size, the same problems exist.

Because of years of engineering success stories and financial success through mergers and acquisitions, the division's culture had become blind to SCM's importance in overall business performance. The divisional raw material spending at this company was $170 million. The senior buyer, let's call him Matt, was responsible for the highest dollar spent within this division. He failed at his last three positions within this same company. Rather than finding the right fit for Matt or terminating him, local leadership moved Matt into SCM's purchasing department. I was told, "Supply chain people are too expensive" and "How complicated can it be to cut a purchase order?"

Matt was a cordial and pleasant person. However, he was responsible for over $60 million in spending per year without formal education or technical SCM training. As a result, the company was ignoring millions of dollars of potential cost savings. I suggested that we move Matt to another position that better suited his skills and core competencies.

Searching around, I discovered Kathy within the same corporation who had a BS in SCM-Procurement from a nationally recognized university and the client promoted her as the manager of procurement. Next, we hired Quinn as director of SCM. He had seven years of experience and an MBA in SCM from a nationally recognized university. These two well-trained and educated, high-potential individuals brought a new level of professionalism and energy to the team.

The existing team stepped up their game and learned from the new team members. Over the next few years, we established supplier partnerships. We improved customer service on time to ship date promise from 45 to 97 percent, reduced supply base complexity by 18 percent, decreased total inventory by 32 percent, and the raw material purchase price had nearly 10 percent year-over-year improvements. EBITDA improved by $18.5 million annually, and corporate valuation increased by $150 million. All from hiring two SCM professionals and supporting them effectively with consultants, resources, and training.

During prior years, the supply chain's lack of professionalism resulted in little or no improvements, and the total cost of ownership increased. The lack of professionalism in the past held the company back. These outstanding financial results can be typical when a professional team is in place.

Dive Log 2 (Art's Commentary)

I'm adamant about a formal university education or a supply chain certification from a nationally recognized association to drive professionalism. However, I'm not opposed to hiring vocational skilled trade supply chain team members on the team. Nevertheless, there must be a mix. Vocational team members always bring tactical knowledge that is critical for tying together processes to achieve sustainability. Professional university training often adds three crucial elements:

1. SCM's total cost reach is substantial. In most cases, between 50 and 65 percent of COGS. Most people I know do not just allow anyone

to manage their retirement investing. Neither do I. Why would you let an unqualified person manage your supply chain?

2. You will see a higher level of professional behaviors and better business perspectives from individuals who have taken the initiative and time to earn professional degrees and certifications.

3. Formal training and education enhance critical thinking, analysis, and communication skills.

These areas are fundamental to bridge the gaps that come with applying SCM techniques across industries. Additionally, a degreed individual who has dedicated their time and hard work to become an expert has the skills to build enterprise greatness. The same skills are valid for the diver with 100, 500, and 1,000 dives that conquer the seas.

Buddy Check: Questions From Coach Art

- Does your organization hire top SCM talent?
- Are there supply chain professionals in executive roles?
- How do you invest in vocational team members' training and education of SCM?
- What is your process for transforming the supply chain organization into industry-leading professionals?

Art's Deep Dive

Remember, cheap is expensive! In most cases, material cost alone is greater than 50 percent of COGS. Most smart people don't want amateurs to repair their Mercedes Benz or Porsche. So why would you allow a nonprofessional to manage such a significant percentage of your costs that have a direct impact on your ability to meet customer quality and deadlines, your bottom line, and share price?

When transforming your organization, we cannot forget that many of the managers and top performers are already overworked for all the reasons discussed in this book. I've had great success backfilling the easy tasks for managers with college interns and with virtual buyers and expediters from Monterrey, Mexico. But you need the support of leadership.

Without CEO ownership, transformations fail.

Success is achieved when these three elements are combined:

1. Tools
2. People
3. Organization

Art's Gold: Every team member in supply chain roles should be capable of paying for their salaries with improvements to processes they control.

CHAPTER 3

Mastering the Fundamentals: The Bedrock of Supply Chain Management

Whether you're strapping on a scuba tank or taking the reins of a supply chain management (SCM) operation, a rock-solid foundation is your passport to long-term success. In both domains, it's the groundwork that defines your trajectory.

After earning my certifications, I set out to explore the undersea world. At first, I did not venture too far from home, diving in Key Largo, Florida, followed by diving at a repurposed rock quarry and the in-shore wrecks off the North Carolina coast. I was comfortable enough that I had the skill set needed to explore these locations. As the number of my dives increased, I cast my diving sights further and further out: first to the Bahamas, then Cozumel, Mexico, the Caribbean, the Pacific, and as far away as Indonesia. With each new dive excursion, my skills, knowledge, and experience increased, and I built the self-confidence to move on to the next destination.

I used a similar process to develop my career. Growing up in Flint, Michigan, gave me a unique opportunity to witness first-hand the American automotive industry's collapse. I watched while friends and family lost what were once great jobs. This unique perspective shaped my views on life, learning, and career. Determined that this will *never* happen to me, I purposely changed jobs and industries, each building upon one another, broadening my skills, knowledge, and confidence, hence avoiding obsolescence!

My first job fresh out of graduate school was with a startup company experiencing rapid growth with little or no formalized processes.

I worked long hours and then went home and opened my SCM text-books to relearn the theories. The next day, I took those theories back into the workplace to apply them to real-world situations. I literally did this for 10 years. Going through this process, I was amazed at how much I knew and yet how little I knew at the same time. What became evident was that my university education gave me an excellent foundation: critical thinking skills and determination not to fail!

Similar to my scuba journey, and with each new job, I ventured on to bigger and broader challenges. With each change in position, I cemented the foundation that I had started building from my university studies and then learned how to lay the foundation's bricks for application toward the real world.

In this chapter, I want to share a model I've built throughout my career that bridges the gap between classroom education and the core competencies that help supply chain professionals and executive leader-ship navigate toward supply chain excellence.

How Diving the World Helped to Transform My Supply Chain Journey

Completely hooked on diving, I continued my dive training and edu-cation by taking more advanced courses. All the training and education helped me build a body of knowledge on how to be a safer and more competent diver and, ultimately, to have the ability to rescue myself and others.

The same thought process translates to SCM. With professionalism comes intellectual bandwidth for critical thinking, strategy, and execu-tion. Without professionalism, associates often see only the tactical part of their roles and have difficulty achieving sustainable corrective actions. Professionalism adds the required core competencies that connect the cause, effect, and relationships among process, structure, and financial deliverables.

Art Koch's Three "Fs" of Supply Chain Management

Let's dive deeper into the process and methodology I created and called "Art Koch's Profit Chain®—The Three Fs of SCM" (Figure 1.1). It's a hierarchical structure for the supply chain that incorporates the closed-loop problem resolution to apply the plan-do-check-act process.

This chapter focuses on introducing the **people and process foundation**, **structural framework**, and **financial focal point**. Notice the dark gray (green if on digital reader) arrows within Figure 1.1. They indicate there is no single critical path and linear dependencies. It's OK to work between areas and move back and forth as skills increase or the need arises.

Before diving deep into each level of the model, it's essential to understand that I've built my career on improving each of the three Fs of SCM: people and process foundation, structural framework, and financial focal point.

What I currently find disappointing is that many of the basics are broken or not in place. For example, poor inventory accuracy, lead times not maintained, or supplier orders not acknowledged for delivery date and quantity. This realization caused me to become very passionate about building the right foundation with great fundamentals. In its elemental form, the model is straightforward. The difficulties organizations have is a clear understanding of three key areas of expertise that prevent them from pulling the supply chain function together and not achieving the optimum benefits from the pinnacle of sustainability:

1. Understanding what foundation and fundamentals are building blocks.
2. The execution of putting everything into place and plan execution.
3. The organization's ability to attract and retain top supply chain talent.

As already noted, the functional foundation component is what they teach at the university. For students, after earning their education, the expectation is to apply learning to guide employers to reach and maintain financial success, or the pinnacle of sustainability, as discussed in Chapter 1 and repeated below. However, what isn't taught in universities is how to bridge the gap between classroom education and the core competencies, skills, and processes necessary to achieve the pinnacle of sustainability for customer loyalty, corporate culture, and profitability.

An ongoing challenge is finding individuals with leadership skills who are well-versed in supply chain and operations management and can focus on both short-term tactical and long-term strategic game plans.

Often the same skill gaps are seen with divers. They may have earned their certification card; however, they lack the simple skills in executing gear setup, necessary mask clearing, or buoyancy issues. In either case, not knowing the fundamentals can lead to disastrous results.

Many people are not interested in the tactical game plan because it isn't sexy. However, if you can't establish the fundamentals of inventory accuracy, data integrity, or exception-based planning, you will never realize the strategic game plan.

However, the results are transformational. When done effectively, everyone will think you're a genius. In reality, it was the synergy of individuals and teams dedicating time, energy, and hard work to become experts in their specific skills and tasks. The continual trial and error of fixing many small things, in other words, a focus on continual improvement, have culminated into hundreds of little wins that collectively amounted to remarkable successes.

Don't allow yourself to get distracted by the silver bullet solutions, such as a new enterprise resource planning (ERP) system, a new demand planning solution, or the next shiny new underwater camera. Maintain the balance between the fundamentals, keeping up with new technology and being very cautious of being drawn into silver bullet solutions. If you don't have the foundation and fundamentals of SCM in place, you will overdesign and spend too much time and money on a long-term solution that will never solve your problems because you don't have the foundations in place.

We see this happen every year with the NFL draft. How many teams draft a quarterback as their number one pick without building the foundation of their offensive or defensive lines?

To me, the drafting of a star quarterback is a prime example of chasing the new shiny toy without securing the foundation. How many of us have seen a new ERP implemented with hugely anticipated deliverables that never materialize?

In fact, over 80 percent of ERP system implementations fail to achieve results because they attempt to solve the wrong problem. The software vendors won't tell you what the right problem to solve is because they don't know it.

Pinnacle of Sustainability

As discussed in Chapter 1, the top of the model is the pinnacle of sustainability. This is the output of the efforts to build and establish the foundation and structural framework. It comes together to drive the enterprise into a perpetual profit-generating machine—Art Koch's Profit Chain. The supply chain becomes a competitive differentiator by achieving customer loyalty, corporate culture, and profits.

Let's review the base of my model, the foundation of SCM. There are two significant areas within the foundation: the functional foundation and the people and process foundation.

Functional Foundation

Building from the bottom up is the functional foundation that is much like the cement footers of a house. The foundation consists of the primary functions within SCM. These are the courses taught in SCM programs at universities. We will not be going into textbook lessons here, but rather the practical application to achieve profitable and sustainable results.

In general terms, each function looks to be very direct. In principle, it should be easy to transition from the textbook to the real world. However, it's not so simple. With procurement, it's not just magically placing a purchase order and then having parts arrive. In operations it's not as simple as manufacturing takes place, a product is shipped, and as a result, we have happy customers. There are more pieces of the puzzle that need to be considered.

People and Process Foundation

The next level up in the model from the functional foundation is the people and process foundation. Think of it like the bricks that support the structure of the house. In the simplest terms, these are the lessons learned from university teachings that are translated and applied to the real world of business and operations management.

Chapters 4 and 13 discuss the "Swift Yet Meticulous: Rapid Assessment of Your Supply Chain" (Chapter 4), benchmarking of current status, and the "Supply Chain Health Check Advisory" (Chapter 13) to sustain the current state and reach stretch objectives. The emphasis is on using rapid assessment processes to secure a commitment for change and then a structured follow-up process to "health" check the team's ongoing status and the need for corrective actions.

Chapters 5 through 11 discuss:

- The *Planning Fundamentals* of scheduling, replenishment, and demand, utilizing classification methodology to significantly improve customer service and inventory performance.
- *Inventory Is Evil* enlightens the reader on the negative impact of inventory on profits, customer service, and problem resolution.
- *Material Controls Management Fundamentals* explain how to systematically improve your inventory accuracy.
- *Entropy Busters® Introduction, Phase I and II* are the final three chapters of this foundation applying Visual Daily Management to improve communications and teamwork and achieve rapid results.

Structural Framework

The next step is the structural framework, which is similar to a house's frame that holds the structure together. Once there is a solid foundation and framework in place, we can work at an advanced capacity to apply business processes and practices to step functionally improve. Within this framework is where the refinements and details emerge in real-world applications.

Chapter 15 is for *Team Skills and Core Competencies* that help you determine the required skills and competencies within the supply chain to become industry leaders.

The *Supply Chain Framework Builder Assessment* identifies gaps within qualitative and quantitative supply chain practices that keep the organization from becoming world-class.

Chapter 16, *Art's Law of 1 Percent = 50 Percent*, examines how 1 percent of purchases or demand can account for 50 percent of the complexity.

Chapter 17, "How to Create the Supplier Partner," illustrates the importance of transforming your relationships from vendors to supplier partners and how accomplishing this accelerates competitive advantage.

Next, in Chapter 18, we transition into *The Inventory Doctor*® on how to diagnose and improve inventory performance.

Financial Focal Point

The final piece in the model is the financial focal point, which lies below the roof's peak. This part consists of the convergence of the processes and methodologies that catapult the organization ahead of the competition. In doing so, we accomplish the closed-loop model of sustainability, getting leadership to excel by building inclusive teams and the ongoing leadership advisory to break away from industry peers.

Chapter 12 outlines the final *Phase of Entropy Busters* for achieving process *sustainability*.

In Chapter 19, "Are You Finding the Genius and the Castaways," you will learn how to discover hidden stars in the organization.

Next, Chapter 20, "Leadership Advisory," is about how to select and work with experts who help leaders attain professional growth and improve business performance.

Checking the Functional Foundation for Cracks

How do you know whether the supply chain foundation is solid, has minor cracks, or is complete rubble? Below are several questions to help you determine your foundation's structural integrity:

- Not all facilities are perfect within a national or global enterprise. Some sites are usually better than others. Do you struggle with multiple locations that drain resources or significantly reduce the profits of their sister location?
- Before you say your organization is world-class, consider professional sports teams. How would your team's performance stack up against the teams that consistently play for division titles in Major League Baseball's World Series,

NFL Super Bowl, NHL Stanley Cup, Soccer's World Cup, or Red Bull's current F1 team? There are few teams who can consistently lead at this level. Are you sure you're part of this unique group?

- How often do surprises in the organization interrupt the workflow or daily processes? These unexpected events can range from significant parts shortages to inventory write-downs. Too many surprises indicate the lack of control or inability to detect supply chain process failures.
- Is your organization able to attract and retain superior talent? If the answer is no, then I seriously doubt the organization is world-class. It does not mean you're not on the right path, or you can't get there, but you are just not there yet.

After answering the above questions, you will have a clear understanding of your starting point to turn your supply chain into a competitive advantage.

Energy and resources must be added to build and maintain an organization, whether talking about the fun of learning to scuba dive or building and sustaining a world-class supply chain process. I like to say, "anything worthwhile isn't easy, and nothing is for free." It is where the first law of thermodynamics applies to achieve world-class status.

First Law of Thermodynamics. Energy can't be created or destroyed. It can only change forms. The total energy of the universe stays the same. If you need work done to your enterprise, more heat, energy, or resources need to be added from the outside or transferred internally from non-value-added activities.

Suppose you are going to win the battle against entropy—the constant pressure of decline—in your processes. For example, your internal continuous improvement office corrects a decoupled process. Process entropy is the undoing of the correction.

Time, resources, and energy need to be added from the outside or transferred internally from nonvalue activities to keep the process in control. When adding resources, just don't add warm bodies; get some of your best and brightest to help tackle the opportunities.

I am talking about adding supply chain and operation professionalism with energy, drive, and zealots for positive change. Remember, the goal is to change the mindset and behaviors of the people from a cost center to become a sustainable profit chain.

The intent of Art Koch's Profit Chain methodology is to guide corporate leadership and supply chain professionals with a pathway to dramatic improvements which lead to increased inventory velocity (the speed at which inventory moves through the enterprise), improved customer service, and corporate profits.

Overall: Supply Chain Management

Let's look at five areas to evaluate the stability of the functional foundation:

1. Does each area have relevant key performance indicators?
2. How well do the functions work within peer groups and the team? Are they siloed, or do they play well together?
3. Is SCM considered procurement, a singular department? Or a philosophical mission led by degreed professionals within various operational functions?
4. Is there a process to pull the tactical and strategic factors together?
   - Do you have policy deployment and strategic plans for one and two years? Does your long-term planning drive tactical initiatives for the next 30/90/180 days?
   - Are there daily tactical activities aligned with long-term goals?
     ○ Are there visual daily management systems?
     ○ Are there weekly staff meetings?
     ○ Do monthly and quarterly sessions focus on long-term strategy?
5. Does the organization manage for complexity and variation?

Can you review your organization and empirically say yes to all the above? Consider how well these five areas are under control. If so, you likely have a solid foundation. If not, read further ahead to learn the processes and methodology for improving the supply chain foundation and framework.

Dive Master Briefing (Client Example)

A six-billion-dollar tier 1 automotive supplier retained my consulting services. The production facility was just over one million square feet, with nearly $175 million in annual revenue. The goal was to rescue a facility that had lost its true north and had forgotten what "good" looks like, customers placed them on a no bid list and profits were well below expectations. The organization did not invest in supply chain leadership and thought the ERP system could guide the organization. Additionally, the facility was without a supply chain manager for over one year.

To make matters worse, Kevin, a vital member of the organization, took an extended vacation (four weeks), causing the facility to lose the few controls they had in place. With deficiencies in multiple areas and the facility already skating on thin ice for quite a while, this vacation put them over the top, and the internal supply chain processes crashed, causing on-time deliveries to drop to the mid-80s percentile.

To further set the stage for the challenges that lay ahead, within my first two hours at the facility, I chartered a plane to deliver parts to a major customer's assembly plant and avoided a line-down situation. If you shut down an automotive customer, they can charge you $25,000 per minute, which can quickly turn into $1,500,000 per hour!

Another challenge to overcome was that the supply chain team was spread throughout the facility without a method to keep them aligned. Some of the team's office areas were the bleakest I had ever seen. The ceiling tiles were falling, there were broken light bulbs, and everywhere, piles upon piles of paper and rat droppings. At the time of my arrival, here were the key indicators of how badly the facility's performance had declined:

- On-time delivery had dropped to an appalling low of the mid-80s percentile.
- Premium freight costs had skyrocketed to over $100,000 per month.

- Inventory accuracy was horrific. The stock rooms doors were wide open without any guidelines on who was authorized to enter, and there was no monitoring of parts movement activities.
- Multiple inaccurate bills of material routings caused backflushing of parts from the incorrect work center locations, creating $2.5 million of negative inventory. Because there were so many part numbers with negative work center location balances, accurate cycle counting was impossible, resulting in material planners being forced to guess inventory balances, leading to surprise part outages.
- Defective material was not correctly transacted in the ERP system and placed in reject locations, and not reworked or scrapped. This transaction error created significant data integrity issues, which resulted in painful part shortages.
- The manufacturing plant also was a supplier to sister facilities. Because of the chaos, the parts did not get scheduled or were used internally, resulting in dissatisfied customers at the sister facilities.
- The supply chain team was burnt out and had excessively high overtime of 20 to 25 percent.
- Plant safety was nonexistent.

There were several barriers blocking progress everywhere I turned. Since I was hired by corporate, the existing leadership team did not trust me. They were not receptive to any outside criticism of their supply chain organizational design and leadership style. The location was fast approaching a "No Bid" list from their primary customers, which meant the facility would be out of business in four years.

It was an exercise in brute force, tenacity, and willpower for me not to give up on this seemingly hopeless situation.

As with all barriers, there are opposite positive forces. You need to find them. I found many bridges for progress.

Dolores, the plant manager, joined the company one week before I arrived. Together we won over several vital influencers. The supply chain team was thirsty for leadership, even though leadership was not. I'm a scrapper, and I love this type of fight! Barring an on-site fatality, this facility was at rock bottom, and there was no place to go but up.

Establishing People and Process Foundation

The first step needed at this facility was to start establishing the foundations of leadership. I focused on bringing Christina and Patricia from the materials management team into the picture. They had been pushed aside by past leadership. Their new voices helped to empower them as part of the solution rather than part of the problem. We integrated daily Gemba walks of manufacturing with the materials team (previously, they had not engaged in this process).

> Gemba means "actual place" in Japanese. Lean thinkers use it to mean the place where value is created.[1]

Making this minor yet impactful change, we helped the supply chain team identify and resolve issues as they occurred. This effort significantly increased their team shop floor presence and raised the team's morale. As a result, the team felt respected and part of the solution.

Next, I combined the offices of two production planners (Debbie and Francis) into the same office as the production buyers (Susana and Julio) and materials control supervisors (Molly and Laura). As I had mentioned earlier, the office was in rough shape. We 5S'ed the area (see Figure 3.1), scrubbed surfaces, cleared away the junk, and installed proper lighting. 5S is a workplace organization methodology that uses five words: sort, straighten, shine, standardize, and sustain.

By performing the 5S method regularly, workplace performance improves.

In this instance, the team immediately started to feel like the facility was a better place to work.

We implemented a visual daily management team review for safety, quality, delivery, inventory, and productivity within the materials department and a shift change hand-off meeting.

Next, we started weekly staff meetings and monthly one-to-one meetings with all three shifts to discuss open items, problems, and successes.

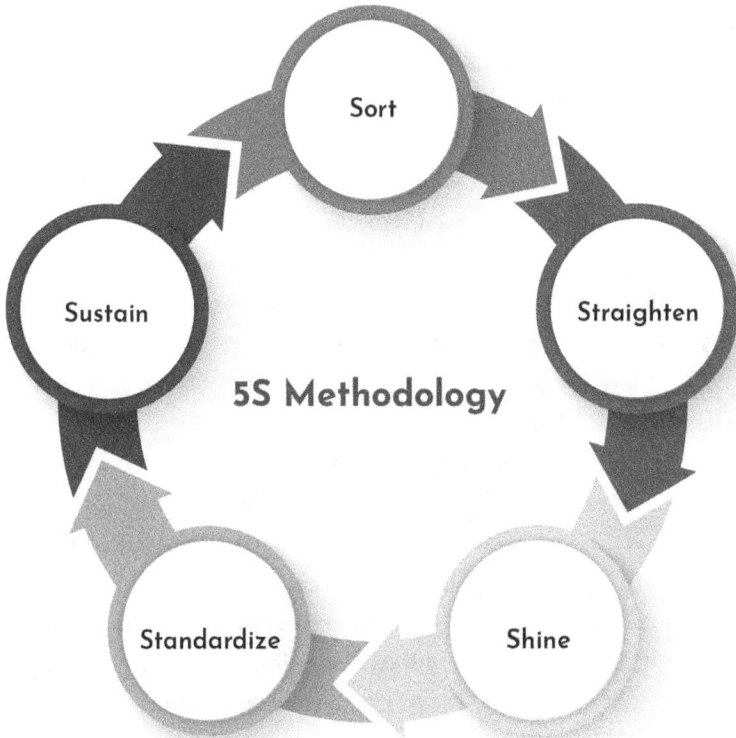

Figure 3.1 5S methodology

To highlight what needed to be accomplished, we created a visual management board and established meaningful key performance indicators (KPIs). These actions dramatically increased the materials team engagement, improved morale, and created urgency within the supply chain team.

We hired Joseph and Juan to be the materials group leaders for managing shipping, receiving, and production inventory control. Because other functional areas were picking up the slack for the organization's neglect in backfilling these roles, the materials group leaders' addition allowed the rebalancing of workloads across all supply chain functions. The additional professionalism allowed for increased leadership and focus on inventory control, and we were able to gain traction in implementing corrective actions.

The materials team led the efforts to 5S all the operations, which earned them excellent reviews from senior leadership and a well-deserved confidence and credibility boost.

We implemented daily Gemba walks with manufacturing and then added all supply chain areas. Also, we introduced the five whys and plan-do-check-act, the fundamentals of operational excellence.

The 5 Whys is a method of getting to the root cause of a problem or opportunity by asking a minimum of five questions.[2]

Here is an example of the five whys to help you see the process in action, in the example it took six ways to get to root cause (Figure 3.2).

We assessed the team's proficiency of their ERP system. As a result of the assessment, all supply chain and many operations members needed retraining. They were then required to pass a proficiency test to demonstrate how to complete the systems tasks of their roles. In addition to cultivating their new skills and knowledge, we also engaged corporates' internal ERP expert to help resolve the negative inventory situation.

With renewed confidence and increased positive exposure to leadership, the SCM team started to thrive. They reintroduced improved tugger routes for material delivery. The team also enhanced material presentation

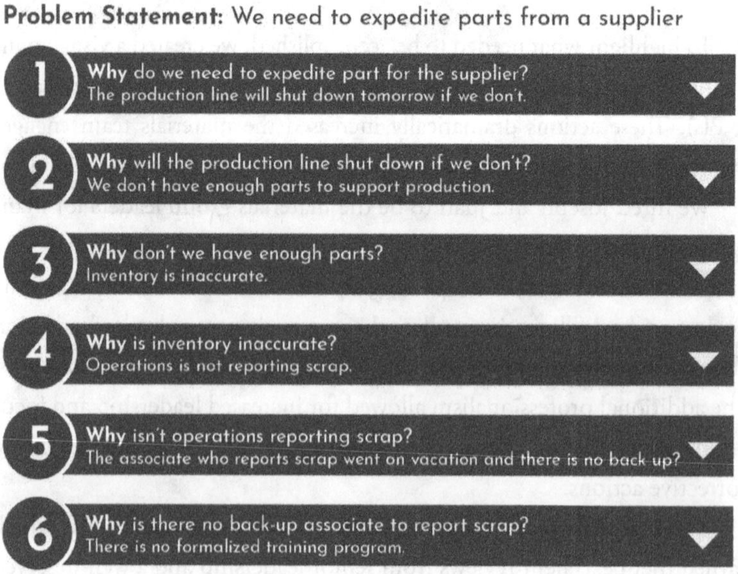

Problem Statement: We need to expedite parts from a supplier

1. **Why** do we need to expedite part for the supplier?
   The production line will shut down tomorrow if we don't.

2. **Why** will the production line shut down if we don't?
   We don't have enough parts to support production.

3. **Why** don't we have enough parts?
   Inventory is inaccurate.

4. **Why** is inventory inaccurate?
   Operations is not reporting scrap.

5. **Why** isn't operations reporting scrap?
   The associate who reports scrap went on vacation and there is no back-up?

6. **Why** is there no back-up associate to report scrap?
   There is no formalized training program.

Figure 3.2 Six whys analysis

at supermarkets and assembly cells so machine operators had better access to the parts they used. We used these learnings to design and implement a model cell for best visual materials control practices: FIFO, sequential pull lanes, and Kanban. Kanban is a just-in-time inventory pull process based on parts usage and triggered by empty parts bins or movement cards.

- **FIFO (first in, first out)**—The principle and practice of maintaining accurate production sequence is that the first part entering a storage location or process is the first part to be consumed. FIFO processes help to ensure parts don't become obsolete, quality defects don't become hidden in inventory and are a prerequisite for pull system implementation.[3]
- **Sequential pull lanes**—Used when there is a high part number count for pull inventory processes. Very practical pull process in make-to-order manufacturing.[4]
- **Supermarkets**—Holds a set amount of each product it produces. Each process simply produces to replenish what is consumed from its supermarket. Typically, the material is consumed by the downstream customer process.[5]
- **Tugger routes**—A material delivery route utilizing a small tractor to pull a train of "cars" loaded with parts to their assembly destination. Very practical in medium to large manufacturing facilities.

Professional leadership and addressing SCM fundamentals will reward those who take the time and expend the energy. As outlined in the client example earlier, these efforts led to stabilizing manufacturing operations and SCM during a crisis period. Within only 90 days, the team was able to achieve the following substantial results.

Results

- Improved on-time delivery by 14 points to +99 percent.
- Reduced negative inventory from $2.5 million to $184K and reduced rejected inventory from +$275K to $76K.

- Reduced premium freight of $100K/month to below $5K/month.
- Improved overall equipment effectiveness by 9 percent.
- Improved supplier on-time delivery performance from 88 to +99 percent by reducing past due line items from +500 to 139.
- Improved machine downtime due to purchase parts availability from 4 to 8 hours per day to 45 minutes or less per day.
- Reduced safety incidents from 4.6 incidents per month to zero per month.
- Reduced unnecessary hourly overtime and balanced work hours, took team members out of unnecessary meetings, and focused on value-added activities.
- Established a future model for what "good" looks like; increased supply chain's team engagement and focus.
- Dramatically improved employee engagement, performance, and commitment to the company.

Client Testimonial

Brian Keyser, VP of Operations, stated,

> Art's leadership provided a crucial contrast to the "Command and Conquer" management style in the Automotive industry. Focusing on team capability, visual management, and Gemba walks, Art swiftly enhanced delivery and customer relationships, leaving a lasting benchmark for effective supply chain management.

Dive Log 3: (Art's Commentary)

This book is about getting the foundation and fundamentals correct within SCM and operations. Without the prerequisites in place, it's nearly impossible to achieve the focus necessary to accomplish the bigger-picture goals of world-class inventory performance, complexity rationalization, and supplier partnerships.

My experience has shown that fundamentals don't just fall into place. The constant firefighting and the lack of process sustainability suffocate progress by not allowing team members to perform their work without interruption and manual checks. The single most significant root cause is lack of management due to not attracting and retaining good people, not using basic process controls, and lack of timely communication.

Most often, the barrier to moving forward is when one or two key individuals in leadership deny there is a problem. Many managers want to manage from behind a computer monitor through weekly meetings or trend reports instead of dealing directly with people.

Ever seen the "rubber band" effect? Take a manager to the factory floor to show them an opportunity. Often, they will have one foot pointed toward their office, ready to go back to e-mail or a meeting. We need to remind ourselves to go to where the problems are, and to take the necessary time to hear and learn from the shop floor team and get away from the comfort of offices and e-mails.

I've heard from executive leadership, "We only need to hire better people!" Though this is partially true, you still need to lead them and build sustainable processes. Just hiring good people isn't enough. Most people want to be part of a winning team. Executives and managers need to be the leaders the company needs and the employees want.

Art's Gold: Fixing the fundamentals takes perseverance and the tenacity to dig in before moving on to the next challenge.

I've seen individuals who get sucked into a minutia quagmire, and they are unable to find their way out. They don't complete a project before moving to the next one.

The amateurs look for the silver bullet or a big shiny toy to solve all their woes. When data and inventory inaccuracies go unresolved in today's environment, a new ERP will only become an expensive trophy with negative return on investment (ROI) for the effort.

Art's Gold: Amateurs look for the silver bullet or a big shiny toy to solve all their woes.

The world of SCM is fast-paced and unforgiving. Many issues can't wait until the next day. To break the failure spiral, leaders need to lead by contact and participation, physically working with team members to resolve problems. They need to create a process of rapid communication and problem resolution to increase urgency. Great leaders stop and take the time required to fix problems immediately that achieve wins for the team.

Buddy Check: Questions From Coach Art

- Are you successful in using visual daily management to achieve rapid improvements, build employee engagement, communication, and cultivate teamwork?
- Do you manage variability and complexity effectively?
- Are the incidents of surprise parts issues decreasing?
- Is the team better at reactive firefighting or proactive problem resolution?
- Does the organization struggle with one or more sites' poor performance, draining resources and negatively impacting overall enterprise profits?
- Is the organization looking for a silver bullet solution to fix its legacy problems?

Art's Deep Dive

As you will see, Art Koch's Profit Chain and the three Fs of SCM support the board's responsibility of increasing shareholder value through increasing inventory velocity and leveraging the supply chain as a strategic competitive advantage to improve financial performance.

It's the coupling of processes, people, and organizations that create success.

For additional information and free tools, please scan the code.

CHAPTER 4

Swift Yet Meticulous: Rapid Assessment of Your Supply Chain

In scuba diving, mastering buoyancy isn't just a skill; it's a quick but crucial assessment of your capabilities, surroundings, and equipment—a process that ensures your safety and enhances your underwater experience. Likewise, in supply chain management (SCM), the ability to rapidly assess your operations, from procurement to distribution, is not an optional expertise but a necessity. This capability enables you to identify bottlenecks, optimize resources, and strategize effectively, all contributing to a more resilient and profitable supply chain.

> Excellent buoyancy control is what defines skilled scuba divers. You've seen them underwater. They glide effortlessly, use less air and ascend, descend or hover almost as if by thought. They more easily observe aquatic life without disturbing their surroundings.[1]

When I was a new diver, seeing a stingray, turtle, or something for the first time, or when I stopped swimming to observe my surroundings, my buoyancy was all over the place. Since breathing controls most of your buoyancy, when seeing something new, you get excited, and your breathing changes, causing you to go up and down in the water. Most instructors like to add a "couple" of extra pounds to a new diver's weight belt because of the buoyancy issue. It helps to keep the diver from bouncing up and down in the water.

This bouncing up and down is the same type of behavior happening in organizations that don't have control of their processes. Their lack of control sends them running all over the place, trying to put out fires, often not knowing which way is up, resembling a poor buoyancy problem in the water.

Over the years, I have developed considerable experience in helping clients assess their supply chain baseline quickly. To accomplish this goal, I've created the supply chain foundation rapid assessment, adapted from a 2002 Harvard Business Review article by Eugene Goodson, titled "Read a Plant—Fast."[2] Using the assessment results, we can determine a benchmark for the company's supply chain processes and then develop a necessary improvement plan.

Supply Chain Foundation Rapid Assessment

The supply chain foundation rapid assessment is quick, accurate, repeatable, and defensible. After all, the client is an active participant in the process.

The assessment process allows the client to slow down and evaluate their operations to benchmark them against easy-to-follow scoring guidelines. The assessment rates 10 key fundamental categories in just one to two hours, including developing an action plan to make necessary improvements.

The areas outlined in Figure 4.1 follow the three "Fs" of SCM: people and process foundation, structural foundation, and financial focal point. I recommend following the physical process and starting with the people and process foundation: Stores—5S, then finishing with sustainability: commitment to quality.

Art's Gold: Don't get caught in analysis paralysis, waiting to plan until you have 100 percent of the data. Achieve forward progress.

The supply chain foundation rapid assessment is like the weight check for a diver's buoyancy status. Either you're too heavy or light. It is a benchmark for the buoyancy weight checks of the operational supply chain

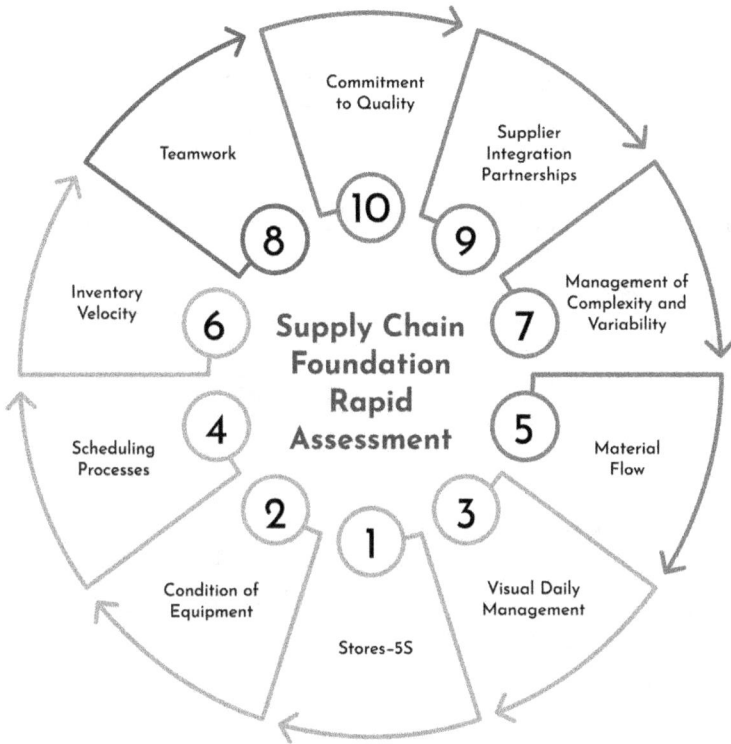

Figure 4.1 Supply chain foundation rapid assessment

practices, processes, and the team's readiness to support current business transformation initiatives.

There are three to seven questions in each of the 10 categories, and the scores shown are the average for each category. Figure 4.2 is an example of the people and process foundation assessment form.

Below are the scoring guidelines that are easy to follow, quick to evaluate, and none subjective.

Scoring guidelines are as follows:

- Not found = 0
- Only found in some locations (25 percent) = 1
- Commonly found, but not in a majority (50 percent) = 4
- Very typical (75 percent), with some exceptions = 7
- Found everywhere (100 percent) = 10

	0	=	Not found
Plant: ACME Enterprises	1	=	Only found in some (25%) locations
Tour date: April, 28, 2022	4	=	Commonly found (50%), but not in
Rated by: A. Koch	7	=	Very typical (75%), with some exceptions
	10	=	Found everywhere (100%)

Categories	(0)	(1)	(4)	(7)	(10)	Total Points	Possible Points	%	Weight	Category Score
People and Process Foundation										
Stores - 5S (Materials Controls and Management 1. Store/Supermarket/Cleanliness and order - 5S						39	90	43.4%	15.00	6.5
Condition of Equipment 9Materials Control and Management) 2. Condition and maintenance of equipment and tools: Ford Trucks/Pallet Jacks/Tuggers/Carts, Trailers						42	90	46.7%	10.00	4.7
3. SCM/Materials - Visual Management System						35	90	38.9%	10.00	3.9
Scheduling Process (Planning Fundamentals) 4. Exception Based Planning and Established Pull Scheduling Process						15	30	50.0%	5.00	2.5
Material Flow 5. Material only advances with a Kanban or FIFO lanes						20	50	40.0%	10.00	4.0
Structural Framework										
Inventory Velocity 6. Levels of inventory and work in progress						33	60	55.0%	10.00	5.5
Management of Complexity and Rationalization 7. Management of complexity and variability						21	30	70.0%	5.00	3.5
Team Work (Team Skills and Core Competencies) 8. Teamwork and motivation - SCM/ Materials Integration with Operations						27	70	38.6%	15.00	5.8
Supplier Integration and Partnerships 9. Supply chain integration						22	40	55.0%	5.00	2.8
Financial Focal Point										
Commitment to Quality (Sustainability) 10.Commitment to quality						29	80	36.3%	15.00	5.4

Figure 4.2 Supply chain foundation rapid assessment sheet

As earlier stated, I always complete the assessment with the client. Because of the simplicity of questions and nonsubjective scoring guidelines, the client's "blind spots" with their current problems or opportunities quickly disappear. When clients are physically able to walk through the processes as a team and rate themselves, they challenge one another, are typically harder on themselves, and there is no debating the results.

Buoyancy: It's All About Knowing if You Need to Lose or Add Weight

As a diver, adjusting your weight for peak buoyancy isn't a one-time correction. Neither is the improvement of business processes; it's ongoing. It's essential to keep your dive gear simple with as little variation as possible, and it is the same for business process improvements. Simplicity wins the game.

My experience has shown that a simple radar chart for benchmarking makes it visually easy for individuals to understand the process and identify opportunities for improvement. Using the radar chart as the model, the sequential steps are:

1. Conceptualize the current state baseline—actual (red line).
2. Determine the top two or three priority areas (and no more, or the lack of focus will stall results).
3. Brainstorm plans to improve the top two or three priorities.
4. Discuss what success would look like when you achieve your priorities.
5. Establish the targeted goals based on your analysis and discussions from above.
6. Develop a plan to move the priority areas from the baseline to the targeted levels.

You know you've completed this important planning task when the radar chart shows where you are now, where you want to go, and your team has discussed a plan on how to get there.

It's all about getting the client's attention by creating a decisive moment to lead people forward. The radar chart has worked wonders for me in getting clients focused on potential opportunities. Once you have their attention, securing the team's commitment to making positive changes is much easier to achieve.

In this example, Figure 4.3, the red graph line is a baseline for the current process conditions. The blue line is the team goal for improvement, and the green line is the new score, 36 months later, after implementing corrective actions.

SCM Rapid Assessment Results—Current State

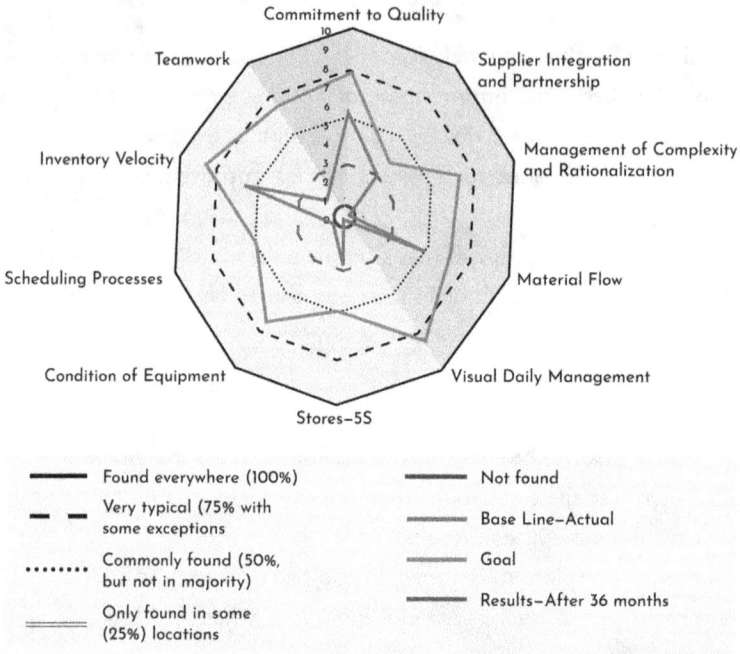

Legend:

- Found everywhere (100%)
- Very typical (75% with some exceptions
- Commonly found (50%, but not in majority)
- Only found in some (25%) locations
- Not found
- Base Line—Actual
- Goal
- Results—After 36 months

SCM Rapid Assessment Results—After 36 Months

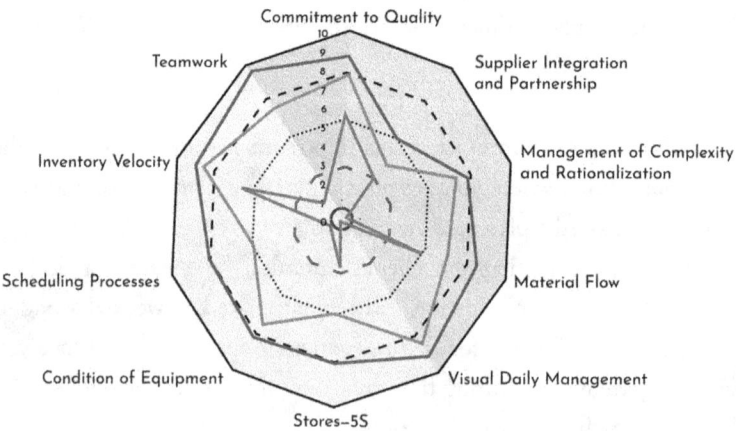

Figure 4.3 Supply chain rapid assessment current versus 18-month results later results

After completing the assessment, the natural tendency is to dive in and try to fix everything all at once. Don't do this! It leads to paralysis.

The key to sustainable success is to tackle a few priority areas and do them well. Ensure you have addressed the root cause of the problem and established sustainable processes before moving on to the next area requiring change or improvement.

Dive Master Briefing (Client Example—Food Products Manufacturer)

The client was a $26 billion international corporation that manufactured food products. The facility I was consulting with had annual sales of $225 million per year. Once the corporate flagship, the facility had become undermanaged and underfunded due to competing resources for international site expansion (where the goal was to manufacture products closer to customers). The supply chain and operations teams had lost their "true north," and it was negatively impacting the organization. As a result, this site had the lowest production efficiency, the highest scrap within the corporation, and they were losing an average of $500,000 per month.

As a team, Sharon—plant manager, Georgia—operations manager, and James—maintenance manager completed the supply chain rapid assessment and discovered seven significant deficiencies:

1. **Store 5S:** Stockrooms and supermarkets lacked leadership and engagement skills. Worksites were cluttered and disorganized, open boxes were strewn everywhere, and parts were not properly put away. The team did not understand the importance of an adequately staffed stock room for service parts or the importance of having the right leadership for long-term success. *Score 2.2/10.*

2. **Teamwork:** Several supervisory changes had taken place, and the current supervisors lacked the essential knowledge and education to lead the team. Much of the training the supervisors had received was inadequate, negatively impacting the organization. Their frustration spilled over to their direct reports, which created workforce tension and division within the ranks. The facility needed to have a dedicated process and area for education and training. *Score 0.8/10*

3. **Management of Complexity and Variability:** Due to the facility's age, unused old service parts needed to be scrapped, sold, or shipped to another location. Additionally, the ERP system needed significant

cleansing and purging of outdated data to improve data accuracy. *Score 0.5/10*

4. **Condition of Equipment:** Team members were scattered through-out the building because past managers lacked the understanding of proper workspaces for the pipefitters, electricians, and heating, ventilating, and air-conditioning (HVAC.) These maintenance indi-viduals set up independent work areas that were not colocated and inadequate for the type of work to be completed, causing chaos. *Score 1.1/10*

5. **Visual Daily Management:** None present. *Score 0.0/10*

6. **Supplier Integration:** Several suppliers were doing vendor-managed inventory (VMI) programs. After thoroughly reviewing the process, we concluded that the client's inaccurate data in the ERP system caused most of the supplier issues. *Score 2.5/10*

7. **Scheduling Processes:** The scheduling of planned maintenance activities with supply chain and operations was hit or miss, resulting in frustration among all departments and machinery downtime lon-ger than necessary. *Score 0.9/10*

Seven of the 10 rapid assessment areas had unsatisfactory (<5/10) results. The natural tendency was to fix all areas simultaneously.

Rather than trying to solve everything at once, we focused on four areas that needed the most significant improvements and quickly applied implementable solutions.

Step One—Teamwork and Visual Management: Georgia and James cleared a large office area and created daily visual management processes using safety, quality, delivery, inventory, and productivity (SQDIP) methodology: safety, quality, delivery, inventory, and produc-tion, as illustrated in Figure 4.4. Then, Sharon set up six 15-minute meetings at the beginning and end of each shift to communicate the current day's production activities and maintenance project's status. This daily communication pulled the group together as a team and eliminated an "us vs. them" mindset.

Step Two—Management of Complexity and Variability: The com-pany had lost the effective application of their ERP system due to multiple changes in leadership with managers and supervisors. With the fundamen-tals of maintaining data integrity absent, this caused inventory to increase.

	Calendar or Fiscal Month	J F M A M J / J A S O N D	Value Stream: BR 54-9

Safety	Quality	Delivery	Inventory	Productivity
1 2 3 4 5 6	1 2 3 4 5 6	1 2 3 4 5 6	1 2 3 4 5 6	1 2 3 4 5 6
7 8 10 11 12 13	7 8 10 12 13	7 8 12 13	7 8 9 10 11 12 13	7 8 10 11 12 13
14 15 16 19 20	14 16 17 18 19 20	14 15 16 17 18 19 20	14 15 16 17 18 19 20	14 15 16 17 18 19 20
21 22 23 24 26 27	21 22 26 27	21 22 24 25 26 27	21 22 23 24 25 26 27	21 22 24 25 26 27
28 29 30 31	28 29 30 31	28 29 30 31	28 29 30 31	28 29 30 31
KPI Legend	**Goal**	**Goal**	**Goal**	**Goal**
Achieved Goal	100% 1st Step Inspection	Meeting Master Production Schedule	Zero Part Shortages for Current Production Schedules	Meeting TAKT Time
Missed Goal	100% First Pass Yield	100% on-time to next internal customer		
✖ Not in Current Month/Observed Holiday	Internal PPM < 25			< 15 Minutes total Down Time
Counter Measure Legend	◯ 0% No Progress ◑ 25% Under investigation	◑ 50% Identified Counter Measure	◕ 75% Counter Measure Implemented	● 100% Counter Measure Completed

Figure 4.4 SQDIP key performance indicators

At the same time, part shortages were growing significantly. Georgia, James, and their team members implemented my Entropy Busters® methodology to clean up the ERP database for open purchase orders, purchase requisitions, and work orders and set new safety stock parameters.

Step Three—Scheduling Processes and Visual Daily Management: There was little to no communication between the production and maintenance departments. Production was reluctant to schedule maintenance work because they were usually behind schedule or over budget due to lost productivity associated with machine downtime. When the maintenance department started preventive maintenance on schedule, the project took two to three times longer due to needed parts that were lost or not ordered. Also, the inability to repair or rebuild the equipment and the outside repair technician's unavailability compounded the problem. Georgia and James implemented the following corrective actions to counter the aforementioned deficiencies:

1. The maintenance planners cleaned up the ERP data and processing integrity using the Entropy Busters methodology and visual daily management to track their progress.

2. Locked in maintenance schedules four to nine months ahead of time and used a visual scheduling board to track kitting parts on hand, ordering and tracking special-order purchase parts, noting vital team members' vacations, and listing outside technical resources needed.

3. Identified gaps in organizational design and developed a corrective action plan to fill the gaps.

4. Sharon brought in an outside expert from SAP and initiated critical machinery training and ERP education to increase skills.

Step Four—Condition of Equipment: The teamwork areas were an absolute disgrace. Sharon led by example. With Georgia and James's help, they 5S'ed the area (Figure 3.1), scrubbed the floor, cleared away junk, installed proper lighting, and located the necessary tools for team members to complete their work. The team responded immediately to better working conditions with increased sharing of issues and improved teamwork. Plans were developed with the team members' input addressing long-term workspace conditions, inadequate workspaces and training stations, and creating a service manual library.

Results

- Reduced recordable safety incidents by 95 percent.
- Reduced surprise machine downtime by increased daily communication.
- Achieved a cost-saving of $375,000 per year by reducing emergency expenses due to surprise equipment downtime.
- Reduced maintenance and supply expenses by $250,000 per year by working less overtime.
- With better inventory replenishment parameters and practices, we reduced store's inventory by one million dollars and generated annualized savings of $350,000 per year.
- A more effective maintenance department improved plant efficiency by two percentage points, an ROI of $500,000 per year.
- By canceling purchase orders, purchase requisitions, and work orders for unnecessary parts and aged-out tasks, the maintenance team avoided four million dollars in purchases.

- Maintenance, supply chain, and operations organizations felt that they were now part of the solution rather than being victims of daily fire drills.
- The facility's team no longer felt the humiliation of being the lowest-performing facility.
- Overall, the associates became more engaged and much less combative.
- Total financial benefits were $1,475,000 per year, and increased business valuation conservatively by $7,375,000 using a five-times earnings multiple.

Client Comments About This Case Study

Knute Hankins, plant manager, reflected:

In two major internal operations endeavors across different companies, Art assessed positive systems and areas for improvement. His direct approach delivers unfiltered truths with leadership, all while prioritizing a people-first approach to build trust, credibility, and compassion among team members.

Dive Log 4 (Art's Commentary)

When used correctly, the supply chain rapid assessment encourages the team to quickly and easily take stock of what is happening around them. When they assess their situation, they will take responsibility for their situation and focus on what they can control.

When the results are unfavorable, the radar figure's visceral response creates a knot in the gut and will unite the team to focus on a common enemy. The questions are purposely designed to highlight gaps in the foundation and framework, as teams tend to want to run before they can walk or even crawl. It helps to keep solutions simple, grounded, and root cause-oriented.

Buddy Check: Questions From Coach Art

- Do you or the team bounce from one short-term priority or crisis to the next?

- Are there "blind spots" to the current opportunities?
- Is there a clear benchmark of the supply chain process with a plan to address deficiencies?

Art's Deep Dive

It's easier to let daily firefighting and deflection of responsibility become the normal operating mode. Leaders understand that the path to success can be a difficult road paved with many obstacles. However, the rewards of success are boundless.

CHAPTER 5

~~Inventory Is Your Security Blanket.~~ Inventory Is Evil!

Picture yourself decked out in the latest scuba gear, from state-of-the-art knives to an array of safety signaling devices—mirrors, air horns, safety sausages, reels, you name it. While some of these tools are vital, an overburdened buoyancy control device (BCD) creates unnecessary drag, reducing your efficiency and expediting your air tank's depletion as seen in Figure 5.1. The goal of diving isn't to carry the oceanic version of a Swiss Army knife; it's to immerse yourself in the underwater world as efficiently and enjoyably as possible.

In a strikingly similar fashion, an overstocked inventory acts like a boat anchor to your business—weighing you down and slowing your responsiveness. The clutter of excess inventory not only curtails your operational agility but also consumes valuable resources for its maintenance. Just as a diver must carefully choose gear based on specific dive conditions, businesses must ascertain the optimal level of inventory to meet market demands without hampering performance.

We need to practice lean methodologies to efficiently navigate the current business environment.

Dive Log 5-A (Art's Commentary)

At this point in my career, I'm very proud that my accomplishments include reducing inventory by more than $250 million, an average project improvement of 28.3 percent. Simultaneously, clients have increased their customer service by an excellent average of 18.5 percent. Most people don't think this is possible, but it truly is.

Art's Gold: Too much inventory causes poor customer service and increases the total cost of ownership, driving down profits.

"I think it's time to reduce the amount of gadgets you use."

Figure 5.1 Too many gadgets

How are inventory reduction and an increase in customer service accomplished? Both are accomplished by following the processes and methodologies of this book.

Most methods are intuitive, and some are counter-intuitive.

The concept that inventory is evil is counter-intuitive.

These aren't abstract theories; all these methodologies have worked for my clients to reduce inventory while simultaneously improving customer service and profitability.

Please keep an open mind, enjoy the journey to streamlining your supply chain processes, and it's perfectly fine to seek assistance from outside experts with any questions.

Why Do We Care About Inventory?

Inventory is the lifeblood of many organizations. Without inventory, you would have a hard time satisfying customer demand. Inventory also has several essential functions and objectives. It functions as a buffer for anticipated and fluctuation of customer demand. Also, lot and batch sizes are necessary for certain physical operations like heat-treating or plating. And inventory is required when transporting the product to customers. Finally, inventory can act as a hedge against currency changes and inflation.

At the same time, inventory objectives align with overall business objectives, including the best customer service and low-cost operations with minimal inventory investment.

We care about inventory because inventory costs money.

But all is not good with inventory. Inventory, unintentionally, also hides problems Figure 5.2.

Inventory hides: inefficiencies, poor planning, poor organization, and poor execution. I would hope that everyone would agree with this fact. However, I know it's not the case.

Clients will frequently ask me to work with their teams to dispel the myth that inventory is their security blanket.

Let's take a moment to discuss why inventory isn't our security blanket. In today's highly competitive market environment, we are playing to win! Customers demand high-quality, innovative products, responsive service, and competitive prices.

Many organizations still believe that high inventory is necessary for businesses to achieve excellent customer service, broad product offerings, responsiveness, high manufacturing efficiencies, and low total cost of ownership (TCO).

We are talking about TCO here because it fits in the context of the security blanket. We will discuss TCO in full detail in the next chapter. Again, it's still a common belief that to provide a high level of service, all segments of inventory must be increased and that the following myths are given for excellent service:

- High finished goods inventory.
- High work in process inventory.
- High raw material inventory.
- Many warehouses and distribution centers.
- Full truck, rail car, and sea container loads.

The same organizations also believe more myths such as land is cheap, machines should have full utilization, and all purchases should be at the lowest piece price.

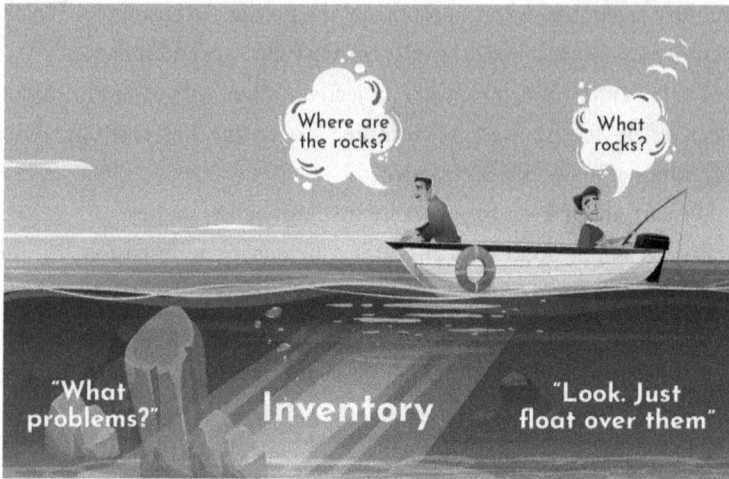

Figure 5.2 Inventory floating over rocks

They falsely believe that the chosen transportation mode should be the lowest cost factor and that there should be ubiquitous product offerings. They believe maintaining higher inventory levels allows them to "float" over problems and creates a false sense of security that customer service will be excellent and profits will be limitless.

These myths and beliefs, hard-wired into many organizations and leadership teams, are all wrong.

I talk with leaders who believe that nothing is wrong with their business model or inventory beliefs. They feel their models just need to be executed properly to be profitable.

It is just like saying the weight loss diet failed due to incorrect implementation. In reality, it was the lifestyle transformation and behavior change that failed.

The error in thinking is their emphasis on individual cost center optimization. I repeat: individual cost center optimization is a misguided management concept that hurts overall business performance. This mindset leads to siloed decisions, with little regard for inventory levels, resulting in higher TCO for the entire organization.

Divisional accounting makes these problems even harder to find.

My passion is to help clients and executive leadership reshape their understanding of TCO, which, in turn, transforms their supply chain and operational strategy from a cost center into a profit chain. In my experience, many client's assumptions are often misguided when assessing the TCO.

TCO includes all the direct and indirect costs associated with an asset or acquisition over the product or service's entire life cycle. These attributes include the purchase piece price and the cost of transportation, handling and storage, damage and shrinkage, obsolescence, spoilage, taxes, insurance, labor, and redistribution costs.

Why do we care about inventory?

Look at these inventory principles, which are based on decades of results.

- Inventory costs money and lowers profits.
- Inventory consumes needed capacity.
- Inventory negatively affects service.
- Inventory hides problems.
- Inventory delays fixing problems.

Inventory left unchecked has many negative and unintended consequences on profitability Figure 5.3.

Inventory hides problems. Therefore, it delays or prevents fixing problems.

Why Inventory Is Evil

There are several myths about inventory. These falsehoods keep organizations from achieving greater financial success.

Myth #1: Fixed inventory levels. Leaders make the mistake of believing that inventory levels are fixed and that the current level is essential to support their customers. High inventory levels reduce customer service. Solution: We need to become disruptors by blowing up the existing inventory paradigms and belief systems. We need the right amount of inventory, based on professional analysis and planning.

Myth #2: Inventory is an appreciating asset. A common misconception is to think of inventory as an investment similar to capital equipment or factories. It's correct to think of inventory as an asset. However, inventory does not increase in value over time, like the stock market (on a good day) or hard real estate investments (over the long term, hopefully).

Inventory decreases in value over time due to damage, theft, shrinkage, obsolescence, and spoilage. When inventory sits motionless in a stockroom or warehouse, it is negative value-added. Solution: Understand that inventory is a rapidly depreciating asset.

Myth #3: Low inventory equals poor service. Leadership believes this myth to be true because of a lack of root-cause corrective actions, and the team does not have the proper skills to complete a plan for every part (PFEP). Then, when management mandates an inventory reduction and cuts it across the board, customer service suffers. Solution: Develop a PFEP to identify optimal inventory levels.

Myth #4: Excellent service equals fast delivery. Suppliers or manufacturing can't be fast today and late tomorrow. Customers want predictability, especially when it comes to running logistics networks and manufacturing. As variability increases, so does TCO. Solution: Excellent services mean predictable and reliable delivery, not fast delivery.

Art's Gold: Excellent services mean predictable and reliable delivery, not fast delivery.

Myth #5: Many stocked locations equal excellent service. It's common for organizations to want to cover the "map" with inventory stocked nearly everywhere or to fill their warehouses (WH) and distribution centers (DC) to 99 percent capacity to minimize costs. However, too much inventory also causes warehouses and distribution centers to overflow, compromising their ability to find items and diminishing efficiencies. Solution: Less is more; reduce inventory levels to what is needed.

Get the Facts About Inventory

Here are the facts about inventory.

Fact #1: Minimal inventory system designs are more responsive to customer needs. A well-executed PFEP followed by a root-cause

Figure 5.3 Inventory increase, so does the total cost of ownership

problem resolution will help improve inventory performance by establishing a consistent plan for each part number when aligned with management objectives. Having the appropriate part number, quantity, and stocking location plan will enable your inventory systems design to be more flexible and responsive to customer needs.

Fact #2: Reliability. Reliable and predictable customer delivery dates and times are more valued than the speed of delivery. Remember, as variability increases, so do complexity and supply chain costs. Expediting, premium freight, and safety stock are some of the expenses incurred when reliability is not satisfactory, hence increasing the TCO.

Fact #3: Inventory hides substandard internal operational performance. Everything from insufficient supply and demand planning, inventory accuracy, and weak data integrity to manufacturing first-pass yield and operator cross-training requires additional inventory to hide poor performance. Additionally, poor operational performance can rob capacity by building too much of product "B" for forecasted demand or safety stock while customers are waiting on product "A."

First-pass yield is the number of defect-free, requiring no rework, parts produced from a process divided by the number of units going into that process over a specified period.

Fact #4: Inventory conceals poor supplier delivery and quality performance. Poor operational performance, such as low first-pass yield, inadequate scheduling, or high absenteeism, requires additional inventory to hide the problems.

What to do? Excellence, reliability of service, and lower costs go hand in hand. Combining these factors with the service equation: short-cycle times, flexible manufacturing, responsive suppliers, and clear communications enables the company to have low inventory and higher-standard customer service and loyalty.

The objective is to get organizations to understand the importance of reducing inventory by producing the correct amount of the right products at the right time.

This takes hard and important work of thinking and planning.

Art's Gold: Avoid the easy work of buying too much inventory.

A trait of world-class organizations is high inventory velocity. Increasing inventory performance correlates with higher customer service and lower TCO. These same world-class corporations consider service improvements, inventory improvements, and cost reduction to be mutually supportive of each other.

When we think of world-class corporations, Amazon and Apple are at the top of many people's lists.

Both have exceptional customer service and excellent inventory velocity, 11 and 20 turns per year, respectively. Remember that these inventory turns are averages and that analyzing specific product turns is more important to improving the averages.

Breaking Paradigms

So why aren't other corporations achieving similar performance? What are some of the barriers? From my experience, it starts with the misunderstanding of inventory carrying cost.

How is inventory carrying cost determined? Ask your chief financial officer, "what is the number to use for carrying cost of inventory for capital approval or budgeting of annualized savings?"

It is an important question!

Most of you will get an answer somewhere around "Prime +1," which is the lower range of the incremental cost of borrowing capital and not close to the carrying cost of inventory.

Art's Gold: The total cost of carrying inventory is much higher than the cost of capital.

We discover a more revealing definition of inventory carrying cost after thorough research.

Inventory Carrying Cost

One of the elements comprises a company's total supply chain management costs.

Inventory carrying costs consist of the following:

- **Opportunity Cost:** The opportunity cost of holding inventory should be based on your company's capital cost standards using the following formula:
    - Calculation: Cost of Capital × Average Net Value of Inventory
- **Shrinkage:** Shrinkage is the cost associated with breakage, pilferage, and deterioration of inventories. It usually pertains to the loss of material through handling damage, theft, or neglect.
- **Insurance and Taxes:** The cost of insuring inventories and taxes associated with holding inventory.
- **Total Obsolescence for Raw Material, Work in Process, and Finished Goods Inventory:** Inventory reserves are taken due to obsolescence and scrap, including products exceeding shelf life, that is, spoilage and products that can no longer be used for their original purpose.

Channel Obsolescence

Aging allowances paid to channel partners and provisions for buy-back agreements include all material that becomes obsolete while in a distribution channel. Usually, a distributor will demand a refund on material that goes bad (shelf life) or is no longer needed because customer needs have changed.

Field Service Parts Obsolescence

Reserves taken due to obsolescence and scrap. Field service parts are those inventories kept at locations outside the manufacturing plant walls, in a distribution center or warehouse.

Source: Council of Supply Chain Management Professionals (CSCMP)[1]

Let's break down inventory carrying cost into four categories, Figure 5.4:

1. **Capital costs**—Money tied up in inventory.
2. **Storage costs**—Warehouse space, personnel, insurance, and equipment.
3. **Opportunity costs**—What could you do with the cash?
4. **Risk costs**—Obsolescence, damage, pilferage, and deterioration.

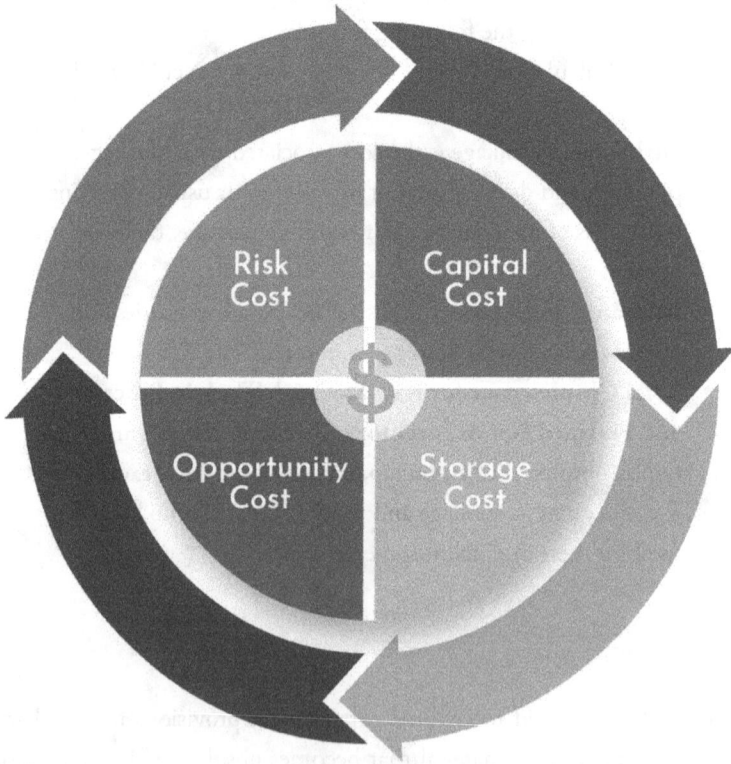

Figure 5.4 Inventory carrying cost categories

The four categories are straightforward. Now let's break this down into incremental costs.

As you can see in Figure 5.5, below, these values are very reasonable percentages for each area. We have quickly surpassed prime +1. Inventory incremental cost of somewhere between 30 and 60 percent is very logical. When considering carrying inventory, we must also understand the consequences of not having inventory.

It's essential to balance the costs of carrying inventory versus the costs of not having inventory. Not carrying inventory effects:

- Customer service—the cost of lost sales (but too much inventory also reduces customer service, so it's important to strike a critical balance here).
- Production/Manufacturing changeovers—the cost of machine changeovers, especially when you overproduce one product while another product is in short supply.
- Placing orders—the cost of placing and administering purchase or work orders.

	Low	High
Interest (Prime +1% - Finance)	3%	10%
Opportunity (What could you do with the cash?)	10%	15%
Handling (How many people, full time equivalents?)	3%	5%
Space (Square footage)	1%	3%
Damage (Scrap)	1%	2%
Shrinkage (Reserves, write-off, and obsolete product)	1%	2%
Taxes (Personal property)	1%	2%
Insurance	1%	2%
Transactions (Counting, moving, retrieving, issuing, reconciling)	5%	10%
General & Admin. Staff (Managers, planning, physical mgmt.)	5%	7%
Total Incremental Cost of Inventory	31%	58%

Figure 5.5 Incremental cost of inventory as a percent

The sum of the costs of carrying inventory and not having inventory should be as low as possible. We are in the business of providing goods and services to customers while simultaneously returning profits to shareholders. Balancing inventory is key to generating positive customer service and profits.

Remember when I asked you to walk down the hall and ask the CFO about the cost of carrying inventory? What number did you get? Most, if not all of you, were told something around "Prime plus one."

So why are CEO, CFO, and COOs not taking the larger picture into account? It's because they are only looking at the incremental cost. But why?

1. Because most inventory is added or taken away incrementally.
2. Additionally, there is a knowledge gap across critical disciplines of accounting, finance, operations, and supply chain management who default toward cost center optimization and not the TCO. It is such an essential point because only considering one-quarter to one-third of the cost significantly changes our inventory velocity improvement decisions.

Think about how different your solutions and decisions would be if you considered an inventory carrying cost of 30 to 60 percent of inventory book value or more.

Using the correct inventory carry cost will result in:

- Fewer vendors and more supplier partnerships focused on the lowest TCO, not just the lowest price. That's how I define Art Koch's Profit Chain˚: Better suppliers provide less variability, more predictability, and higher quality. How would this improve your manufacturing? It leads to greater responsiveness and flexibility and shorter lead times.
- Increased professionalism within the supply chain team.
- Smaller and more frequent deliveries from suppliers and to customers.
- Swifter and more accurate receiving and shipping.
- Better trained material control team members.

- High inventory velocity through facilities requires fewer cycle counters. (Think about this one.)
- Smaller and more focused distribution centers.
- Frees up significant floor space and transforms the space into value-added production.

Dive Master Briefing (Client Example)

Some years ago, a client struggled with the management and obsolescence costs associated with the last 1 percent of purchases. The company was experiencing excessive stock outages and significant obsolescence write-offs. Working with the company's financial team, Elaine and Clark were skeptical of my inventory-carrying cost methodology. I challenged them to calculate their inventory carrying cost for the last 1 percent of purchases. In just 45 minutes, they had hard proof of $0.71 of cost for every $1 spent or 71 percent of $1,000,000 per year. This realization significantly shifted their frame of focus to potential solutions. We were able to fast-track the approval and implementation of third-party logistic providers (3PL) for their commercial purchases, resulting in a hard savings of $3.1 million dollars per year.

I'm confident that when breaking the incremental paradigm, the actual inventory carrying cost will be closer to one dollar for one dollar of inventory. That's 100 percent. That's a lot more than prime +1.

Client Testimonial

I, as an Operations Director in a new role, first met Art when tackling On-Time Delivery issues. While the management team relied on intuition, Art guided us to use data to identify the root cause. Under his guidance, we implemented a Plan for Every Part (PFEP) methodology, addressing inventory levels for supplied and internally made components. Contrary to assumptions, the issue wasn't lack of inventory but having the right one. Art's method, making us delve deep, was pivotal, leading to a shift in our thinking. Annualized savings exceeded $5 million.

—David Hilditch—Vice President of Operations for $2 Billion Industrial Manufacturing Corporation.

My Friends, This Is Why Inventory Is Evil!

Inventory left unchecked has many negative and unintended consequences on customer service, profitability, and valuation.

Buddy Check: Questions From Coach Art

- Does your organization think of inventory as a security
  blanket?
- Does the organization only consider incremental inventory
  carrying costs when making financial decisions?
- Who is responsible for inventory performance? SCM or the
  entire organization?
- Do inventory levels increase over time after reduction
  initiatives?

Art's Deep Dive

As inventory increases, costs increase faster than most organizations can
respond, often resulting in ineffective task forces working to reduce excess
inventory. The task forces typically have short-term success in inventory
reduction. Often, quickly assembled task forces don't dive deep enough
into the "whys" of excess inventory, shortcut complete root-cause analysis, or don't have the authority and managerial support to properly implement the necessary solutions for long-term success.

For additional information and free tools, please scan the code.

CHAPTER 6

Art Koch's Profit Chain®— Beyond the Surface: The Total Cost of Ownership

Imagine the intricate costs of scuba diving—it's not merely the upfront investment in high-quality equipment or the boat trip that takes you to your underwater destination. The equation is far more nuanced. To fully and safely savor the scuba experience, you must factor in continual training, regular equipment upkeep, and even lifestyle choices that maintain your fitness. The adventurous among us might also add international travel, lodging, and specialized insurance to the tally. This cumulative financial commitment paints a comprehensive picture—the total cost of ownership (TCO) for your diving pursuits. Interestingly, while we may diligently calculate these expenses for our personal hobbies, this crucial concept often gets sidelined or underestimated in the business landscape.

That's why I created a methodology called Art Koch's Profit Chain; to highlight the significance of TCO and educate how to use the supply chain as a competitive differentiator.

TCO includes all the direct and indirect costs associated with an asset or acquisition over the product or service's entire life cycle. We covered TCO in detail in the previous chapter. TCO consists of the purchase price and the cost of transportation, handling and storage, damage and shrinkage, taxes and insurance, and redistribution costs as seen in Figure 6.1.

During my years in SCM, I've observed that most organizations make procurement and sourcing decisions based solely on the purchase price and not on TCO. This is shortsighted and inaccurate. It leads to bad purchase decisions, poor inventory management, and weaker financial performance.

Art Koch's Profit Chain®
Total Cost of Ownership Model

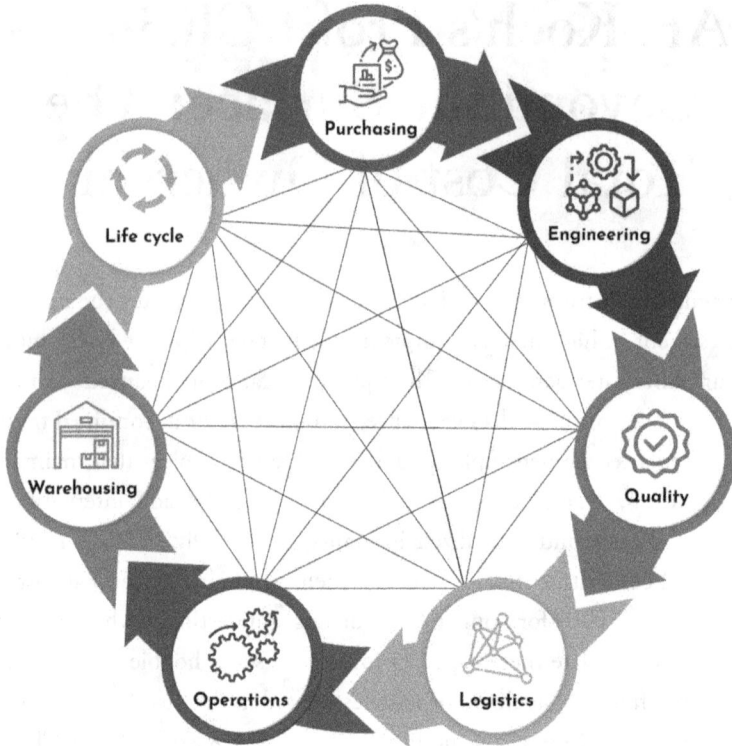

Figure 6.1 Total cost of ownership model

The top 10 percent of the iceberg, which we can see, shows the only costs traditionally used to make TCO decisions. The iceberg illustration, Figure 6.2, highlights the fundamental differences between professional and amateur leaders.

Professionals build their models to include *all* costs.

Leaders should use the TCO to make better more informed decisions. Few, if any, use a TCO calculation or model that determines an accurate TCO. When using a model, the numbers are usually off by at least 25 to 40 percent because they underestimate the hidden cost of carrying inventory and the hidden cost of purchasing offshore.

Additionally, many organizations have only used incremental inventory carrying cost of prime +1 percent when assessing make versus buy

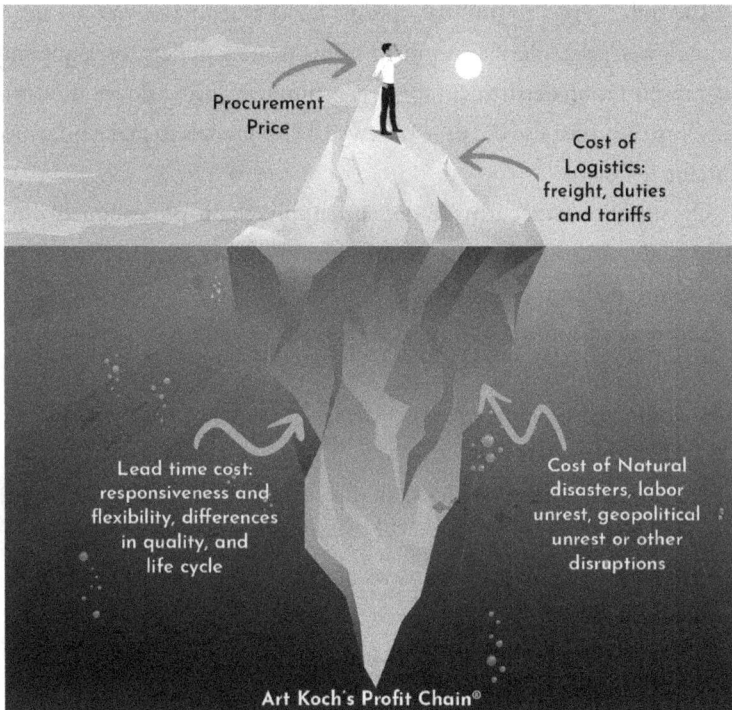

Procurement
Price

Cost of
Logistics:
freight, duties
and tariffs

Lead time cost:
responsiveness and
flexibility, differences
in quality, and
life cycle

Cost of Natural
disasters, labor
unrest, geopolitical
unrest or other
disruptions

Art Koch's Profit Chain®

Figure 6.2 Total cost of ownership iceberg

decisions. Throughout my career, I've calculated the actual inventory carrying cost to be between 31 and 58 percent, depending on the industry, of the cost of goods sold (COGS) when considering all costs. These numbers are the precise cost metrics to use when determining the internal rate of return (IRR) for long-term inventory carrying cost when calculating the TCO. Refer to Figure 5.5, The incremental cost of inventory.

Breaking the Cycle

It's time to break the cycle of being misguided by antiquated costing and incorrect performance indicators. It's no longer a matter of paying the lowest price for goods purchased from a supplier. That's an amateur move.

We can no longer assume the relevance or accuracy of accounting assumptions and costing models from the 1960s and 1970s when attempting to strategically reduce today's TCO.

The only "levers to pull" or options for cost reduction are *not* negotiating lower prices, longer payment terms from suppliers, or requesting the transportation department for larger shipments using slower modes of transport. We must use the peer-reviewed TCO models to make informed sourcing decisions.

Organization's executive leaders or supply chain professionals often vastly underestimate the cost of carrying inventory and the impact of significantly reduced lead times.

Shorter lead times result in:

- Improved responsiveness and flexibility to customer demand and design changes.
- Diminished rework and scrap due to higher inventory velocity.
- As inventory velocity increases obsolescence and slow-moving inventory reduce.
- Implementation of phase-in and phase-out of new part numbers becomes more manageable and quicker because there are fewer variables and inventory to consider and manage.
- Forecasting solutions become more straightforward, easier to maintain, and less costly.
- When total inventory decreases, customer service and profits improve.

The model displays the seven functions that make up the TCO and the components for each of their cost elements, useful for creating and understanding TCO models, Figure 6.3.

The TCO model also illustrates how 90 percent of the costs are out of view and traditionally not considered for make versus buy and outsourcing decisions.

Rely on Facts and Data

Personally, I am never one to shy away from a good debate. However, be careful of the critics who can't back up their statements with facts

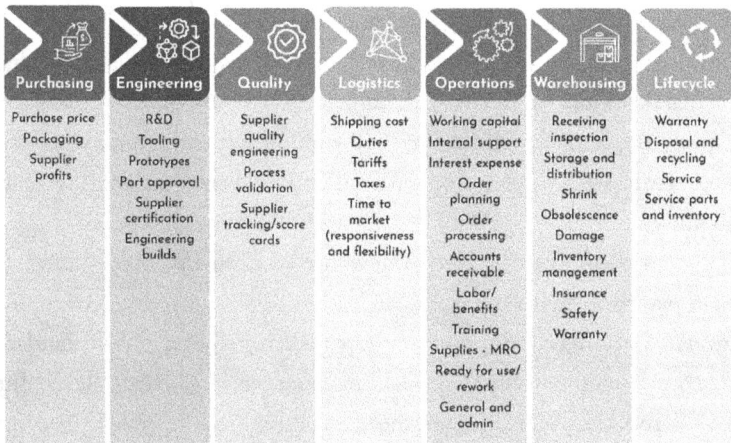

Purchasing	Engineering	Quality	Logistics	Operations	Warehousing	Lifecycle
Purchase price	R&D	Supplier quality engineering	Shipping cost	Working capital	Receiving inspection	Warranty
Packaging	Tooling	Process validation	Duties	Internal support	Storage and distribution	Disposal and recycling
Supplier profits	Prototypes	Supplier tracking/score cards	Tariffs	Interest expense	Shrink	Service
	Part approval		Taxes	Order planning	Obsolescence	Service parts and inventory
	Supplier certification		Time to market (responsiveness and flexibility)	Order processing	Damage	
	Engineering builds			Accounts receivable	Inventory management	
				Labor/ benefits	Insurance	
				Training	Safety	
				Supplies - MRO	Warranty	
				Ready for use/ rework		
				General and admin		

Figure 6.3 Building a total cost of ownership model

and data. The transportation department leadership often is one of the most common critics of reducing order size and having frequent deliveries. They argue, that if we start to receive items more frequently, costs will increase.

We need to reframe the argument.

The amount of freight over time doesn't change, just the frequency of deliveries. The predictability and accuracy of delivery times, dates, and weights significantly improve with shorter lead times and more frequent deliveries.

Art's Gold: Remember, variability is the enemy of cost containment.

Executive leadership must demand the same professionalism from support organizations as they do of Operational Excellence practitioners.

Be cautious of cost center accounting. To break this cycle of erroneous antiquated costing, shift the paradigm by focusing on TCO and not just on a few localized costs.

Dive Log 6 (Art's Commentary)

It's essential to understand why inventory is important, dispel the myths associated with it, and appreciate the people and process foundation of

Art Koch's Profit Chain Model and the three F's of supply chain management. I will debate with anyone that inventory costs are dollar for dollar of actual inventory on hand on an annual basis. If you have $100 million in inventory, and it's reduced by $50 million with the same sales volume, your inventory-related operational costs will potentially decrease by $50 million.

I've helped organizations achieve world-class inventory turns of 55 per year for total inventory, which leads to sizable improvements to the corporate bottom line. Suppose your organization does not use a standard range of 35 to 60 percent of annual carrying costs to calculate TCO. The TCO is too low. Senior leaders need to rethink their strategy and the financial impact on corporate performance.

Join me in becoming a zealot for operational excellence!

Dive Master Briefing (Client Example)

The client was a medium-sized Tier 1 automotive electronics manufacturer specializing in populating circuit boards and electromechanical assemblies. The material was manufactured in the United Kingdom, then shipped to and warehoused in the United States for North American customers. The long lead times and substandard manufacturing quality significantly impacted customer delivery performance and quality ratings. The company was near a customer no-bid status that could result in a loss of over $20 million in annual sales.

Before my arrival, the primary transportation mode for shipping was sea containers. To minimize freight costs, the manufacturers in the United Kingdom were manufacturing significantly into customer information-only forecasts. When the customer requested design changes, the client either ate the obsolescence cost or had to renegotiate with the customer, neither of which were good for the business or customer relationships. Between the inventory stored in the U.S. warehouse and in-transit inventory, there were nearly five months of inventory on hand.

Additionally, the manufacturing plant was struggling with quality issues, and in many cases, the root cause was ocean freight damage or warehouse handling issues. We implemented sorting and reverse logistics processes to contain quality issues, but that only addressed the symptoms of poor quality and ocean freight damage.

With the high inventory levels and the number of quality issues, it was impossible to contain defects by 100 percent. All these challenges combined amounted to a high expedited freight cost. Unplanned next-day air freight from the United Kingdom to the United States can be costly. Then, add charter jet and helicopter service to assembly plants, and the transportation portion of TCO was enormous.

After working on the program for a short period, I assessed the root causes and most of the cost of ownership: standard ocean freight, expedited freight, obsolescence cost, sorting, other indirect costs of managing the process, and reverse logistics cost of goods returned. With this new information, I knew we needed to compress lead times to reduce inventory to detect actual problems rather than reacting to symptoms.

I negotiated a new freight agreement with our carrier:

- Next-day delivery to our warehouse or customer for 15 percent of annual demand weight.
- Three-day delivery to our warehouse or customer for 15 percent of annual demand weight.
- Seven-day delivery for the remaining 70 percent of the annual demand weight.

Because I could guarantee the weights of shipments, pick-up days, and give the carrier a delivery window, they came up with an extremely competitive costing structure for air freight. Interestingly enough, because they were shipping a tremendous amount of unplanned expedited freight, subject to capacity-constrained spot-buys, the new logistics model of 100 percent preplanned air freight was nearly the same cost as the old model excluding the additional expedited freight.

Art's Gold: This was an excellent example that perfectly illustrated the high cost of variability versus the lower cost of predictability.

We implemented the plan, then drew down inventory and eliminated six weeks of transit and six weeks of safety stock for a 60 percent inventory reduction that represented a $4.6 million annual cost improvement.

During this period, the manufacturing site stopped over manufacturing items, and they were now building to actual customer planning data instead of inaccurate internal forecasts. On-time deliveries increased from 84 to 98 percent.

After reducing lead times dramatically, manufacturing could no longer blame sea carrier conditions for defective material. They were able to tackle quality and delivery problems at their root cause and implement corrective actions. Sorting costs and reverse logistic costs were reduced by 70 percent. This reduction alone gave the project a significantly positive return on investment (ROI). Finally, we were able to transform the warehouse space into a value-added manufacturing cell.

Art Koch's Profit Chain

Effective supply chain management creates dramatic improvements to inventory velocity, increased customer service, and corporate profits.

Client Testimonial

I first met Art in the early 1990s when we were part of a young interdisciplinary management team that transformed the performance of a components manufacturer using leading wave lean management thinking. Not only did we transform the business, but in the process, we also transformed ourselves, and the lessons learnt have influenced our views on all aspects of business ever since.

We quickly realized that inventory was the enemy. Draining the inventory swamp not only improved cash flow, but also exposed the real underlying issues facing the organization. These we were then able to tackle one by one in a systematic way. This is not easy as it requires belief, collaboration, commitment, and focus.

—Adrian Billingham FCMA, CGMA, BA, MBA

Buddy Check: Questions From Coach Art

- What is the TCO model used to make financial decisions?
- Suppose your organization has a TCO model. Does it consider the seven functions identified in Figure 6.3?
- Are there departments that block TCO efforts by focusing on outdated cost center accounting and localized costs?

Art's Deep Dive

Whether your role is as a strategist, an adviser, or an executive leader, the goals are to maximize customer service and shareholder and company valuation. Striving for optimum inventory velocity allows you to achieve these goals.

We must stop thinking of the process only as supply chain management and reframe the process as one that requires the entire organization's participation, as per Art Koch's Profit Chain. You might remember the phrase, "Measure me, and I'll tell you how I'll perform." If you only measure and reward prime +1 results, you'll get poor results because you're using the wrong TCO.

CHAPTER 7

Forecasting Is Always Wrong: Plan for Every Part

After diving for about five years, I had yet to see a whale shark. Whale sharks are the largest fish in the ocean, reaching 55 feet or 17 meters in length and weighing 40,000 pounds or 18,000 kilograms. They are elusive and majestic creatures and rank at the very top of most diver's bucket list of must-see animals.

Over the years, I have talked to other diving friends and have read about the best places and times to dive for the best chance of seeing whale sharks. While personally forecasting the best time to have an encounter, scheduled the trip accordingly, only to see a whale shark tail! I was losing hope.

It took 18 years of diving for me to finally spot a whale shark in Cebu, Philippines. Since that day in the Philippines, I have seen whale sharks on six different trips! What changed? I quit relying on long-range forecasting to estimate the best time and place for an encounter, and I went on trips to locations that nearly guaranteed a sighting, places like Isla Mujeres, Mexico, and West Papua, Indonesia.

Is your business relying on long-range forecasting to determine product mix for a period of 8, 12, or 16 weeks?

This chapter will outline the planning parameter foundations to maximize your planning processes and impact and discuss how to reduce the dependency on forecasts. I will present my 80/15/4/1 rule, which improves planning and inventory control performance, affecting higher inventory velocities while delivering better customer service.

Why Do We Forecast?

We use forecasting to anticipate customer's future requirements, then we use demand output data for planning and the prevention of using costly resources unnecessarily.

It is necessary to break down the administering of demand data into two functions: demand management and demand planning. Demand management is on the front end of sales and operations planning. Demand planning is the tactical execution of the sales forecast's consensus agreement. Below are the definitions for each demand function:

- **Demand Management:** The proactive compilation of requirements information regarding demand (i.e., customers, sales, marketing, and finance) and the firm's capabilities from the supply side (i.e., supply, operations, and logistics management). The best-led organizations build consensus around the ability to match the requirements, capabilities, and an agreed-upon synthesized plan that can most effectively meet the customer requirements within the constraints imposed by supply chain capabilities.
- **Demand Planning:** The process of identifying, aggregating, and prioritizing all sources of demand for the integrated supply chain of a product or service at the appropriate hierarchy level, time horizon, and time interval. The following concepts comprise sales forecast:
  1. The sales forecasting level is the focal point in the corporate hierarchy where the forecast is at the most generic level, that is, corporate forecast, divisional forecast, product line forecast, stock-keeping units (SKU), and SKU by Location.
  2. The sales forecasting time horizon generally coincides with the developed plan's time frame, that is, annual, one to five years, one to six months, daily, weekly, and monthly.
  3. The sales forecasting time interval generally coincides with how often the plan is updated, that is, daily, weekly, monthly, and quarterly.
- Definitions adapted from the Council of Supply Chain Management Professionals (CSCMP).[1]

- **Forecast:** An estimate of future customer demand. Scientific techniques based on historical usage and adjusted to accommodate various life cycle attributes, cyclical usage patterns, promotions, and pricing actions predict future demand.

Let's skip over the topics of forecast accuracy, different types of demand patterns (stable, seasonal, lumpy, and intermittent), and dependent versus independent forecasts because they are beyond the scope of this book. There are many excellent books, white papers, and publications available on these topics.

I want to discuss how to use the forecast to improve inventory velocity and customer service better.

We must discuss the differences in qualitative and quantitative forecast processes. The qualitative forecast method is valuable, based on intuition or informed opinion, and it is very subjective. This method is best applied to new product introductions when there is no "like" product to model.

The quantitative forecast method is based on historical data and assumes the future will repeat the past based on certain assumptions. I often encounter individuals who believe they can create a far more accurate forecast than the complex multi regression algorithms provide. If you behave accordingly, make sure you track the raw unchanged forecast to the consensus forecast. This will help keep individual biases in check.

Forecasts are necessary, and it is crucial to have the most accurate estimates possible. However, forecasts are always wrong…!!! So, get over it…!!!

Let's discuss a few techniques and alternatives that minimize the need for prediction and improve accuracy when a forecast is necessary. To reduce the dependency on forecasting, we need to:

- Reduce complexity.
- Reduce lead times.
- Reduce "cost" per setup.
- Reduce lot sizes.

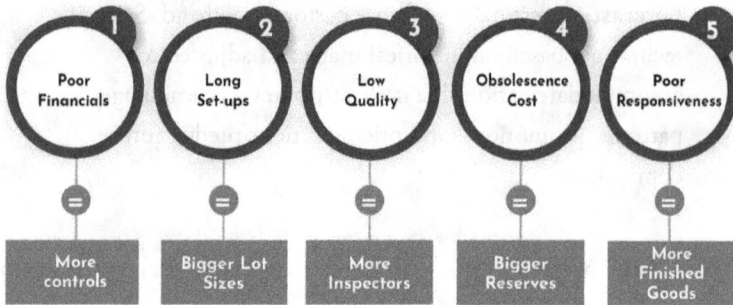

Figure 7.1 Dirty five copying mechanisms

We must establish objectives and processes with the long-term goal of eliminating the need for forecasting by envisioning utopia: building to order in lot sizes of one and with a lead time of minutes.

Become zealots for reducing the dependence on forecasts. This is the model of Art Koch's Profit Chain®: inventory reduction, improved customer service, and improved total cost of ownership. Avoid what I like to call the dirty five coping mechanisms that attempt to compensate for or cover up problems (Figure 7.1).

The most significant opportunity for reducing the need for forecasts is to reduce lead times and improve operational flexibility. Reducing lead times improves operations by shortening the forecast window and the need for long-range projections. As the forecast window shrinks, it becomes more accurate. With more forecast accuracy, variability decreased. As variability diminished, operations become more efficient.

Break down lead-time reduction into five components: supplier, manufacturing, setup, replenishment, and distribution.

With suppliers, I've had tremendous success in establishing two to three-year long-term agreements. Because of the length of the contract, we build a trust and partnership mindset. We implement raw material, work-in process, and finished goods authorization windows within a 52-week forecast horizon (Figure 7.2). This methodology eliminates the "spot buy tax" by giving suppliers the long-term security of a two to three-year agreement and delays adding value to the product until the final configuration is more clearly defined.

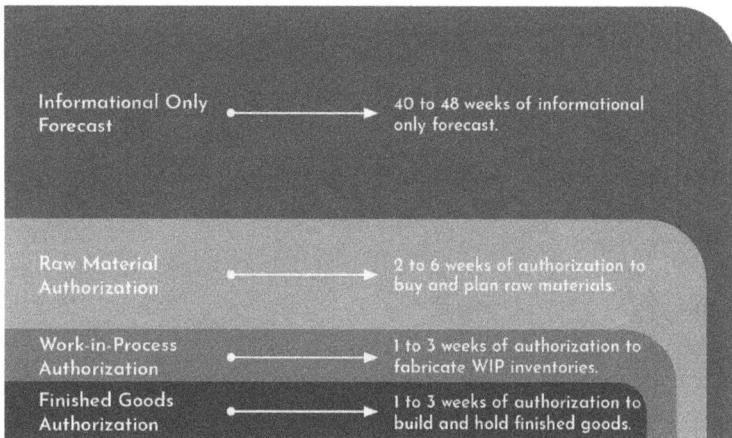

Figure 7.2 Raw material, work-in process, and finished goods authorization model

Manufacturing and setup lead-time reduction is accomplished by following lean manufacturing methodologies of Kanban pull processes for scheduling and "single minute exchange of dies" or "SMED."

Merely by changing the carrier, transportation and distribution costs can be reduced. Remember, we are transitioning from an incremental cost center mindset to reducing the TCO.

By increasing the frequency of ordering, replenishment lead times will be reduced. We will discuss more on this topic in the next section.

Within the five components that make up lead time, it is critical to become increasingly flexible (Figure 7.3). Breaking flexibility into six components allow teams working on lead-time reduction initiatives to better understand starting points and key areas for further analysis (Figure 7.4). Increasing flexibility reduces lead times and dependency on forecasts. Having more cross-trained team members enables the operation to be flexible and responsive to customer demand changes because they have more diverse skill sets. Standardized processes facilitate cross-training and ensure more mistake-proof processes, improved quality, and first-pass yields.

Planning to have ready-to-serve capacity permits the team to build what is required for the customer on the right day and time with the right

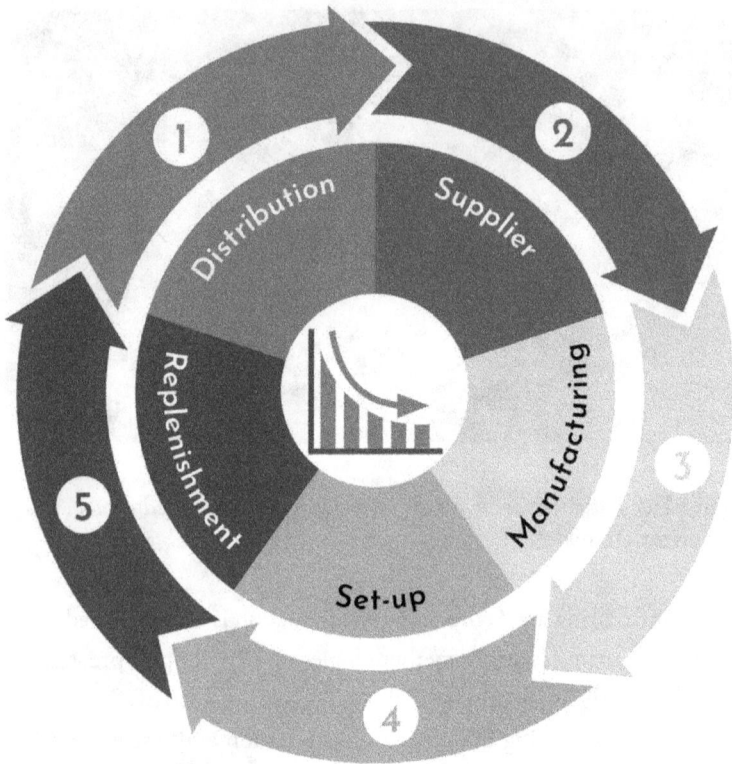

Figure 7.3 Five components of lead-time reduction

quantity and product mix. Inventory at standardized levels aids in delaying value-added processes until the last possible minute.

Make-to-order is a manufacturing process strategy where the trigger to manufacture a product is an actual customer order or release rather than a market forecast. More than 20 percent of the value-added takes place for make-to-order products after receiving the order. All necessary design and process documentation are available when the order is received.

Earlier, I suggested that we aspire to thoughts of Utopia when it comes to reducing dependency on forecasting: make-to-order, lot sizes of one, and a lead time of minutes.

Now, think of the ideal product to forecast. The perfect product has three essential parts. Customers want the product to meet their expectations. From the manufacturing point of view, the product would not

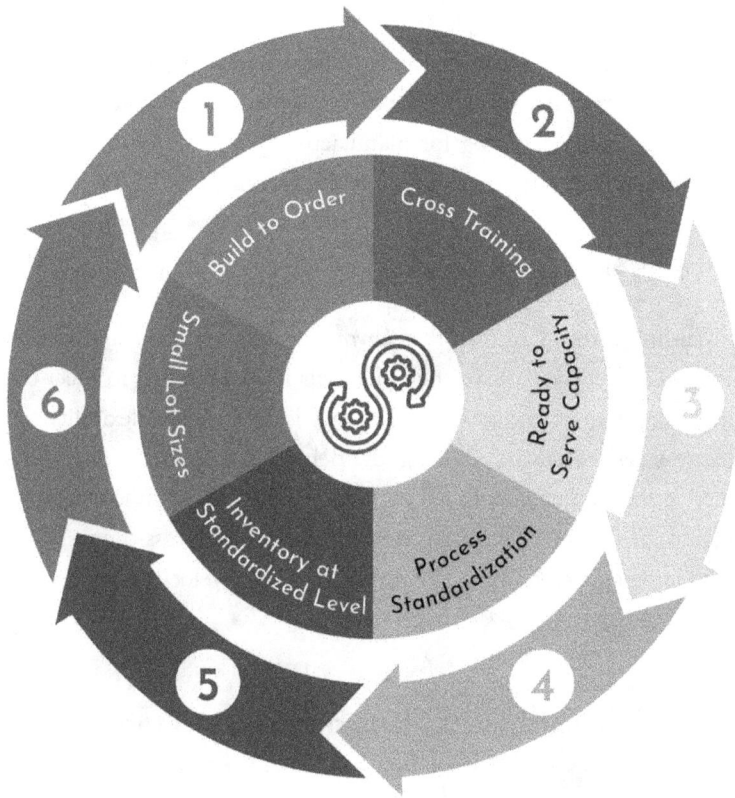

Figure 7.4 Six components of flexibility

waste material or labor, have an extremely short setup time, low cost, and is already being manufactured. From the design point of view, every feature will add value for the customer.

Additionally, reductions in complexity have a significant impact on reducing the dependency on forecasting. Three methods to reduce the dependence on forecasting:

1. Eliminate the last 1 percent of items with demand.
2. Hold raw material of blanks rather than finished goods.
3. Make use of new technologies such as 3D printing/additive manufacturing to reduce lead times and fill the demand for low-volume, lumpy, and intermittent demand items.

Today, we can buy eyeglasses in an hour, download e-books to our Kindles and iPads in seconds, check-in for airlines online, and produce paperless boarding passes. It's time to break free of the traditional models of long-term forecasting for manufacturing operations and become zealots for reducing the dependency on forecasting.

Dive Log 7 (Art's Commentary)

Early in my career, I learned that *forecasts are always wrong* and that it's up to us, as leaders, to have the right tools in our toolbox to meet customer expectations consistently. The key is to increase flexibility and responsiveness to customer demands. Being proficient at meeting customer demands is accomplished by reducing complexity, lead times, setups, and lot sizes and increasing standardization and cross-training. This methodology directly impacts increasing inventory velocity and customer service and reduces the TCO.

Replenishment Planning and Inventory Control—Plan for Every Part

When working with clients, too often, the replenishment planning team has no strategy for segmenting parts classification, or entropy creep has taken over, and their data integrity is a complete mess. I like to start with the notion of a plan for every part (PFEP), a component of lean strategies for purchased parts.

To introduce such a system, one must understand everything there is to know about every part: how each part is purchased, received, packaged, stored, and delivered to its point of use. Most of this information exists in your organization, held in many places under the control of several managers, and is mostly invisible. The first step in creating a lean material handling system for purchased parts is to collect all of the necessary parts information in one place.

I start with the concept of 80/20 or my adaptation of the 80/15/4/1 rule for planning and inventory control. The premise is a small number of items represent the most critical to manage. 80/20 planning and inventory control maximize planning impact by separating significant items

Art's Law:

1% = 50% as an aid to PFEP
Typical Segmentation

Classification	Percent Demand	Percent Total Items	Demand Variability
"A" Items	80%	5–15%	Low
"B" Items	15%	10–20%	Low-Moderate
"C" Items	4%	10–20%	Moderate - High
"D" Items	1%	35–55%	High

Figure 7.5 Art's Law: 1% = 50%

from the less critical and determining the degree and level of control required for each stratification class (Figure 7.5).

What if I were to tell you that I completed the following analysis for every business I have worked with, and all had the same outcome?

Art's Gold: The last 1 percent of customer demand represented 50 percent of finished goods part numbers and dramatically increased complexity.

There is a myth that many managers believe. "If you focus on the top 80 percent of the 80/20 rule, the results will come." In the short term, you can make the argument that this is correct. However, the results are not sustainable in the long term because the last 1 percent of demand is significantly draining the team's resources.

The last 1 percent of demand or purchases represents 50 percent of business complexity, and if left unchecked, it will consume more than 50 percent of your resources and energy. We must shift the focus on eliminating the complexity drivers for the last 1 percent of demand.

Many managers also have the myth that there should be lots of inventory for "A" items and very little on "C" items. Otherwise, service will suffer. That method doesn't work, and it should be just the opposite. **We need a Process!**

The Process

Let's begin the stratification process by compiling the past 12 to 18 months of quantities used multiplied by the purchase price or standard cost. As a side note, it's common to use the same stratification process considering material scarcity and quality issues. Classify the items into their desired groups and determine a degree of control and importance for:

- Annual dollar usage.
- Scarcity of material.
- Quality problems.
- Classify items based on the criteria established.
- *Apply a degree of control in proportion to the importance of the group.* For example, if a group of parts have quality problems, there is an argument for stratification based on the severity of each. From this stratification, it's possible to apply differing significance to root cause problem analysis.

Before getting too far into the process it's important to understand two key definitions: **Inventory turns** and **days on hand** of inventory; these are terms businesses use to measure inventory in relation to time and velocity.

- **Turns**—the rate at which inventory is moving, typically measured in times per year.
- **Days on hand**—how long the current amount of inventory will last.

Either can be used. I prefer to use this method of days of inventory on hand because it's easier for most people to understand.

The Process—Key Principles "A" Items

Here are the steps.

Set safety stocks at the lowest possible level to achieve the desired quality of service by item or bill of materials level before manufacturing adds value/complexity. Don't use fixed safety stock quantities. Use dynamic methods such as safety stock days. Don't allow high-safety stock quantities to become a crutch.

Strive to solve root causes of problems that will enable high inventory velocity for "A" items.

When possible, establish an order review policy at the lowest level (daily/weekly) and order in the smallest quantities possible.

Challenge suppliers on minimum order quantities, lead times, and delivery times.

Don't let the status quo influence your long-term goals.

"A" items need to be the focus of your management resources!

The Process—Key Principles "B" Items

Set safety stocks for "B" items at two to three times that of "A" items.

Taking this action will help to maintain a slightly higher level of safety stock (days) to compensate for the typically more elevated levels of demand variability verses that of "A" items.

Establish order review policies to take place slightly less frequent than "A" items; weekly or bi-monthly.

The Process—Key Principles "C" and "D" Items

Set safety stocks for "C" items at three to six times, and for "D" items at six to twelve times that of "A" items. Taking this action will help to maintain a significantly higher level of safety stock (days) to compensate for the typically more elevated levels of demand variability of "C" and "D" items.

Establish order review policies to take place infrequently, monthly, or bi-monthly.

Set the order size for "C" items at four to eight times (in days), and for "D" items, eight to sixteen times (in days) that of "A" items. Again, the larger reorder quantities will help to compensate for typically higher levels of demand variability of "C" and "D" items.

The key to "C" and "D" items is to let inventories replace management time by ordering less frequently and in larger quantities (in days).

Additionally, is it efficient to have a supplier partner manage all of these items or specific families? Yes. Examples of supplier partners for hardware and fasteners are Optimas Solutions, Fastenal, and Wurth. These companies do an excellent job of managing the supply chain's complexity for "C" and "D" items.

The Process—Key Principles for New Items

Manage new parts as you would an "A" item, set safety stock and reorder quantities, and review parameters after three to six months. It's essential to manage new items carefully if you're unclear how they will behave. Once there is a clear understanding of their volume and variability, align them with the correct ABCD ranking.

The Process—Key Principles—Get the 80/15/4/1 Facts

Segmentation is dynamic. It applies to a specific part number or SKU, not a group, and it is only useful if your inventory policies and procedures differ from one another. Stratification permits resources to be applied where the impact is the greatest. It is one of the key drivers to reduce inventory and increase service.

Inventory Velocity—The Impact of Order Frequency

Weekly Order Frequency

Scenario	Method	Average Inventory	Inventory Turns Per Year	Day's Inventory on Hand	Activity Weekly (Work)	Activity Annually (Work)
#1	Weekly	$115,385	34.7	6.9	900	46,800

Figure 7.6 Scenario 1: weekly order frequency

Let's walk through an example: Should we plan weekly, monthly, quarterly, or with 80/15/4/1 segmentation? The data set consists of 900 items, annual usage of $4,000,000, and one-week safety stock (Figure 7.6).

Scenario 1—Weekly Order Frequency

In this example, inventory turns of 34.7 and 6.9 days on hand are very respectable. However, since every part number is ordered every week, the 900 orders per week and 46,800 orders per year are excessive and could strain the buying organization. Let's see what the results are of ordering monthly (Figure 7.7).

Scenario 2—Monthly Order Frequency

Monthly Order Frequency

Scenario	Method	Average Inventory	Inventory Turns Per Year	Day's Inventory on Hand	Activity Weekly (Work)	Activity Annually (Work)
#2	Monthly	$243,590	16.4	14.6	225	11,700

Figure 7.7 Scenario 2: monthly order frequency

As we see, inventory has more than doubled, turns reduced by more than 50 percent, and work is more respectable at 225 orders per week. Let's see what the results are of ordering quarterly (Figure 7.8).

Scenario 3—Quarterly Order Frequency

Quarterly Order Frequency

Scenario	Method	Average Inventory	Inventory Turns Per Year	Day's Inventory on Hand	Activity Weekly (Work)	Activity Annually (Work)
#3	Quarterly	$576,923	6.9	34.6	69	3,600

Figure 7.8 Scenario 3: quarterly order frequency

With quarterly ordering, inventory more than doubled, inventory turns dropped to 6.9, while days on hand rocketed to 34.6, with weekly orders of 69 being the only respectable number here.

Scenario 4—80/15/4/1 Segmentation

Let's now apply the 80/15/4/1 segmentation methodology utilizing the following criteria stratification (Figure 7.9).

80/15/4/1 Segmentation
900 Items Ranked on Annual Dollar Usage

Class	Percent Demand	% Total Items	Number of Items	Annual Usage
A	80%	7.9%	71	$3,200,000
B	15%	15.1%	136	$600,000
C	4%	16.9%	152	$160,000
D	1%	60.1%	541	$40,000
	100%	100%	900	$4,000,000

Figure 7.9 Scenario 4: 80/15/4/1 segmentation—900 items ranked on annual dollar usage

And the following criteria for ordering parameters of safety time inventory and order review policy (Figure 7.10).

Typical Order Parameters of Safety Time
Inventory and Order Review Policy

Class	Safety Time (Days)	Order Review Policy (Days)	Order Review Policy
A	5	5	Weekly
B	5	10	Bi Weekly
C	15	30	Monthly
D	25	60	Bi Monthly

Figure 7.10 Scenario 4: typical order parameters of safety time inventory and order review policy

80/15/4/1 Segmentation and Planning Parameters

Scenario	Method	Average Inventory	Inventory Turns Per Year	Day's Inventory on Hand	Activity Weekly (Work)	Activity Annually (Work)
#4	80/15/4/1	$142,308	28.1	8.5	209	10,893

Figure 7.11 Scenario 4: 80/15/4/1 results

With scenario 4, 80/15/4/1 segmentation, we gain the benefit of planning the "C" and "D" items (77 percent of the total items) less frequently, which dramatically reduces the number of orders placed weekly and monthly. Then, by planning the "A" and "B" items (95 percent of total demand, but only 23 percent of the total items) weekly, the average inventory only slightly increased. Using the 80/15/4/1 planning methodology, we can achieve inventory velocity goals while keeping the order workload reasonable (Figure 7.11).

Review Figure 7.12 to see the side-by-side comparisons of all four scenarios. 80/15/4/1 wins by achieving excellent inventory velocity while maintaining moderate order workloads.

Comparing Traditional Planning Process to 80/15/4/1
Stratification Planning

Scenario	Method	Average Inventory	Inventory Turns Per Year	Day's Inventory on Hand	Activity Weekly (Work)	Activity Annually (Work)
#1	Weekly	$115,385	34.7	6.9	900	46,800
#2	Monthly	$243,590	16.4	14.6	225	11,700
#3	Quarterly	$576,923	6.9	34.6	69	3,600
#4	80/15/4/1 Planning	$142,308	28.1	8.5	209	10,893

Figure 7.12 *Comparing traditional planning process to 80/15/4/1 stratification planning*

The Process—Key Principles—All Items

There is a significant difference between safety stock versus safety time of inventory:

- **Safety Stock**—is static and does not change with changing schedules and forecasts.
- **Safety Time**—is dynamic and changes with schedules and forecasts.

The vast majority of the time, I recommend using a dynamic calculation to determine safety stock rather than a fixed quantity. The quantity of safety inventory will move up and down with forecast and demand changes.

However, with a static or fixed safety stock, the amount must be manually adjusted with demand and forecast changes.

Too often, when working on inventory obsolescence challenges, I have heard, "The demand was 10,000 pieces per week, and when demand started to decline, someone forgot to reduce safety stocks." I recommend using safety time, which helps to avoid this problem.

The Key to Getting Results—Increasing Inventory Velocity—PFEP

Follow lead times, and don't order any sooner than necessary. Use time parameters versus quantity where possible. Review, challenge, and negotiate lead times and minimum order quantities to achieve the shortest times and the smallest quantities.

When **placing an order late**, there is the possibility of a **stock out**. When **placing an order early**, there will be **extra inventory and costs**. Don't combine quantities. Ordering triggers (can be physical—Kanban or systematic—MRP) provides the information that signals us when to order.

Control orders based on 80/15/4/1 segmentation. There are two general rules to follow: (1) Have plenty of low-value items and (2) use control mechanism efforts to reduce the inventory of "A" items.

- "A" items: Tight control.
- "B" items: Normal control.
- "C" and "D" items: Looser controls.

This is a critical step. When working in supply chain management, there will always be **demand fluctuations** and **part shortages**. It's crucial to avoid knee-jerk overreactions. Ask **Why, Why, Why, Why, and Why?**

Walkthrough the processes that lead to the shortage. Were the order parameters accurate? Were the parts ordered on time? Resist making changes to safety stock and lead times for every fluctuation and focus on finding the root causes of the shortages.

Managing and maintaining parameters:

- Update order review policy parameters/Kanban triggers for your safety stock and stocking program before and after seasonality.
- Make adjustments that support lead times so that inventory is in place before peak season.
- Review and update order review policy parameters/Kanban triggers for safety stock and stocking program inventories quarterly.

To Kanban or not to Kanban? That is the question.

I'm an advocate of utilizing Kanban pull processes. Kanban is the Japanese word for "visible record," roughly translated means card, billboard, or sign. Popularized by Toyota Corporation, it uses standard containers or lot sizes to deliver needed parts to the assembly line "just in time" for use. Empty containers are then returned to the source as a signal to resupply the associated parts in the specified quantity.

Some modern IT systems use "Electronic Kanban's," which are messages to the upstream step advising of the need for parts downstream.

Typically, I use a two-card/bin pull system to get clients started. While you work from a bin, the opposite bin is replaced. Kanban is different from materials requirements planning (MRP). MRPs are push systems. The MRP does not know if you're ahead or behind and will keep pushing inventory even if production is behind schedule.

Kanban is a pull process. It physically pulls inventory as it is consumed, based on actual usage. Therefore, I recommend the Kanban pull method because it reflects your production status and doesn't keep pushing inventory into a bottleneck.

Where Do You Start and How Do You Decide Which System to Use?

Start with an 80/15/4/1 stratification of the data you want to analyze. I typically analyze purchase parts, manufacturing assemblies, and finished goods to improve inventory performance and customer service to determine the number of stock-keeping units (SKU).

Next, complete a PFEP. PFEP, combined with the 80/15/4/1 analysis, will evaluate physical size requirements. The ABCD analysis and PFEP provide you with the requirements for a 100 percent understanding of choosing the correct material replenishment process for specific parts.

But you're not done yet. **Review each item with internal experts from purchasing, planning, and operations for** (listed in my preferred order of importance):

1. Demand variability
2. Supplier issues
3. Delivery lead times
4. Manufacturing complexity
5. For any supplier stocking programs, minimums, and multiple ordering requirements
6. Frequency of use
7. Uniqueness or custom to order
8. Physical size and cost

Remember, you're deciding the best fit of Kanban, MRP, min/max, reorder point, and vendor managed inventory (VMI) replenishment methodologies to each specific item number. Yes, every SKU.

Those are the steps to achieve the optimum inventory performance, customer service, and customer loyalty.

When starting your lean journey, typical ordering methods are as follows:

- Classification "A" items are Kanban with low demand variability and higher volume repetitive usage.
- Classification "B" items can be a mix of Kanban and MRP, min/max, re-order-point.
- Classification "C" items are typically MRP, min/max, and re-order-point due to higher demand variability and lower usage.

- For Classification "D" items, I prefer having supplier managed programs, and at the very least, using min/max or re-order-point strategies.

Why is there a need for PFEP?

Every item needs a physical home, we need to understand its space requirements, the location items are delivered and so on. What is often forgotten in PFEP is the reorder method, system parameters, safety stock quantities, and so on. The stratification of 80/15/4/1 as an aid to PFEP allows us to focus resources on the optimum replenishment trigger, which then allows the team to spend valuable time-solving opportunities with a higher net return on investment, such as developing supplier partnerships or part number rationalization.

Use continuous improvement methodologies to maximize the TCO improvements. Focus resources on:

- Reducing complexity
- Improving inventory velocity
- Increasing flexibility
- Reducing cost per setup
- Reducing lot sizes
- Reducing lead times

Art's Gold: Complexity is reduced by eliminating unnecessary part numbers and combining multiple parts and raw materials into a single item.

Rationalize or eliminate suppliers that have redundant part numbers or processes. Typically, the last 1 percent of purchases are from 50 percent of the supply base. Remember, it's okay to rationalize the number of customers and finished goods part numbers. Simplify!

It's not about "Dumbing it down." The real deep work comes from the elegance of simplification.

Increase flexibility and responsiveness by manufacturing in smaller lot sizes, cross-training teams, standardization of processes, maintaining ready-to-serve capacity, holding strategic inventory at a standardized level, and transforming operations to build to order or assemble to order.

Improve inventory velocity by compressing:

- Manufacturing setup times;
- Supplier lead times;
- Replenishment cycle times; and
- Distribution times.

Work with suppliers to establish long-term agreements utilizing authorizations for finished goods, fabrication, and raw materials. Forecast the remaining demand. When possible, for both manufactured and purchased parts, have safety stock only on the raw materials and avoid keeping safety stock on finished assemblies or make-to-order components. One-part number of bar stock could satisfy 20 final assemblies.

Know the difference between efficient and effective:

- Efficient—Doing things right, exclusive of wasting materials, time, or energy. The tactical side of the business.
- Effective—Doing the right things. The strategic side of the business.

An individual can be efficient but not producing a result that is needed (not effective). We are busy professionals, and so are our teams. Therefore, they must know the difference between efficient and effective.

It is critical to understand that eliminating variability, non-value-added steps and processes are the keys to success. You are generating sustainable cost reductions. In supply chain management, decreasing the dependency on forecasts, lead-time reductions, part number, and supplier rationalization all reduce variability.

Non-value-added waste is avoided by eliminating extra processing steps, excess material moves, and redundant or unnecessary paperwork through elegant yet straightforward automation and avoiding complexity. If manual processes work, keep them, and don't discard what works!

Setup Costs

Reducing setup costs has a direct correlation to reducing lot sizes. When working to reduce setup costs, strive for SMED by utilizing kaizen events to improve changeover time. Complete as much of the changeover as possible offline, re-engineer the part to reduce changeover times, and change manufacturing equipment to types that can complete rapid changeovers. Finally, remember changeovers only matter at bottlenecks. As changeover times are improved, costs will reduce, and lot sizes should also reduce. Strive for make-to-order or assemble-to-order methodologies and establish a continuous reduction program to improve setup times.

Supplier Lead Times

For supplier lead-time reductions, when possible, source local, source standardized items, and use merchants. Ask your supplier partners what you can do to help reduce lead times. Become quick!

Inventory Obsolescence

There will always be inventory obsolescence. The key is understanding the five leading root causes of obsolescence:

1. Forecast dependence and overly optimistic forecasting
2. Consumer and market changes
3. Style changes
4. Shelf life
5. Ordering more than dependent demand

The net impact is lost profits.
Preventing obsolescence requires the minimization of:

- Forecasting dependence;
- Purchase commitment times;
- Safety stock and lot sizes; and
- Strict adherence to exception-based planning.

Inventory Pull

Next, maximize the use of inventory pull processes such as Kanban. Tighten management controls over engineering change orders and engineering change notices. Make the process visible and part of the daily visual management changes. And lastly, avoid large buys.

As mentioned earlier, obsolescence can and will occur. Once you have it, dispose of the items promptly, find substitute uses, discounted sales, donate to a local high school or trade school, and hold a "Fire" sale, and, finally, scrap on time.

*"Something's got to go, Sam.
You, me or this scuba inventory, and it's not going
to be me."*

Figure 7.13 Something's got to go, Sam

The key to success is toughness. Supply chain management is a tough job!

Play to win by doing something differently. Make systemic changes backed by real solutions, and accept no trade-offs, so that everyone wins! (Figure 7.13).

We cannot allow ourselves or our teams to become guilty of doing the same thing repeatedly and expecting different results. That is Albert Einstein's definition of insanity!

We need to challenge ourselves by creating a world-class operation that is responsive to customer demands, operates with fast cycle times, maintains low inventories, and has excellent supplier partnerships. Let's break the current cycle of outdated inventory management techniques and focus on the utopian vision.

The utopian vision for supply chains:

- Daily receipts;
- Daily production;
- Daily shipments;
- Zero plant inventory at the end of the day;
- Replenish distribution centers with minimal inventory;
- +300 inventory turns.

Imagine the positive cash flow and the competitive differentiator for your business when accomplishing the utopian vision.

The Lean 5S Model

I like to use the lean 5S model.

Sort—Keep what's needed and eliminate the unnecessary items.
Straighten—Place required items in the correct place for easy retrieval.
Shine—Keep the workplace neat and clean.
Standardize—Make sort, straighten, and shine consistent habits with standard processes throughout the business.
Sustain—Maintain and improve your processes to aid in implementing PFEP.

As represented in Figure 3.1.

Typical Steps of 5S for 80/15/4/1 and PFEP

1. **Sort:** Complete the ABCD analysis of 80/15/4/1 for sorting items into their proper stratification.
2. **Straighten:**
   - Select groups of parts for Kanban, MRP-driven, or VMI.

- **Kanban items:** I like to start with the most uncomplicated part numbers to build a model of excellence cell for the organization to gain confidence (Figure 7.14).

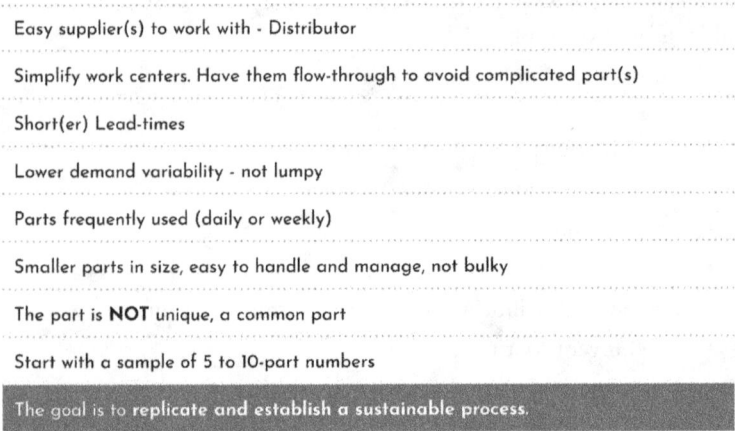

Easy supplier(s) to work with - Distributor
Simplify work centers. Have them flow-through to avoid complicated part(s)
Short(er) Lead-times
Lower demand variability - not lumpy
Parts frequently used (daily or weekly)
Smaller parts in size, easy to handle and manage, not bulky
The part is **NOT** unique, a common part
Start with a sample of 5 to 10-part numbers
The goal is to **replicate and establish a sustainable process.**

Figure 7.14 Eligible purchased and manufactured parts for Kanban's

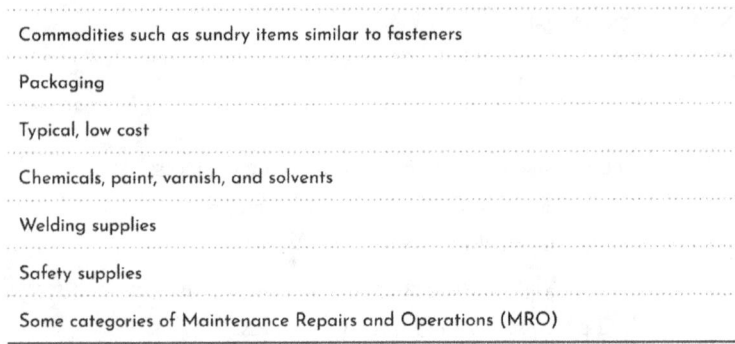

Commodities such as sundry items similar to fasteners
Packaging
Typical, low cost
Chemicals, paint, varnish, and solvents
Welding supplies
Safety supplies
Some categories of Maintenance Repairs and Operations (MRO)

Figure 7.15 VMI eligible items

- Physically moving or building new supermarkets and new material line-side locations.
- After defining Kanban, MRP, and VMI part number groupings (Figure 7.15), create standard work to sustain processes.
- Work through the remainder of both purchased and manufactured parts to complete the PFEP and use either Kanban, MRP, or VMI to manage the process.

3. **Shine:**
   - Keep the supermarkets and processes clean and orderly.
   - Multiple Gemba walks per day.

4. **Standardize:**
   - Make sure standard work reflects the process for all parts.
   - Be sure there are standard reports for Kanban and the calculation process.
   - Automate the replenishment process with barcoding, radio-frequency identification (RFID) chips, and so on.
   - To ensure process integrity, use Gemba walks.
   - To keep sustainability, team members need to be ZEALOTs about process integrity.

5. **Sustain:**
   - Rerank the ABCD 80/15/4/1 items every quarter.
   - Maintain Kanban and MRP parameters.
   - Set up a calendar of activities that need to be audited, corrected, and monitored.
     - Lead times
     - Order modifiers
     - Safety stock overrides
     - Distribution center redistribution
     - Inventory accuracy
     - Order accuracy
   - Gemba walks must be part of the operational excellence process and the DNA of the business.
   - The goal is to establish a sustainable process.
   - Follow "The Planning Commandments (Figure 7.16)."

Create your vision of utopia: A process that supports a one-day customer order receipt to shipment cycle, with *no* inventory!

To be successful, you must develop new techniques to give customers something that they have never had before, which will disrupt your competitors' lives. Having a competitive advantage means understanding what customers need better than they do and delivering it to them. Doing this well requires building a high degree of trust with your suppliers, customers, and internal processes and creating a new working relationship pattern between companies.

1	Review and designate service classes regularly.
2	Have written standard work and policies for planners that will guide them in determining the order quantity and safety stock.
3	Have individual policies for different ABCD classifications.
4	Review and reset supplier lead times regularly.
5	Review and reset order minimums regularly.
6	Ensure purchase orders are placed no sooner than necessary based on lead times.
7	Have separate policies for each inventory segment.
8	Have written goals for desired inventory turnover ratios for each inventory segment.
9	Have written inventory objectives that define how much the inventory investment should be for each inventory segment.
10	Monitor performance versus these objectives.

Figure 7.16 The planning commandments

Figure 7.17 Manufacturing before

Figure 7.18 Manufacturing before

Success today requires the agility and drive to rethink, reinvigorate, react, and reinvent constantly.

—Bill Gates

As leaders of any organization, we need to break the entropy cycle. People do what's inspected, not expected.

Establish visual daily management (VDM) processes with visible KPIs, implement daily Gemba walks to review results, utilize safety, quality, delivery, inventory, and productivity (SQDIP) as part of day-to-day visual management, safety quality, delivery, inventory, and production. Figures 7.17, 7.18, 7.19, and 7.20 illustrate that going from bad to good looks like. Often teams only need to see what good looks like in one area for the model to become the catalyst for long-term sustainable improvements.

Create a culture of friendly competition. Develop a quarterly "good wins-bad losses" report for key metrics. Make TCO a high priority for teams to accomplish and use KPIs to help find the hidden problems or "rocks."

Figure 7.19 Manufacturing after

Be the solution. Create the energy for change, involve everyone, communicate openly and frequently, visualize performance, and celebrate successes.

Remember, if this were easy, someone would've done it already! The critical thing is to: Just Start It!

Dive Master Briefing (Client Example)

Several years ago, I received a request to assist Angeles, the General Manager, with inventory reduction and service level improvements. Her company was a recently acquired South American division of a company that

Figure 7.20 Manufacturing after

produced $50 million in revenue, and they had just become part of a $4 billion multinational consumer products company. Because of ultra-high local interest rates and warehousing costs, their inventory carry cost was completely eroding profit margins. If they could reduce inventory and close a warehouse, the business could be highly profitable. I worked with the planning manager Joaquin to implement the corporate solution for demand and replenishment planning, applied my 80/15/4/1 item stratification and finished goods/work-in process/raw material authorization methodologies, and trained and coached the team on the key to getting results.

Within six weeks of being onsite, Angeles, Joaquin, and the team reduced inventory by $5,200,000 or 47 percent. Additionally, with the significant inventory reduction, they could afford to stock several subassemblies that supported lower demand finished goods items, which significantly improved their customer service and improved total sales by as much as 10 percent.

Dive Log 7 (Art's Commentary)

This chapter's material is part of the People Process Foundation because the methodologies outlined are fundamentally critical to simplifying processes. Supply chain management can be complicated if you let it. Mastering the methods in this chapter will simplify processes and help achieve step functional improvements.

When working through change management and process improvements, seek out decoupled links, anything requiring manual intervention, e-mail, telephone orders, external spreadsheets, and so on, within the supply chain. Information flow should be that of electronic data exchanges (EDI) and not from e-mail or spreadsheets.

Dispel the myth: Adding inventory improves customer service. Far too often, organizations believe that their only option to improve service is to add inventory. Leaders must avoid those knee-jerk reactions and drive toward establishing fundamental processes, 80/15/4/1 planning stratification, reducing reliance on forecasting, adopting postponement strategies, and adhering to sustainable parameters management. These fundamentals will help our valuable team members to succeed. It's all about the fundamentals.

Buddy Check: Questions From Coach Art

- Are you taking steps to reduce the dependency on forecasting?
- Do you have coping mechanisms in place that cause forecasting dependency?
- Are you using 80/15/4/1 stratification to separate the most critical items from the less important?
- Does your organization subscribe to the myth that it's beneficial to have lots of inventory for "A" items and very little on "C" items?
- Do you default toward safety stock over safety time inventories?
- Are you using established guidelines in determining different planning methods for Kanban, MRP, and VMI items?
- Do you find the organization overreacting to demand changes?
- Are you using a 5S methodology to assist PFEP sustainability?
- Do you have written planning guidelines, and are they reviewed/audited regularly?

Art's Deep Dive

Consider adding a fifth stratification class of Super "A." Often, the top 25 to 50 items can represent up to 50 percent of demand.

Why do I say forecasts are always wrong? Has anyone been able to forecast the weather or the stock market? No! If they were able to, they would be worth billions of dollars!

Most students are taught economic order quantity (EOC) models. They want to apply their knowledge when they get into a work setting. However, most can't be relied upon because they don't calculate the trade-off between ordering and holding costs, especially with finished goods.

For additional information and free tools, please scan the code.

CHAPTER 8

The Art of Equalization: Achieving Balance in Materials and Inventory Control Success

In scuba diving, mastering the technique of equalization is nonnegotiable. This essential skill involves adjusting the pressure in your ears and sinuses as you descend, allowing you to adapt to the changing underwater environment. Fail to equalize, and you'll face debilitating sinus pain that halts your dive altogether. While this might be a sensation you've casually encountered on a descending airplane, in the realm of scuba diving, the stakes are significantly higher.

The principle of equalization finds its business parallel in supply chain management (SCM), particularly in materials and inventory control. Think of inventory as the "life-support" of manufacturing—akin to a diver's air supply. It sustains production cycles and enables the timely delivery of physical products to your customers. However, this "life-support" system must be meticulously equalized to ensure a free-flowing, unhindered production line. Failure to identify and eliminate bottlenecks or maintain accurate inventory levels disrupts this equilibrium. The consequence? A halt in production, disappointed customers, and a serious blow to both your reputation and profitability.

Universities and certification agencies do an excellent job of teaching supply chain fundamentals. However, they lack the time and tactical knowledge to "knit" together the details that explain how to achieve 99.9 percent inventory accuracy. They just know that it's needed but don't know how to achieve it.

This chapter discusses what SCM is and isn't and the important distinctions. Then we review how SCM is oversimplified by many when it's an interwoven network of processes that create an elaborate framework. SCM becomes too complex because of inventory inaccuracies, data integrity issues, and human tendency to make things complicated. In this section, I introduce six personal strategies to conquer inventory problems and strengthen the framework for simplified materials control.

Supply Chain Management

What exactly is SCM?

From the birth of the Industrial Revolution, there has always existed some form of SCM. Only in recent times has SCM become more integrated throughout the corporate enterprise.

During the early years of the Industrial Revolution, Henry Ford tamed his supply chain by utilizing vertical integration management, where he acquired ownership of the different suppliers and stages of production, from rubber plantations to tire and iron ore mines to casting facilities. However, the capital investment cost of vertical integration was exorbitant.

Additionally, vertical integration becomes a barrier to innovation and new technology development because the focus is on efficiency.

When the early industrialists such as Ford and General Motors vertically integrated with steel production, a new technology emerged from other companies that could produce steel at a significantly reduced cost, higher quality, and reduced lead times. The cost of retooling typically was considerably increased and created a barrier to innovation. However, with horizontally integrated supplier partners, the cost of adaptation is minimal.

The vertical integration model worked well until:

- Competition increased, forcing the need for quick responses to consumer trends.
- Technology advancements accelerated, and vertically integrated enterprises could not keep up with intellectual property changes and capital investment requirements.

- Enterprise resource planning systems matured, which enabled businesses to horizontally integrate with suppliers and supplier partners, reducing the barriers to entry for new technologies.

When I started my career four decades ago, my MBA was in Materials and Logistic Management (MLM)—Operations. At the time, there were also MLM degrees available for Purchasing and Transportation. The focus was on pulling together the functions of purchasing, forecasting, replenishment planning, inventory control, and logistics to leverage materials requirement planning (MRP) systems.

The management directives of the day were to buy at the lowest price, never shut-down manufacturing, keep inventory at a minimum, and contain indirect costs.

About 20 years ago, the term supply chain management became the trend for describing the coupling of procurement, demand and replenishment planning, and logistics. At the time of this writing, many of my SCM peers, myself included, view SCM as inclusive of all functions of the manufacturing process:

- Everything from extracting raw materials from the earth or via recycling.
- Getting the product to the customers, including any reverse logistics.
- To the combined efforts of engineering, manufacturing, and customer service functions.
- All working toward the goal of total cost of ownership improvements.

How do you know if your organization has the right vision of the complete process of SCM integration? Let me ask you a straightforward question: Are the SCM disciplines fully integrated into the operational excellence of the business?

SCM cannot function in isolation.

It is integrated throughout the entire enterprise. It means working with engineering and suppliers in the early stages of design to achieve the lowest total cost product and making sure it meets fit, form, and function requirements. It means establishing line-side material delivery at manufacturing assembly lines and working with suppliers, internal operations, and customers to compress lead times.

The discipline of SCM is a process not unlike manufacturing; it is very complicated. However, too many people, including experts and consultants, oversimplify the supply chain as: (a) buying from a supplier, (b) receiving from the supplier, and (c) shipping to the customer, with each function occurring within their individually siloed departments.

The myth of supply chain simplicity, as seen in Figure 8.1.

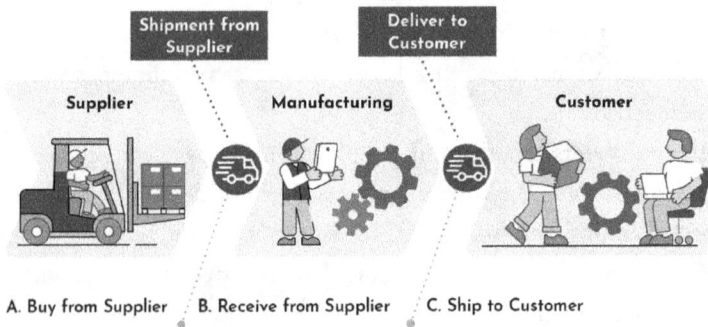

Figure 8.1 What many people think supply chain management is…

However, in reality, the supply chain interrelationship is more complex, as seen in the illustration in Figure 8.2.

To explain SCM in more detail and to further illustrate the functions of the SCM process, I've added a few critical tasks within SCM that are essential for achieving success:

Strategic Sourcing: The role of strategic sourcing is to strengthen supplier relationships into partnerships, establish horizontally integrated partnerships, implement supplier rationalization initiatives, and mitigate supply chain risk. The goals of strategic sourcing are delivering TCO and inventory velocity improvements. Relevant

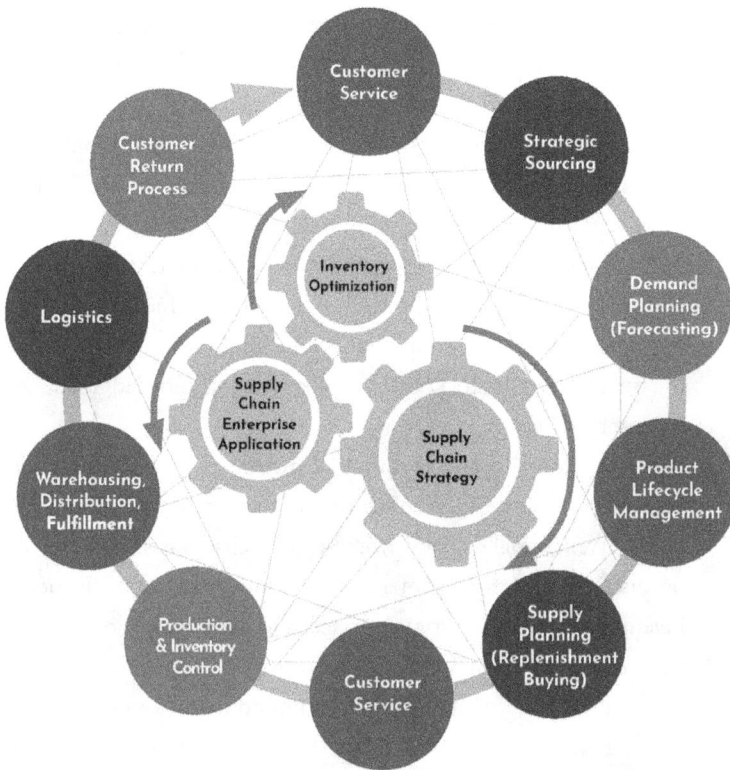

Figure 8.2 The supply chain management process

KPIs for this function include supplier performance, lead time, raw material price indexes (London Metal Exchange), and inventory velocity.

Demand Planning—Forecasting: The role of demand planning is to improve forecast accuracy. Successful teams accomplish this by reducing the dependency on the forecast and leading the sales and operations planning process by managing collaborative forecasting with sales and customers. Relevant KPIs include forecast accuracy, mean absolute percentage error (MAPE), forecast bias, and inventory velocity to determine effectiveness.

Product Life Cycle Management: The role of product life cycle management is to manage new product introduction and end-of-life dates while increasing enterprise responsiveness during the transition. Relevant KPIs include excess and obsolete inventory and improvements to TCO and inventory velocity.

Supply Planning—Replenishment Buying: The role of supply planning is to buy materials based on dependent demand. The team or systems should execute automatic replenishment buying with little or no manual adjustments and implement and maintain ABCD (80/15/4/1) stratification. Relevant KPIs include plan buying adherence (buying early, late, following lead times, adjusting the quantity), part stockouts, supplier order acknowledgment, and inventory velocity.

Production Planning and Inventory Control: The role of production planning and inventory control is to accurately manage in-plant inventory, material delivery processes, capacity constraints, and plan production to meet customer requirements. Relevant KPIs include inventory accuracy, customer service, and inventory velocity.

Warehousing and Distribution: The role of warehousing and distribution is to manage inbound and outbound receipts and shipments, ensure inventory accuracy, update the warehouse management system, and picking customer orders for fulfillment. Relevant KPIs include customer service, inventory accuracy, and velocity.

Logistics: The logistics role is to manage all freight carrier partnerships, scheduling, freight damages, shrinkage, shortages, and costs. Relevant KPIs include TCO and delivery variability.

Inventory Optimization: The inventory optimization team's role is to analyze, recommend, and implement inventory network changes that optimize inventory, customer service, and TCO. Relevant KPIs include TCO, inventory velocity, and customer service.

Supply Chain Enterprise Application: The application team's role is to make sure enterprise tools are used effectively. They should manage and control all supply chain parameters: lead time, order frequency, minimum and multiple order quantities, Kanbans, and so on. Relevant KPIs include percentage of exceptions and overrides to system processes.

Supply Chain Strategy: Supply chain strategy sets the vision and direction of SCM, the type of ERP, demand planning, and warehouse distribution systems to use and MRP versus pull processes. Relevant KPIs include inventory velocity, number of supplier partners, number of supplier VMIs, inventory accuracy, TCO, and on-time delivery to customers.

As you can see, there is a lot of complexity to SCM. It is as complicated as most manufacturing processes, and the larger the enterprise with greater international reach, the more complicated. Yet, at the same time, SCM is as simple as the processes described in Figure 8.1: Buy from a supplier, receive the materials, manufacture into products, and then ship to customers. Because supply chain processes are extensive and intersect with most enterprise functions, they must be part of an operational excellence program.

Building the Foundation of Materials Management and Production Inventory Control

Materials management (MM) encompasses the inbound logistics from suppliers through to the production process—the movement and management of materials and products from procurement through the production stages. MM includes production and inventory control (PIC) functions, the discipline of planning the manufacturing processes, and controlling the inventory of raw materials to be produced into finished goods.

I associate MM and PIC with the enterprise's cerebral cortex that decides when, how much, and where materials need to be for the organization to be successful. The physical flow of materials is like the circulatory system and the air that we breathe: The fuel ensures that materials flow to the proper locations in the correct quantity at the proper time.

The absolute most critical KPI for MM, logistics, and warehousing is inventory accuracy. Without near-perfect inventory accuracy, the enterprise will never be capable of sustaining high inventory velocity and customer satisfaction. I've often heard that the purpose of safety stock is to cover inventory inaccuracies. It's my position that safety stock is needed to support supply and demand variability and not accuracy. Inventory accuracy should have a minimum of 99.7 percent accuracy by location.

The importance of inventory accuracy				
Example	Inventory accuracy	Bill of material size	Formula	Probability of success
#1	98.0%	25 parts	0.980^{25}	60.3%
#2	99.9%	25 parts	0.999^{25}	97.5%

Note: 0.999^{25} is the calculation of 0.999×0.999 ... a total of 25 times will equal 97.5 percent.

Art's Gold: Safety stock is needed to support supply and demand variability and not inventory accuracy.

If the inventory accuracy is 98 percent, and a production bill of materials has 25 discrete components: Then $0.98^{25} = 60.3$ percent is the probability of having all the necessary parts available to complete a production order. When increasing inventory accuracy to 99.9 percent, the probability increases to 97.5 percent. These examples demonstrate how critical inventory accuracy is to order fulfillment.

Achieving inventory accuracy isn't rocket science. It's about simplifying the fundamental processes of production inventory control at key critical points of failure and then sustaining them.

Six World-Class Hacks to Inventory Accuracy

1. Lock and secure access to materials stores. Banks don't allow us to go into their vault to cash checks. Why should we let just anyone into a stock room with millions of dollars of inventory? Make sure that pick and place processes are flawless and accurate by utilizing barcoding and radio frequency identification (RFID) tags for high-value items.

2. Lock access to scrap, salvage, and rework areas. Too often, I've seen many incidents of material and parts just disappearing, only to find them in the scrap bin. Remove the opportunity.

3. Receiving needs to be automated. Make sure suppliers have labeling and barcoding guidelines to follow. The best KPI for receiving is invoices without physical receipts. This we when the supplier contacts account payable weeks or months later requesting payment and

there is no receipt in the ERP system. Once validating the supplier claim with freight carrier proof of delivery and cycle counting the suspect part number, payment is often made. This one measure tells the truth about receiving accuracy.

4. Bill of materials (BOM) accuracy. Make sure there is a process to measure BOM accuracy. If BOMs are not accurate, this will wreak havoc on the work-in-process inventory accuracy during backflushing.

5. Production reporting must be a systematic process utilizing precision scales or counts and tied to items of record, such as the master production schedule.

6. Shipping accuracy. There must be an automated system that can verify weights and counts with the package contents.

Besides inventory accuracy, here are five KPIs that focus on the correct areas:

1. **Invoices without physical receipts** identify receiving opportunities.

2. **Inventory accuracy as to quantity by location** identify unlocked stores and transaction opportunities.

3. **Negative inventory** identifies bill of material opportunities.

4. **Measure the number of shortages due to inventory inaccuracy or BOM errors.** By tracking surprise shortages, we learn two key pieces of information. First, how good is the team at early detection of problems? Second, as processes improve, the interval between surprises should always be expanding. If the interval frequency isn't increasing, more work needs to be done.

5. **Production worker visits to the warehouse, stockroom, or supermarket.** This highlights material delivery opportunities to materials control's internal customers and potential supply quality or planning issues. Assembly associates should never need to go to the warehouse, stockroom, or supermarket to get parts. The parts needed should be delivered by water spiders or material handlers to the location where value is added. In world-class manufacturing sites, a water spider is the most highly cross-trained operator. They are responsible for covering for their team members when they need a break and ensuring all point-of-use material bins are fully stocked.

Finally, remember cycle counting is not for maintaining inventory accuracy. Cycle counting is rework that should be used to direct managers to hidden problems.

Keep problem resolution simple. When it comes it inventory and MM, it's easy to overcomplicate solutions by implementing some crazy "off the wall" solution such as cycle counting 100 percent of each part every month.

Dive Master Briefing (Client Example)

Years ago, I received a request to assist a plant manager of a $125 million revenue facility that was part of a $2 billion multinational electronics manufacturer with opportunities to meet manufacturing schedules and on-time delivery to customers.

I met Cory, the plant manager, who had just joined the company earlier that same week. In that meeting were Adrian, the materials manager, Matt, the manufacturing manager, and Amy, the customer service manager. We exchanged the typical standard greetings, made introductions, and small talk. After a few minutes, I asked a simple question, "In what way do you need help?"

Well, the flood gates burst open!

Amy, the customer service manager, said, "I just need customers' orders built, forget on-time, just build them!"

Adrian, the materials manager, said, "I can't schedule production when you keep changing orders."

Matt, the manufacturing manager, chimed in, "if we could stop running out of parts, I could complete an order." Then Amy said, "I only move the schedule and reschedule orders when the customer calls and needs something that we are late on."

This exchange could have gone on for hours. I called a cease-fire and said, "We, as a team, are going to tour the facility before we go any further." Matt said, "We don't need to do that. They just need to do their jobs right."

It was plain to see that none of the managers were pleased with each other.

I explained to everyone that we are going to the plant floor to review 10 items (as outlined in Figure 8.3) from the Supply Chain Foundation

Rapid Assessment, after which we will rate each area again: 0 = Not found, with the highest score of 10 = Found everywhere.

During our shop floor review, their tone started to change. The managers went from pointing fingers at each other and denying their problems to total acceptance that something had to change. Each manager was guilty of:

- In the heat of the battle, trying to manage the symptoms and not addressing the root causes.
- Working within the lanes of their departmental silos and using localized solutions to make their individual KPIs look favorable.
- They were not operating as a team on TCO solutions.
- Remember the rating criteria: 0 = Not found and 10 = Found everywhere. Their actual scores are below.

The rapid assessment score of the five worst areas:

1. Stores 5S = 0.75
2. Visual management = 0.2
3. Material flow = 1.0
4. Inventory velocity = 0.8
5. Teamwork = 1.3

Reference: Figure 4.1, Supply chain rapid assessment and Figure 4.3, SCM rapid assessment results.

It was abundantly clear that we had our work cut out for us. Once the scores for the five worst areas finally registered with the managers and the denial subsided, the managers became more accepting of the necessary changes that needed to take place. We quickly outlined a six-step action plan.

Step One: Getting on the Same Page—The Plant Tour

We needed to get everyone on the same page. It was essential that manufacturing be able to complete a production order without interruption.

To resolve this issue, we implemented 15 to 20-minute daily visual production meetings.

Addressing the first issue was simple. We needed to figure out what products we could build for which we already had all the raw materials, blueprints, and machinery available. We outlined the status of each production order on a whiteboard in the middle of the plant floor. Next, we looked at what we could build for the next 8 hours and then added items for the next 12 and 24 hours, eventually progressing to the next 72 hours of the schedule.

Step Two: Figuring Out 5S

The 5S and flow were terrible in material stores. The accuracy by inventory part number and location was approximately 50 percent. Finance claimed that in the last physical inventory, the accuracy was recorded at 99.9 percent. It might have been in total net dollars, but you could never find parts within the plant's four walls. Net dollar inventory accuracy is a misleading KPI, because when taken out of context, it doesn't reflect location accuracy that is the prerequisite for pick sheet and manufacturing order completion.

When I asked what they thought were the next steps, it was like the Fourth of July with fireworks everywhere. All too often, I see individuals overcomplicating situations and working themselves into analysis paralysis. To simplify the process, I outlined a model that I started to use in 1992. It's never failed me before, has stood the test of time, and has worked for multiple industries. Refer to Figure 8.3.

In MM, there are six critical areas to control for inventory accuracy success:

1. Receiving;
2. The issuing of materials from stores to manufacturing;
3. Scrap, salvage, and rework control management;
4. Bill of materials accuracy;
5. Production reporting;
6. Shipping.

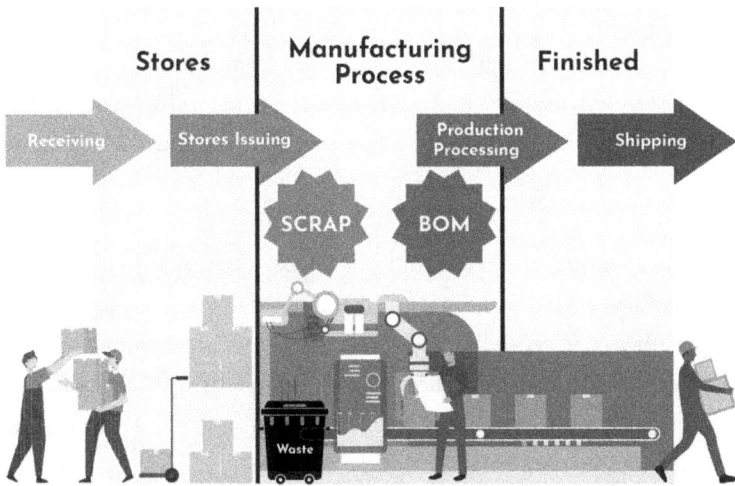

The simplicity of Materials Control

Figure 8.3 The simplicity of materials control

To address the inventory accuracy issue, we first closed the stores to anyone other than the materials team members. We placed a check-out person at major gateways leading to manufacturing. Next, we kitted major parts for production to ensure we had everything we needed before scheduling the order and starting manufacturing. The kitting step helped us to regain control of material stores. Additionally, we built trust and confidence within the manufacturing team to schedule the assembly lines effectively. With newly found confidence, the materials team was able to work on 5S'ing their store. Refer to Figure 3.1, 5S methodology.

Step Three: Who Is the Customer?

We reframed our focus on who was materials' internal customer. They had lost track of the fact that it was manufacturing. For many years, there had not been a good relationship between materials and manufacturing. As of late, the relationship has become very adversarial. We also needed to teach manufacturing how to be a better partner with their sole source supplier.

After building bridges, mending fences, and having people under-stand they were on the same team, that is achieving the above goals, the materials team shifted their mindset to become the best supplier possible. If a manufacturing person came to the store for material, it was considered a failure or breakdown in service. We also needed to reiterate that manufacturing could not do whatever they pleased and that the stores were CLOSED to them.

Again, a bank does not allow you to enter their vault or cashier registers to cash your check. So unauthorized individuals should not be permitted into a stock room with an inventory worth millions of dollars. The materials team started to understand the importance of their role and how they needed to service their customers. We then implemented an inventory pull system based on Kanban processes on the assembly lines for all commonly used parts.

Step Four: Production Reporting

We implemented a production reporting system that verified the part count by using the item of record.

The finished product was placed on a weight scale at the production reporting area, and the operator scanned the packaging label for part number and count. A computer program validated the item record locator with the standard part weight and piece count. If the weight and piece count met the parameters, production was reported. If the variance was too large, the box or pallet was rejected and required reverification. This reduced reporting errors from approximately 15,000 PPM to less than 50 PPM.

Step Five: Barcoding

We implemented barcode transaction reporting for receiving, parts put away, part picking, and issuing to plant work orders and work-in-process. As part of this process, we scanned a bar-coded pick sheet that verified the correct parts were picked to the BOM and from the proper location. Additionally, we used a mobile scale to confirm the accurate counts of small pieces. Figure 8.4 illustrates the bar-coding process flow that allow for near zero defects in data entry and production reporting.

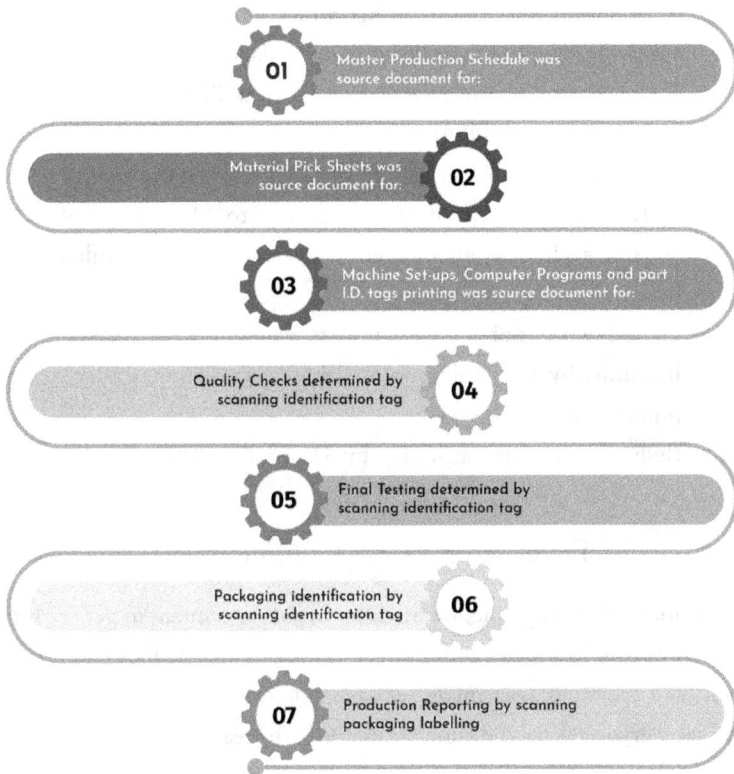

Figure 8.4 Process flow

Step Six: Bill of Materials

We completed a deep dive into both scrap reporting and BOM accuracy. The team identified several BOM inaccuracies, which significantly improved work-in-process inventory accuracy. Additionally, we needed to lock and secure the scrap bins and highly monitor scrap tickets to actual parts. As is common, they were never able to get accuracy using the honor system; too many foxes in the hen house, and no controls or accountability previously existed.

Year-Over-Year Results

- Improved inventory accuracy to 99 percent+.
- Eliminated a two-week physical inventory, which enabled the addition of two weeks to the production calendar.

- Annualized $850,000 in profits, which enhanced company valuation by more than five million dollars.
- Reduced production reporting errors to 50 PPM—annualized savings of $2.5 million.
- Eliminated production disruptions that allowed the facility to achieve a 100 percent line rate and 97 to 99.5 percent of customer schedule, an annualized cost savings of two million dollars.
- Closed two out-of-state just-in-case warehouses. Reduced inventory by $3.5 million or to 13.5 days on hand, a $1.75 million annualized savings.
- Reduced inventory shrinkage by $1.3 million annually.

Dive Log 8 (Art's Commentary)

In the above client example, we used the Rapid Assessment to get the team focused on the basics and to see what was occurring. By focusing for one hour with the rapid assessment, we were able to freeze a moment in time and get everyone to see the same issues. Once the team was seeing the problems in the same light, you could almost hear their egos and self-protection dissolve, with the collective recognition all departments were at fault.

Nonetheless, the early going was still tough.

The team had not bought into my approach and methodology. From prior experience, I knew the changes we were making would get us there. We just needed to accomplish several small wins. After a few weeks, the small wins started to come.

The kitting and visual production meetings enabled the team to begin stringing together several good production days. They completed the Kanban of an assembly area. Several people started to notice this wasn't just another "flavor of the month" program.

There was one event in particular that pulled the team together.

We received an air delivery of a keg of screws needed for production in a few days. The materials manager saw the parts, as did most of the team. Then, in the middle of the production order, the time came to use the parts, and they were not to be found anywhere. Well, Max, the manufacturing manager, was old school and yelled and shouted. That didn't help matters.

They could not find the parts. The production line went home. More screws were air freighted in for the next day. The next day, the line ran again.

Do you know where the parts were found? They found the keg on the same line, used as a footrest!

From that point on, we had the full and undivided attention and support of the entire team.

There must be a structured and foundational approach with a conscious effort to lead the team toward inventory accuracy and utilize the critical KPIs outlined earlier. If you're managing operations, these principles need to be the foundation of visual daily management and part of the KPI cadence reviewed. Then, as required, the appropriate corrective actions are taken.

The rapid assessment set the stage for an unbiased review of their processes. By utilizing this methodology, we shifted team members away from the non-value-added deflection of issues into a professional issue-resolution mindset. This allowed them to dive deep into the people and process foundation fundamentals for Entropy Busters® I and II and materials controls management.

Buddy Check: Questions From Coach Art

- Has purchasing rebranded themselves SCM, and nothing else in the organization has changed except for their name?
- Does your organization view SCM as a singular department or a complete enterprise-encompassing function?
- Are you using cycle counting to maintain inventory accuracy?
- Is inventory accuracy considered vital for total enterprise process integrity?
- Can the team simplify SCM processes, or are there too many complex solutions to straightforward functions?

Art's Deep Dive

Does your bank let you into the vault to cash a check? I don't think so! Why should your stockrooms be open to just anyone?

Do suppliers call four or five months after delivery requesting proof of delivery and payment? If the answer is yes, then you have two concerns. First, there is no useful KPI for an invoice without a physical receipt. Second, there is a material process issue that allows parts to be received, put away, and picked without physical receipt of the part.

The materials team cannot forget they are the supplier to operations. If the operation's team members are coming to the stores requesting parts, there is probably a breakdown in the delivery process. Use this process breakdown as an opportunity to build more robust material delivery processes utilizing pull processes and visual management.

CHAPTER 9

Turbocharging Supply Chain Sustainability

Fans of Jacques Cousteau have heard of "the bends." The bends occur when nitrogen gets absorbed into body tissue and cannot escape fast enough as a diver surfaces. Have you ever opened a carbonated beverage and seen the bubbles escaping to the surface? The same thing can happen to the human body. Only bubbles get trapped in body tissue or the bloodstream, causing embolisms, painful tissue damage, and even death. This is something you want to avoid!

Divers use an underwater dive computer to calculate safe dive times and maximum depths and to avoid the bends. The U.S. Navy perfected a mixed gas combination called Nitrox to increase dive times safely. The typical Nitrox mixture consists of 30 to 32 percent oxygen. The increase in oxygen allows a diver to enjoy their dives longer if they follow the proper dive computer recommendations for time and depth and don't use up their air supply.

My goals as a diver are to experience the underwater environment for as long and safely as possible, capture beautiful images to share, and have fun! Nitrox allows me to accomplish these goals. It's like turbocharging your diving.

How does this relate to business? In business, I aim to reach the pinnacle of sustainability by two methods. First, earning a fair and sustainable profit. Second, creating an inclusive corporate culture that allows every team member to be part of the success story by leveraging their strengths and acquiring loyal customers. Nitrox accomplishes this goal for divers, and Entropy Busters® assures this goal for the business.

Here's an example of entropy.

When driving through the country, remember seeing the old farmhouse or barn in dire need of paint, new shutters, and fields that needed tending? The farmhouse, barn, and fields are moving to a lower energy state and increasing disarray. That is entropy.

You can see entropy in SCM in many places: an unorganized and messy warehouse and data inaccuracies such as inventory accuracy or lead times.

When entropy creeps into your supply chain, it will lead to firefighting, rushed orders, late shipments, unhappy customers, stressed employees, and increased costs.

Entropy doesn't occur overnight within business processes or nature. It can take weeks, months, or years to develop. I call this entropy creep.

To combat entropy creep, I've developed the three-phase methodology of Entropy Busters business processes leveraging visual daily management for the critical skills of:

1. Problem identification and resolution by increasing team involvement.
2. Operational excellence driven by visual daily management.
3. Team building and empowerment.

Are You Managing the Process, or Is the Process Managing You? Getting Supply Chain Management Fundamentals Right

The old farmhouse and barn are excellent examples of entropy in everyday life. Before reviewing typical work examples, it's essential to understand that entropy is the second law of thermodynamics, a natural law of the universe.

Second Law of Thermodynamics: The universe is expanding or moving toward a lower energy state, or increasing randomness—increasing entropy—Lack of order or predictability; the gradual decline into disorder.

This is important to comprehend because the adage of working harder and not smarter cannot win against entropy. The organization must work smarter by utilizing internal talent to build processes that prevent entropy creep.

Everyday Entropy Work Examples

We see our organizations slowly moving toward disorder: meetings that start late, messy offices, and KPIs not updated on time or at all. These are all examples of enterprises moving toward lower energy states of entropy. These small changes gradually add up to significantly impact sustainability and profits. Do you see this occurring at your business?

Do you ever start the day with a plan, and before you know it, "Poof!" your plans have vanished? It feels as though the day is managing you rather than you managing your day. How often have you been involved in fixing a problem at work, whether it's a manufacturing line quality check, such as when an operator stopped doing their first piece inspection and sign-off, or a supply chain process issue caused when the person responsible stopped following up on purchase order acknowledgments?

When people don't follow processes or processes don't exist, entropy creep occurs. When the process is working well, we can get complacent and move on to the next opportunity without following up to be sure sustainability checks are in place.

When moving on too quickly to the next problem without sustainability checks in place and stopping following up, the corrected process breaks down far too often. More entropy creep occurs. Just like a diver constantly monitors the dive time and oxygen levels, management must continually monitor adherence to systems and processes to prevent entropy.

How often are you hurried to make a quick decision during your workday without considering the repercussions? The higher number of hurries each day and week proves that fewer fundamental business processes are in place.

If business fundamentals are not in place, it leads to more firefighting, which in turn disrupts the team from completing their daily tasks and minimizes time for future business process improvements. These events are errors that impact the customer, causing a customer shutdown or a visible quality issue.

When a leader hurries, this is equivalent to rework within your processes that the customer never sees, but it impacts the total cost of ownership (TCO). An excellent example of this effect is when a major customer's order is late, and they call the CEO out of frustration.

Typically, this leads to a chain reaction of events, just to keep it as simple as possible, (Figure 9.1).

Oh, I almost forgot. In all the haste, the order gets shipped to the wrong customer location. I think we have all been here!

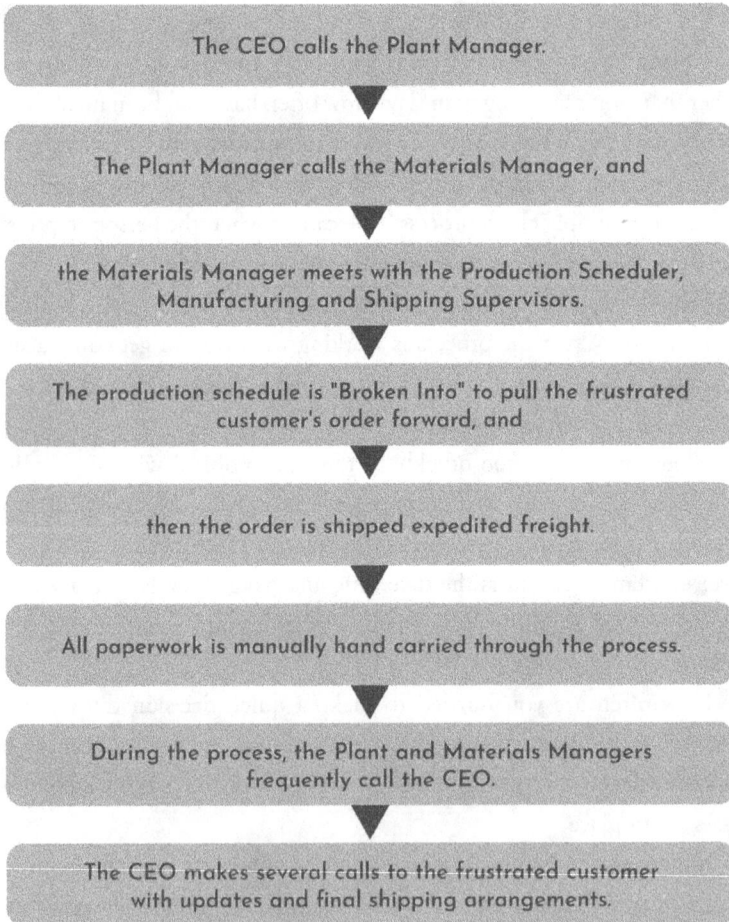

Figure 9.1 Chain reaction of events

Total Cost of Ownership

Let's Review

TCO includes all the direct and indirect costs associated with an asset over the product or service's life cycle. TCO includes not just the purchase price but also the cost of transportation, handling and storage, damage and shrinkage, taxes and insurance, and redistribution costs.

Not having the fundamentals in place is a result of allowing entropy to creep into the process and drive up TCO.

Entropy Is a Profit Killer!

If entropy creep goes unchecked, and it typically does, most teams become firefighters (Figure 9.2). Consider these questions to see if entropy has already crept in:

- Is your team good at the early detection of problems, or are they better at firefighting?

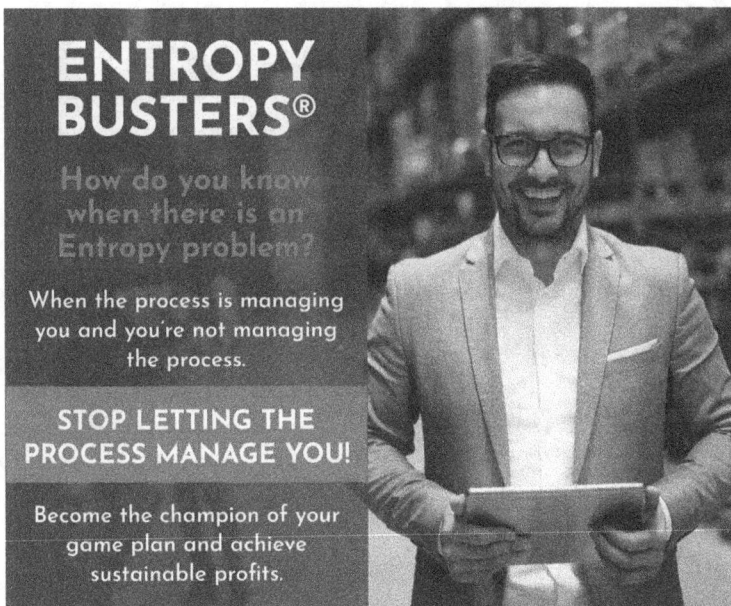

Figure 9.2 Entropy Busters

- How often are there surprise inventory corrections, supplier issues, schedule changes, or pricing issues?
- How good is the supply chain team at managing the supply chain process?
- Suppose there are too many surprises, and there is a sense that the process leads the supply chain or operations team rather than the team managing the process. In that case, critical fundamentals are not correctly in place.

But the problem exists beyond the shop or warehouse floor. It's far too common to see a lack of knowledge of supply chain management (SCM) scope, breadth, and potential as a fundamental misunderstanding among boardrooms, executive-level managers, and leadership.

This common misunderstanding of SCM's functions makes it difficult to administer the proper leadership guidance and KPIs. For this reason, SCM is too often left to its own devices. If nonprofessionals—or no one—run SCM, the consequences can be disastrous for the business.

It all needs to start with establishing the fundamentals.

Going back into my time machine, in 1991, I wrote: "What do managers spend most of their time doing? Firefighting!" But why does a group of trained and educated leaders allow firefighting to take over their professional lives? It happens because of the lack of planning, follow-through, and dedication to process control and management. And some people just like the adrenaline rush of firefighting. (They do not make good leaders, by the way.) Not much has changed in more than three decades!

When I ask clients why they didn't execute their plans, here are the most common and consistent answers:

- "Not sufficient time to plan."
- "Too much chaos."
- "No one followed up."
- "I don't feel empowered."
- "The problem is too big to solve."
- "Limits my creativity."
- "Not my job."

Individuals continue firefighting for many reasons. Here are some of the more common explanations:

- The instant gratification of problem-solving and short-term wins drives decision making.
- It's easier just to put the fire out than to fix the long-term causes and issues.
- Teams follow the path of least resistance and often don't see a need to get other people involved.
- Managers and senior leadership frequently reward the best firefighters with a hero and cult-like status.
- When the culture is built upon these principles, it's common to find that the best firefighters are—unintentionally—also the best arsonists.

It takes energy to challenge the status quo. Therefore, many supervisors, managers, and leaders let firefighting become the norm because they lack faith in their ability to improve things beyond the norm.

To counteract entropy, we must understand and accept the importance of crawling before walking and walking before running. Achieving this goal is an area of significant passion for me, so I designed and developed a three-phase process methodology of Entropy Busters. It highlights business processes that have broken down while revealing what is needed to sustain best practices. If you want sustainable methods, you must add energy to the process to prevent entropy creep.

It makes sense that we need a robust process to keep entropy creep in check.

Each day, we encounter more and more distractions in the form of e-mail, instant messages, and social networks. It's easier to show up at work, hide behind our computers, and close our office doors than to get involved and resolve problems.

No wonder, overwhelmingly, individuals are dissatisfied with their place of employment or managers. The "Franklin Planner/Stephen Covey planning in solitude" is the practice of using the first 15 minutes of each day for solitude and planning tasks that will make the next day or week successful. We need this today more than ever before!!

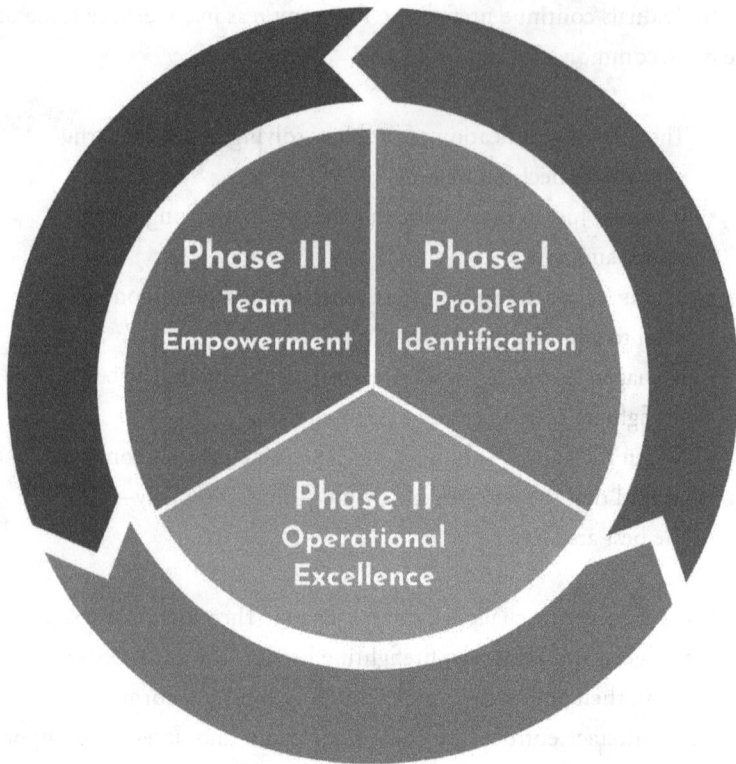

Figure 9.3 The three phases of Entropy Busters

People are often rewarded for timely responses but not for the quality of responses. Too often, broken processes of a formalized enterprise operating system are accepted, and the belief persists that nothing can be done to fix them.

Text messages, e-mails, or phone calls initiated by well-intentioned employees to solve problems have become an inefficient work-around to the existing operating systems. This causes inferior results and is detrimental to business because this information is not captured inside the ERP. The problem may never be identified and cannot be fixed.

In today's ever-increasing drive for cost containment, whether you are conducting business-to-business (B2B) or business-to-consumer (B2C), it's increasingly important to leverage the automation potential of e-commerce and software platforms. Therefore, we need to avoid having people manually transfer information (if this gets done at all) from text messages, e-mails, or phone calls into the enterprise planning system (ERP). We spend millions of dollars of hard-earned capital to implement ERPs that streamline processes and reduce costs. Let's be certain we take full advantage of the ERP capabilities to improve operations and reduce costs.

Now that we understand that entropy creep (after all, it's a natural law of physics) is the root cause of poor SCM performance, management's firefighting—the act of solving urgent short-term problems that could and should be prevented in the first place—must be eliminated.

We need to build a sustainable solution and embrace the concept of a robust process to keep entropy from taking over the business. Time and time again, I've seen continuous failures with attempts to resolve entropy problems within organizations.

A classic example, at least for me, of the inability to keep entropy in check is the morning daily production meetings. I've often seen a manufacturing plant have parts shortages, quality issues, and unscheduled or preventable machine downtime. These all lead to horrible on-time delivery.

Let's say someone establishes a daily production meeting with required attendance from the following groups: manufacturing, materials, quality, engineering, maintenance, and human resource managers and leads. The intent is to outline, track, and take corrective actions on every task required to succeed in the next 8, 12, 24, and 48 hours.

What usually happens, and is supposed to happen, is that on-time deliveries are improved to acceptable levels.

Then, rather than continuing to work as a team to resolve other issues daily, people gradually drop off, assuming the fire has been put out. The positive improvements will continue for a period due to the initial momentum. The people who quit attending the daily production meeting will cry success and say the meeting is now a "waste of our valuable time" and we need to work on something more substantial. However, just as entropy crept into the process before, without daily pushing back against entropy and a constant focus on improvement, entropy creep occurs again.

The Entropy Force Field

From my professional experience, there is a flawed belief that if intelligent and hardworking people get hired and the current team works harder, most problems will be solved. I wish it worked that way. It would make our lives much more straightforward, but it doesn't.

Envision any symphony orchestra without a conductor. Would all the musicians be synchronized in performing and in tune with one another? Most definitely not.

We need a plan to align processes and simultaneously get the entire team working together to break this flawed belief system. It may sound simple. In principle, it is elementary. Here are the five essential management principles that ensure entropy-busting success (Figure 9.4):

1. **Get the team involved.** First, load up the bus with the right mix of team members. Then, later in Phase II, find the best use for each individual's talents. The critical early element of entropy busting is getting team members involved. What can be accomplished by getting just a few team members focused on an opportunity is incredible. It's not about hiring more people. It's about getting the current team members to become part of the solution. It can also be a great learning experience for team members and their managers to better understand everyone's strengths, weaknesses, and natural talents.

2. **Stay focused.** Keep the team focused on the critical few KPIs. It will take discipline, tenacity, and perseverance. This process is similar to building good daily exercise habits and creating a "Deep Work" mindset.

Get the Team Involved	Stay Focused	The Right Path	Play to WIN!	Become a Leader
• Load up the bus • Start to find each individuals best fit seat • Problem resolution	• Keep discipline • Keep tenacity • Develop 'Deep Work' mindset • Operational excellence • Visual daily management	• Don't take the path of least resistance • Don't get distracted • No detours • Everyone on the same page	• Once results start. Don't let off the gas • Go for the WIN! • Don't play 'Not to lose'	• Okay not to know everything • Admit mistakes • Listen and hear • Learn • Build community • Have fun

Figure 9.4 The entropy force field

3. **The right path.** Don't let the path of the least resistance take over. Don't get distracted by the next new idea or shiny object. The state of entropy feeds on these distractions.
4. **Play to win.** Once you start to get results, don't take your foot off the gas. Go for the win! Don't implement the defensive game plan of playing "Not to Lose."
5. **Become a leader.** It's okay not to know everything and to admit mistakes when you have made them. That's what leadership is all about. Teach the team how to make many minor improvements. Educate and train on how to make educated and calculated steps toward improvement. When mistakes occur, they are minor and easily correctable, and you learn something.

Entropy is an opposing force that exists in your enterprise. In fighting entropy's advance, there must be an opposite force of equal or greater value to keep entropy in check. To counteract entropy, I've developed a force field analysis process.

The three-phase operating model called Entropy Busters (Figure 9.3) is a closed-loop methodology to minimize entropy creep. The entropy busters force field analysis model (Figures 9.5) illustrates how the opposing forces of entropy busters keep entropy out of the organization. Additionally, this model allows organizations the flexibility necessary to adjust the steps needed to meet their operational challenges best while establishing structure and methodology for long-term sustainable success.

Dive Log 9 (Art's Commentary)

Three key points set entropy busters apart from other process improvement methodologies.

First, a physical law of the universe causes entropy. My clients who have more easily transitioned through change management know their battle isn't about working longer and harder days but working smarter by building the entropy busters force field.

Second, much of supply chain success is driven by cross-functional teamwork. How does your organization view SCM? Too many organizations incorrectly call the purchasing department the SCM.

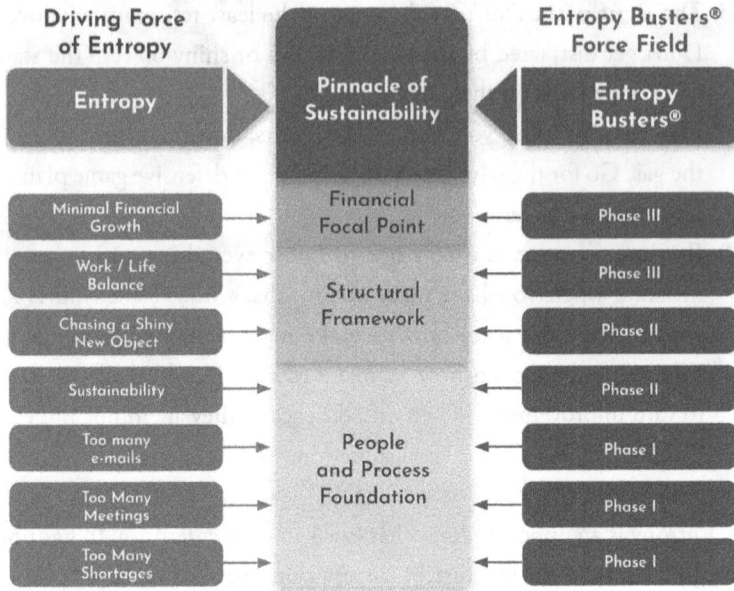

Figure 9.5 Entropy busters force field analysis

If your organization considers SCM by including internal operations such as receiving, shipping, materials and production control, and procurement part of SCM, you're moving in the correct direction. Or do you have supplier partners that work closely with engineering, operations, and procurement to reduce the TCO? World-class SCM organizations have CEOs who once were the head of SCM, such as Tim Cook at Apple.

Third, Entropy Busters is an operational excellence model like The Shingo or Toyota Production System. However, my emphasis is on the three different phases of growth: Phase I, problem identification; Phase II, operational excellence; and Phase III, team empowerment. Ensuring that teams gain traction by crawling before walking and walking before running will help to instill long-term acceptance and sustainability of processes.

Art's Gold: There is a significant underestimation of entropy's ability to creep into your business. It's always waiting for you to drop your defenses.

Buddy Check: Questions From Coach Art

- Are your supply chain processes managing you, or are you managing the processes?
- Do you find yourself rushing from one task to the next, and are you still having surprise problems such as parts outages, expediting, or cost adjustments?
- Are you working harder and harder with little success in solving the root causes of problems?

Art's Deep Dive

Stop letting the process manage you! Become the champion of your game plan and achieve sustainable profits.

For additional information and free tools, please scan the code.

CHAPTER 10

Entropy Busters® Phase I— Overcoming Denial

When scuba diving against a light current, you must keep kicking your fins, or the current pushes you back to where you started or further down. A similar effect occurs with entropy in business. Energy must be added to supply chain processes to reverse entropy and prevent the cycle of entropy creep. To reduce and reverse entropy, we need to break down processes into their simplest elements and rebuild them with simple solutions.

Breaking Denial, Loading the Team Bus, and Problem Resolution

Let's begin with a definition of Phase I: It is not a system implementation but a shift of focus by leadership and an organizational mindset transformation.

Phase I is about getting out of our offices, away from our computers. It's about finding a common enemy, an urgency to succeed, and letting go of the fear that you might not have all the answers.

Leaders must be tenacious, have laser focus, and be committed to involving the team while teaching and educating them in critical thinking skills and problem-solving.

Envision Entropy Busters as your offensive front line, enabling you to manage your daily/weekly/monthly game plan(s). Here are the nine fundamentals of the Phase I framework that must be in place to be successful:

1. **Getting managers and supervisors involved.** I am often asked, "What type of leaders do we need?" We need leaders willing to lead their people face-to-face and have their fingerprints on the solutions. Leading can't be done from an office or behind a computer screen.

Leadership is a contact sport; the team must see your quantifiable contribution. Leaders have to be physically present.

Art's Gold: Leadership is a contact sport.

2. **Significant emotional experience, finding a common enemy, and a heightened sense of urgency.** There must be a powerful emotional experience to get someone's attention and to get them to change. It takes a crisis, such as loss of profits, loss of a significant customer, or loss of a product line. These incidents will affect change. We need a common enemy: **Entropy** or **Inventory Is Evil!** is a good start. This philosophy must be shared across the entire enterprise. During the COVID-19 pandemic, my clients were able to surgically cut through corporate red tape and swiftly turn the organization to course-correct demand changes and supply chain shortages. Without total organizational "buy-in," this would have never happened.

3. **Park the egos and lose the denial**. Ego can be a strength, but as with any strength, once the "volume" is turned up too much, it becomes a weakness. The key objective is to take a hard look in the mirror and ask yourself, "Am I addicted to chaos?" The company fundamentals must be improved if your day is filled with turmoil and regular firefights. As I've mentioned before, companies are usually in dire need of help when they call me. Typically, they are in a severe state of denial, hoping easy improvements are right around the corner. Checking egos at the door is critical to breaking down communication barriers and finding the root cause of problems.

4. **Don't short-cut the process.** The people and process foundation must already be well established while the structural framework takes shape. Be sure considerable progress is being made with the nine points of Phase I before moving forward with Phase II. It's vital to seek critical feedback from peer groups and team members. I've known organizations that have used coaches to ensure that meetings functioned as required. Coaches are an excellent resource for feedback on process compliance across multiple teams. Working with one client, we established a council of coaches to ensure each team had a coach and a consistent application of a visual daily

meeting format, problem-solving tools, and steady quantifiable progress.

5. **Don't become complacent.** I often observe that clients' results will drastically improve, only for them to stop utilizing the exact processes that got them to that point because they thought everything was fixed and could return to "normal." There is no normal. Remember, you are at war with a natural law of nature, entropy, and you must keep pushing back with more energy to succeed in the long term. Keep the focus on the enemy! Good isn't good enough. Push for higher standards and significantly better results.

6. **Keep focused.** You can't bounce around from one "hot potato" or "shiny object" to the next and expect long-term sustainable results. The organization must pick a battle and win that battle. If you have too many priorities, then there are no priorities!

7. **Establish meaningful KPIs.** If you have 100 KPIs, then you have none. Cut the 100 KPIs to three to five of the most meaningful ones. Significantly reducing KPIs will establish a clear vision of the mission that team members must accomplish. Train, enlighten, and educate the team on why these KPIs are essential to the customer and the business and how they will positively impact the organization.

8. **Get everyone on the bus and establish a purpose.** Get everyone engaged and focused on the top three to five KPIs. Clients frequently ask me, "Do we have the right people?" My usual answer is, "Absolutely, they just need to be led!" Don't worry too much about getting individuals or team members into the right seat immediately; just get them involved as part of the solution. Educate your team on the prominent features of your product, who the buyers are, and how it makes the world a better place. Then measure progress daily on the critical KPIs.

9. **Foundations of operational excellence.** Let me emphasize the importance of building the foundation of operational excellence and critical thinking skills in basic statistical process controls (SPC). Operational excellence is the conviction of the continuous improvement methodologies such as the Shingo model and the Toyota Production Systems that embrace team evolvement, visual management, improvement to process flow, and customer focus.

Start simple. We are not building a rocket ship! Basic SPC will significantly improve your profits. Following the plan-do-check-act (PDCA) closed-loop cycle is the simplest and best model to carry out change in any process. The cycle can be repeated multiple times to advance the process continually and thus improve profits with each cycle (Figure 10.1).

The Pareto chart (Figure 10.2) contains both bars and lines; the bars are represented in descending order, and the line is a cumulative total. In simple terms, it's a plain bar graph sorted from left to right, largest to smallest, and it's an essential part of most organizations' root cause analysis. I use a Pareto chart when stratifying part usage, spending, and purchase orders placed. The Pareto chart process allows me to "hone" in on the critical few part numbers that can significantly impact inventory performance and where most purchase orders are placed to improve buyers' workload.

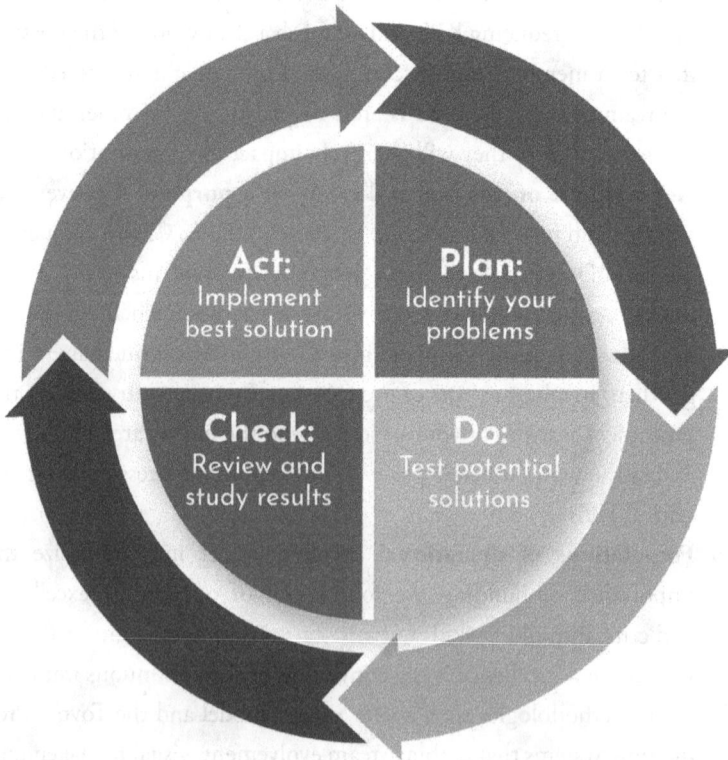

Figure 10.1 Plan-do-check-act process

Typical Pareto Chart—Percent of Total Part Numbers by Class

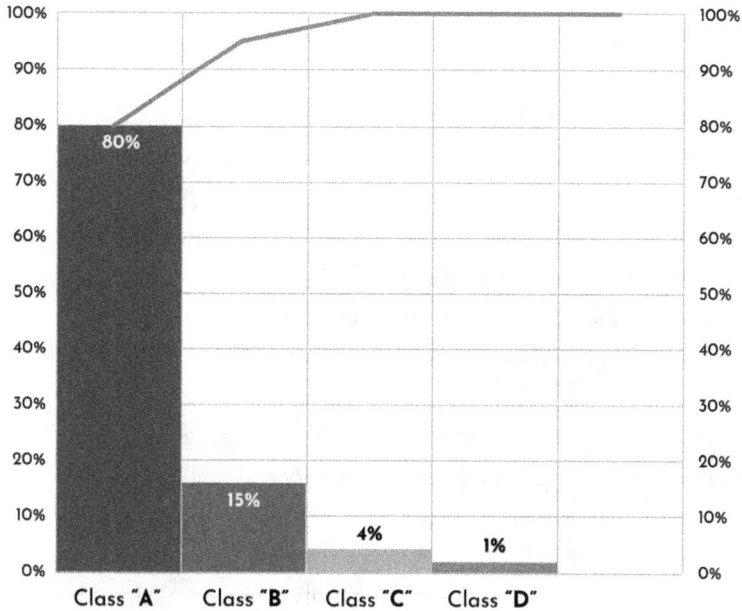

Figure 10.2 Typical Pareto chart

Dive Master Briefing (Client Example)

During one part of my career, I was the head of the supply chain for an automotive tier 1 supplier. We had a good team, and we got everyone on the bus and engaged in improving the business. At one point, we had over 50 KPIs that we reduced to a solid group of five relevant metrics as follows:

1. Supply acknowledgments
2. Supplier late and early deliveries
3. Purchase orders to cancel or defer
4. Compliance with the master production schedule
5. Customer service/requirements—on-time-to-ship requirements

We were functioning at 100 percent of customer requirements and achieving excellent inventory turns of 47 per year.

Even with this momentous success, the days were long and hectic, and we never felt that we had things under control. Something was missing. We achieved excellent inventory velocity, customer service, and respectable profits.

Yet, I still worked 11 to 12 hours/day, six days a week. There was one thing that I discovered that needed to be done differently.

We had these large production meetings that, on a good day, would take 45 minutes. When things were not going well, they could be as long as one and a half hours! The meetings kept critical people off the shop floor and did so at a crucial time, the start of a shift. Also, many tasks were assigned to just a few select people that often were not completed.

During this part of my journey, I learned how critical participative leadership could be. To get the teams motivated, we needed a common enemy.

So, I learned to park my ego at the door and let go of denial. When coupled with driving toward process integrity and keeping our feet on the accelerator of improvement goes a long way toward solving most problems. Additionally, honing in on the relevant few KPIs, achieving team engagement, and developing critical thinking skills help to win critical improvement battles. These critical actions steered us toward excellent progress.

However, to get to the next level of performance, we needed to do something differently. We needed to reframe our focus. That was how entropy busters Phase II was created.

Client Testimonial

Art and I were fellow department managers at a growing and demanding auto supplier. Our environment was like "shoeing a running horse" as we rapidly evolved into an award-winning manufacturing operation with statistical process control, production line teams, bottleneck management, and unheard-of "quality control shutdowns" by line operators. He also skillfully managed the external demands of remote central offices, suppliers, and customers, enabling production to focus on manufacturing tasks. He was instrumental in our organization winning the coveted Ford Q1 award and becoming a key General Motors supplier while more than doubling our workforce and shift operations.

—Charles Phaneuf, Retired TRW Engineering Manager:

Buddy Check: Questions From Coach Art

- Is the leadership team practicing participative leadership?
- Does the organization have a common enemy to motivate transformation?
- Does the team let their egos get in the way of decisions?
- Is there a long-term denial of root causes?
- When improvements begin to gain traction, does the team stop following processes causing progress to slide backward?
- Does the team take their foot off the gas and become complacent and doesn't dig deeper and ask another "why" for a better understanding of root causes?
- Are KPIs streamlined down to the relevant few?
- Is the team engaged, and do they believe they are part of the solution?
- Can team members use PDCA, basic SPC, and Pareto charts to solve problems and improve processes?

Art's Deep Dive

Firefighting results from a lack of communication, planning, and sustainable processes necessitating *change*!

CHAPTER 11

Entropy Busters® Phase II— Making Progress

Operational Excellence Driven by Visual Daily Management and the Same Page

As I noted in Chapter 10, Phase I, a missing piece of the puzzle was getting the team to the next performance level. What I finally realized was that it was all ME! I needed to let the team become part of the solution rather than me driving the entire process.

Entropy Busters Phase II has six fundamentals that focus on sustaining the methods established in the people and process foundation and structural framework, creating visual daily management (VDM) processes that enable transparency, speed of communication, and rapid problem resolution.

Sustain Phase I

Don't become complacent and backslide during Phase I. Keep the focus and the forward momentum going. It's more complicated than it sounds. One barrier to success is that executive leadership must understand entropy busters. They must be informed, be part of the process, and help protect meeting cadence. It's common for different agendas to override the early stages of VDM and its supporting processes. That's why it's important to start small and build a model VDM meeting process. However, it's equally important to include executive leadership and peer organizations as soon as the process begins to gel. Taking this action will build inclusion and shared success.

Getting Everyone in the Right Bus Seat

Many leaders don't know how to get people into the correct bus seat. Too often, people are assigned tasks or roles that match the preexisting beliefs of management. This antiquated belief system is not successful in the long term because there is no buy-in from people who contribute to the process. You'll never discover the people's strengths, weaknesses, or passions unless they are part of the process. Giving everyone on the team a role or task is critical, and I have succeeded in asking volunteers to complete specific and challenging tasks. After implementing this practice, people become engaged in the process, and over time, we can better determine strengths, weaknesses, and particular areas of interest and passion.

Visual Daily Management and Getting Everyone on the Same Page

The goal of VDM is to increase transparency and communication. Management should post VDM information for the teams' review daily and weekly. Team members need to see the good, bad, and ugly results. Increasing communication within departments and cross-functionally will result in swifter problem resolution and fewer missed assignments.

When the entire team is engaged in the VDM process, is on the same page, and knows what must be done right now to make today and tomorrow successful, tactical business processes stabilize, and sustainability develops.

With better communication and team members on the same page, they become more productive and focused and less distracted by e-mails, surprise part shortages, and meetings. With concise and timely communication established, team members become part of the solution, increase their scope of control with the process, are invested in their future, and receive recognition for individual and team contributions.

Working toward this goal is most beneficial by getting everyone to participate in a daily 15-minute review of the most critical and relevant KPIs. These meetings can be production meetings, supply chain status meetings, and so on.

Have the team work on *actions* that must be taken *right now* to make the next 24 to 48 hours successful.

Get everyone focused on the same goal, making the most of the meeting time. Encourage the team to use the meeting to answer questions buried in e-mails and any new issues that must be addressed and invite other key stakeholders to participate in real-time.

Art's Gold: These in-person meetings—not e-mail—must be the heartbeat of all communications.

My experience has shown that conducting one large production meeting lasting 45 to 90 minutes with 40 people is too cumbersome to produce the best results. Production meetings are a more effective and better use of team members' time if they are divided into groups of six to eight people, focusing on a specific line or value stream lasting 15 to 20 minutes.

It's common for the initial meetings to last 20 to 30 minutes until the kinks are ironed out.

Once critical issues are addressed, and everyone is on the same page with a sense of urgency established, each session should be down to around 15 to 20 minutes.

After three weeks, I recommend enforcing a time limit of 20 minutes, understanding that as special situations occur, the session may exceed the goal time of 15 to 20 minutes.

Each departmental function is required to have one representative present at the VDM meeting. The representatives are individually responsible for communicating all relevant meeting information to their peers. The most knowledgeable individuals would attend the meeting if a critical problem needed discussion.

This approach ensures that team members are focused on where they can add the most value, which reduces the time spent in meetings and the total number of sessions and enables better focus and accountability.

When working in a manufacturing environment, I always start by creating a scheduling board (see Figure 11.1 for an example). There is a category for each departmental function. Have team members communicate their corporate roles, be part of the solution, and build team inclusion, ownership, and urgency.

Value Stream / Cell / Production Line: BR -54 -9											Date: 6/1
Model Number	Qty	Due Date	Safety	Quality	Matls #1	Matls #2	Matls #3	Engineering	Maintenance	Production	Clear to Build
			Safety Concerns for work cell	"Prints Jig and Fixtures"	Purchase Parts	Parts from Sister facilities	Part's from Internal Suppliers	All Prints and critical information	All Preventative Maintenance completed	Team Trained Key Employee Coverage	
ACME - NZAB - 001	1 000	6/1	✔	✔	✔	✔	✔	✔	✔	✔	✔
ACME - USAA - 001	500	6/1	✔	✔	✔	✔	✔	✔	✔	✔	✔
ACME - EUAB - 002	1 500	6/2	✔	✔	✔	✔	✔	✔	✔	✔	✔
ACME - USAA - 002	750	6/3	✔	✔	✔	✗	✔	✔	✔	✔	✗
ACME - NZAB - 001	500	6/3	✔	✔	✔	✔	✔	✔	✔	✔	✔
ACME - SAAB - 003	250	6/3	✔	✗	✔	✔	✔	✗	✔	✗	✗
ACME - NZAB - 001	1 500	6/4	✔	✔	✔	✔	✔	✔	✔	✔	✔
ACME - USAA - 001	1 000	6/5	✔	✔	✔	✔	✔	✔	✔	✔	✔
ACME - EUAB - 002	500	6/5	✔	✗	✗	✗	✗	✔	✔	✗	✗
	7 500										

Figure 11.1 Visual daily management—scheduling board

Each time I implement a VDM scheduling board, the team is amazed to observe how hard they have worked and how often different departments have different priorities. In Figure 11.1, the board visually highlights the meeting agenda outline: safety, quality, materials, and so on. This essential tool keeps the meeting focused, to the point, and brief.

Six Positive Outcomes From VDM Scheduling Boards

1. Establishes a meeting cadence.
2. People are on the bus and in good seats.
3. People are on the same page regarding priorities.
4. Creates urgency: What actions are required to make the next 8, 12, 24, or 48 hours successful?
5. People's daily sense of accomplishment.
6. VDM creates a practical visual scoreboard to determine the value stream status.

After successfully implementing a scheduling board(s), the next step is to add an SQDIP board. SQDIP is an acronym for safety, quality, delivery, inventory, and productivity. SQDIP is a tool of VDM that swiftly assesses how the process is performing based on the goals set for safety, quality, delivery, inventory, and productivity. See Figure 4.4, SQDIP key performance indicators.

Common Mistakes

Occasionally, a client will ask me to reimplement failed attempts at SQDIP. To avoid setbacks when implementing this tool:

- Be sure the team knows the process improvement they want to measure. For example, often, there is a quality check to have team members complete a first-piece inspection 100 percent of the time.
- Start with one or two KPI areas—the critical few. If too many KPIs exist, team members cannot implement countermeasures when problems arise.
- SQDIP is a cultural change. Managers and supervisors need to have the proper mindset to support the team, and it will take time for each person to recalibrate their value-added contribution to the process.

Departments included in VDM meetings:

- **Materials Department**—Since materials have a relationship with the external customer and are a vital supplier to internal customers, they typically facilitate VDM by communicating any parts shortages or potential shortages and how they could impact manufacturing orders.
- **Manufacturing**—Critical team members' vacations, machinery statuses, or essential preventive maintenance timing could impact specific orders.
- **Quality**—Any quality issues, pilot order dates, or production part approval processes (PPAP) needed?
- **Engineering**—Any design changes or help needed with the current design or manufacturability questions and support?

- **Maintenance**—Total preventative maintenance questions, staffing support, scheduling for critical technical personnel, or any help needed to address equipment performance issues?
- **Site and Safety**—Any issues with holiday or vacation planning, meeting planning, or following proper environment, health, and safety processes?
- **Operational Excellence Office**—Have a Kaizen or continuous improvement office representative listen to and understand daily challenges for future operational excellence projects.

Understanding of and Focus on Internal Customers

We discussed end-customer delivery, service and fit, form, and product function. However, we often forget that our internal customers can have those exact requirements, so it must be part of our mission statement and process for all customers.

Establish Gemba

Gemba—The Japanese term for "actual place" refers to the shop floor or any place where value-creating work occurs, often also spelt genba.

"The term stresses that real improvement requires a shop-floor focus based on direct observation of current work conditions. For example, standardized work for a machine operator cannot be determined and written up at a desk in the engineering office but must be defined and revised on the Gemba walk."[1]

Gemba Walk—The Gemba walk is a management practice used to assess the current situation through direct observation and inquiry before making a specific action plan. Lean thinkers define it as the place where value is created. Japanese companies often supplement Gemba with the related term "Genchi Genbutsu," essentially "go and see for yourself," to stress the importance of observation. Because value flows horizontally across companies to customers, a productive way to have a Gemba walk is to follow a single product family.

James Womack, the author of *Gemba Walks* and founder of the Lean Enterprise Institute, advocates Gemba starts from product design or customer-facing process, from start to finish across all departments, functions, and organizations. Womack recommends gathering everyone who touches the process to walk together while discussing:

- Purpose (what problem does this process resolve for the customer?);
- Process (how does it work?); and
- People (are they engaged in creating, sustaining, and improving the process?).

The Gemba walk becomes the focal process for organizations to learn real-time issues, communicate actions needed, and reveal the leadership method required to support team members.

Establish Cadence for Tactical and Strategic Tasks

Managers must create a cadence or rhythm for the day. With a known cadence for the day, team members can dedicate time to resolve today's issues and define the deep work focus for tomorrow. I have found great success reserving mornings for *today*—the tasks that make the next 24 to 48 hours successful, afternoons for *tomorrow*, and applying longer-term solutions.

Having mornings set aside for the tactical and afternoons for longer-term solutions reframes the team's focus and reinforces the discipline and structure needed to succeed. Figure 11.2 is a representation of a suggested cadence. Feel free to make any modifications you see necessary to fit your organization.

Dive Log 11 (Art's Commentary)

In my decades of experience, I have witnessed that many companies want to skip VDM steps. They think it is micromanaging their teams, and the team members should know the tasks they are responsible for. The mission of the scheduling board is to get everyone on the same page visually.

Morning - Tactical Cadence	
6:00am	Shift Preparation
7:00am	Shift Start-Up
8:00 - 9:30am	Visual Daily Management Reviews: 15 to 20 minutes each
9:30 - 10:00am	Follow-up
10:00 - 11:30am	GEMBA Reviews
11:30am - 1:00pm	Lunch and Issues resolution

Afternoon - Strategic Cadence	
Weekly	Site and Safety
	Quality and Scrap Analysis
	Kaisen Report Outs
	Training Sessions: Facilitator, Maintenance, Self-Directed Teams, Statistical Process Control
Monthly	Safety Council
	Quality Council
	Materials Council
	Engineering Process Improvements
	Birthday recognition lunch and communications meetings
Quarterly	All hands—Status Reviews, with employee participation/presenters

Figure 11.2 Morning—tactical cadence and afternoon—strategic cadence

Imagine an orchestra without a conductor or a football game without huddling between each play. Within a short period, an orchestra or the football team would be out of rhythm with each other, and a VDM scheduling board prevents this problem from occurring.

Many people think flash reports are the same as the boards used in VDM. Flash reports summarize critical financial and operational measures issued by finance or accounting daily, weekly, or monthly.

Flash reports are typically associated with cash management, operations efficiency, and sales. To me, flash report and VDM are entirely different. Flash reports are sent via e-mail or posted in a cafeteria. Flash reports do nothing more than update the organization on certain information. Flash reports do not highlight priorities or get people working together to solve problems.

VDM boards get people focused on short-term priorities. VDM boards should be four by eight feet in dimension and visible in the organization's communication hub. VDMs broadcast the current statuses, such as production and material availability, and specify what must be accomplished to make the team successful. The VDM meeting functions as the orchestra's conductor, bringing individuals and operations together to create one team focused on common goals.

Many leaders confuse Gemba with managing by walking around. Gemba has a set schedule and route. Nothing is worse than a supervisor or manager appearing at your work area unannounced and looking over your shoulder. Be respectful of team members' spaces.

Supply chain management can quickly become complex and overwhelming with complicated assemblies and far-reaching supplier networks. A crucial fundamental of managing the people and process foundation is the implementation of Entropy Busters Phases I and II to guide the organization toward synchronized communication and materials flow.

Buddy Check: Questions From Coach Art

- Are you able to sustain Entropy Busters Phase I?
- Can you get team members into the most appropriate bus seat that utilizes their strengths and talents?
- Are VDM and SQDIP effective in getting the team working together in harmony?

- Does the organization understand the importance of internal customer focus?
- Are you able to establish GEMBA walks with a predetermined schedule?
- Are VDM and Gemba walk schedules "protected" from others overriding or attempting to change priorities?
- Do all the functions of responsibility actively participate in VDM and Gemba?

Art's Deep Dive

Once the results start occurring and the process gains momentum, include other peer groups such as sales, marketing, and finance. Not involving these departments early in the process risks leaving them behind as the original team matures and has already been through the forming, storming, norming, and performing steps of change management.[2]

When working on problem resolution, don't look for perfection. Try solutions that are practical and quick to implement. The idea is to Fail Fast ... Fix Fast equals success.

For additional information and free tools, please scan the code.

CHAPTER 12

Entropy Busters® Phase III—People Matters

Team Building, Empowerment, Establishing Community, and Having Fun

Note: Entropy Busters Phase III is part of the financial focal point. I've included the chapter here not to lose the cadence of this important discussion.

The three phases of entropy busters are layers built upon one another. At its core, Phase I gets the organization involved, cuts through unnecessary KPIs, and implements the principles for problem resolution. Phase I is like learning how to snorkel.

Phase II emphasizes implementing visual daily management, synchronized communication, and understanding team members' strengths, weaknesses, and talents to get them into roles where they can succeed. Phase II is like learning how to be a competent diver.

Phase III emphasizes tuning the environment so team members can thrive, adding more highly tuned visual daily management for binary data integrity and process controls, and having fun. Phase III is like becoming a dive master.

Whether we like it or not, organizations are bound to their enterprise resource planning (ERP) and material requirements planning (MRP) systems. They are far too often "black" boxes of information, flags, alerts, and multistep settings that confuse the brightest of people. In entropy busters Phase III, you learn how to bring order from chaos by implementing the methodology of entropy busters process and data VDM and unleashing your team's potential.

Team Building

Previously, we discussed getting team members on the bus and finding the best seat for them to thrive. It is vital to recognize a team is not a team until it has completed at least one cycle of forming, storming, norming, and performing, initially developed by psychologist Bruce Tuckman in 1965 to describe group development.

All teams pass through and fluctuate between forming, storming, norming, and performing cycles. It's perfectly normal.

Some of the best teams often need to complete a lot of storming. However, the entire team benefits by forgiving each other for past behaviors and organizational differences, holding each other 100 percent accountable individually and jointly for shared responsibilities, and continuously moving forward.

Don't underestimate team members. Most want to be part of something bigger and better, and building a better team is essential for everyone's identity and self-worth.

Instill a learning mindset among the team. Team members' confidence grows and flourishes when they are better trained and educated on your business processes, philosophies, and methodologies:

- Recognize the team for both good and unfavorable results. Emphasize that "red" is blameless. When a pattern of red KPIs is considered negative and bad news, the numbers might get "sanitized," and the problem might be ignored until it becomes a crisis. Don't let this happen. We need to reframe the team's view of negative or red results as opportunities to fix the root cause of problems.
- Establish friendly team rivalries. We all enjoy sports rivalries between our favorite local teams and teams from other cities. Rivalries between value streams, work cells, and departments can be beneficial if they are healthy and respectful. The goal is to win together; friendly competition helps each "special team" improve performance.
- Make communication meetings enjoyable and establish a family atmosphere. A group I once worked with had the

most productive birthday lunches and dinners for team members. There was no set agenda, just a meeting to recognize and celebrate their birthdays. These events allowed us to create a family atmosphere and meet one-on-one to get to know one another in a nonthreatening setting. Before adjourning, local leadership held a question-and-answer session where team members would ask any questions they desired.

- During quarterly reviews, have hourly compensated team members and all levels of salaried employees participate and present results to their value stream. Recognize the team with the best results from the prior quarter. (Be sure all value streams have matching KPIs and the same evaluation.) The winning team was awarded a trophy that took on the NHL's Stanley Cup persona for best-performing line/value stream.

Give Everyone a Role

By assigning everyone a function, you build inclusion and make everyone part of the solution. You will be amazed at how many hidden geniuses are discovered or the number of organizational castaways that gain a new lease on life when given more responsibility, challenges, and recognition.

Visual Daily Management Process and Data Red/Green

Another area that I'm very passionate about is VDM as a critical element of the entropy busters methodology. Every organization I've worked with has a significant problem with data integrity. This problem can be anything from maintaining safety stock quantities to confirming that purchase orders are acknowledged or promptly disposing of rejected material. What always seems to happen is that individuals are busy taking care of today's issues and never take the time to maintain the process or data integrity. And, before you know it, the data behind Oz's Curtain is in total disarray and useless for management planning or decision making.

When reviewing the root cause behind surprise stock outages, I've found that 90 percent of the time, if we were to practice the fundamentals such as:

- Timely order placement;
- Purchase order acknowledgment;
- Purchase order expediting;
- And establishing that rejected material authorizations are processed accurately and promptly.

Then, surprise stock outages would be a thing of the past.

Because of the common and chronic problem with data integrity, I created the methodology of entropy busters process and data VDM. Earlier, we discussed the VDM of production lines and SQDIP. With entropy busters process and data VDM, we make critical data visual. Figure 12.1, as the VDM name suggests, must be reviewed daily. However, some KPIs will have review cadences somewhere between daily and quarterly. The key is to make it visual and to build the review into your operational excellence process. Since the process report is binary and red-green, the review should take two to five minutes. Understand this is not a red-yellow-green stop light. It's a binary yes-no. The process can also be thought of as an Andon Light for system data. Manufacturing uses Andon systems to alert maintenance, team members and management of quality or process issues within production. The data VDM plays the same function for the ERP and MRP.

Sustaining Phases I, II, and III and Finding Genius and the Castaways, Discussed in Chapter 19

Dive Master Briefing (Client Example)

The most successful team environment I have ever had the privilege to be part of was at an electromechanical assembly plant. Despite their remarkable success, the plant was not improving as quickly as its peer facilities. By falling behind their peer facilities, corporate headquarters would not place new products into the facility, resulting in a loss of an estimated five to ten million dollars in additional sales per year. They had an excellent

Description	Cadence D/W/M	Target for Green	Process and Data Red - Green VDM (1–25)	Calendar or Fiscal Months (Jan Feb Mar Apr May Jun / Jul Aug Sep Oct Nov Dec)
Owner—Replenishment Planning				
Buying to Plan Date	D	3 Lines < 2 Days	●●●●●●●●●●●●●●●●●●●●●●●●●	
Buying to Plan Quality	D	0 Changes	●●●●●●●●●●●●●●●●●●●●●●●●●	
Purchase Order Acknowledgment	D	0 > 2 days	●●●●●●●●●●●●●●●●●●●●●●●●●	
Late Purchase orders	D	5 Lines < 3 Days	●●●●●●●●●●●●●●●●●●●●●●●●●	
Zero Inv On hand (For Stocked Part Number)	D	3 Lines < 2 Days	●●●●●●●●●●●●●●●●●●●●●●●●●	
On hand less than Safety Stock w/o PO	D	< 1 Day	●●●●●●●●●●●●●●●●●●●●●●●●●	
Owner—Quality Assurance				
Hold Location - MRN and or RMA	W	< 8 Days	●●●●●●●●●●●●●●●●●●●●●●●●●	
Owner—Inventory Control				
Negative Inventory	D	0 < 1 Day	●●●●●●●●●●●●●●●●●●●●●●●●●	
Fixed Safety Stock	W	0 < 1 Day	●●●●●●●●●●●●●●●●●●●●●●●●●	
MRP/ERP Network Codes Errors	D	0 < 1 Day	●●●●●●●●●●●●●●●●●●●●●●●●●	
Late Stock Transfers	D	2 Lines < 2 Days	●●●●●●●●●●●●●●●●●●●●●●●●●	
Cycle Count Accuracy	D	2 Items < 98.5%	●●●●●●●●●●●●●●●●●●●●●●●●●	

Figure 12.1 Visual daily management—process and data red—green

team. Renzo, the plant manager, had an operations and human resources background. Lee, the materials manager; Amina, the operations manager; Julie, the quality manager; Charlie, the HR manager; and David, the engineering manager, were all very successful and seasoned professionals. However, their departments were not working well together. It seemed as though they were missing the conductor for their orchestra. Lee, Amina, Julie, and David established visual daily production meetings followed by GEMBA walks to fix this. The day's cadence was divided, reserving mornings for the tactical elements of managing the facilities and afternoons for longer-term strategic focus.

Carlotta, the director of corporate training, with the help of Renzo and Charlie, led a tremendous effort to build inclusion by training and educating everyone on the fundamentals of problem-solving, communication, and working as a team.

Communication was the cornerstone of this process, from the fundamentals of problem-solving to leadership and team facilitation. The group learned how to listen, be heard, and, more importantly, *not* make other people wrong during discussions.

A large part of the process involved the two-way building of communication and trust from hourly associates to senior leadership. Depending on the shift time, we had monthly birthday lunches, dinners, or breakfast meetings. The goal was to recognize and celebrate the team member's birthdays.

However, we gained much more from those meetings. We created a more family-like culture within the organization. There was no agenda other than to gather like neighbors and have cake and ice cream in a pleasant social atmosphere.

The team could ask the leadership team any questions they desired. This exercise gave the team face time with the managers in an informal environment. We learned about team members' lives, and they learned about ours. These meetings built a tremendous sense of community. Everyone was less likely to pass the blame to someone they had gotten to know well.

These measures helped to establish a process improvement mindset and collaborative behaviors rather than settling for the cultural practice of blaming one another.

Also, we initiated the following practice to acknowledge the teams. Referring to Figure 12.2, we measured the five independent value streams on six KPIs, and at the end of an all-employee quarterly review meeting, the team with the best results won the trophy for the quarter (our version of hockey's Stanley Cup). The team name was engraved on the trophy. When a team won, they paraded the trophy around the facility, like when a hockey team won a championship. This simple but meaningful exercise created great pride among team members, friendly internal competition among teams, and bragging rights!

Management could not have achieved this positive reinforcement environment without consistent training on fundamental problem solving, communication, teamwork cooperation among everyone in the building, visual daily management, Gemba, and hands-on leadership.

Figure 12.2 is an example of the banner hanging in each value stream or production area.

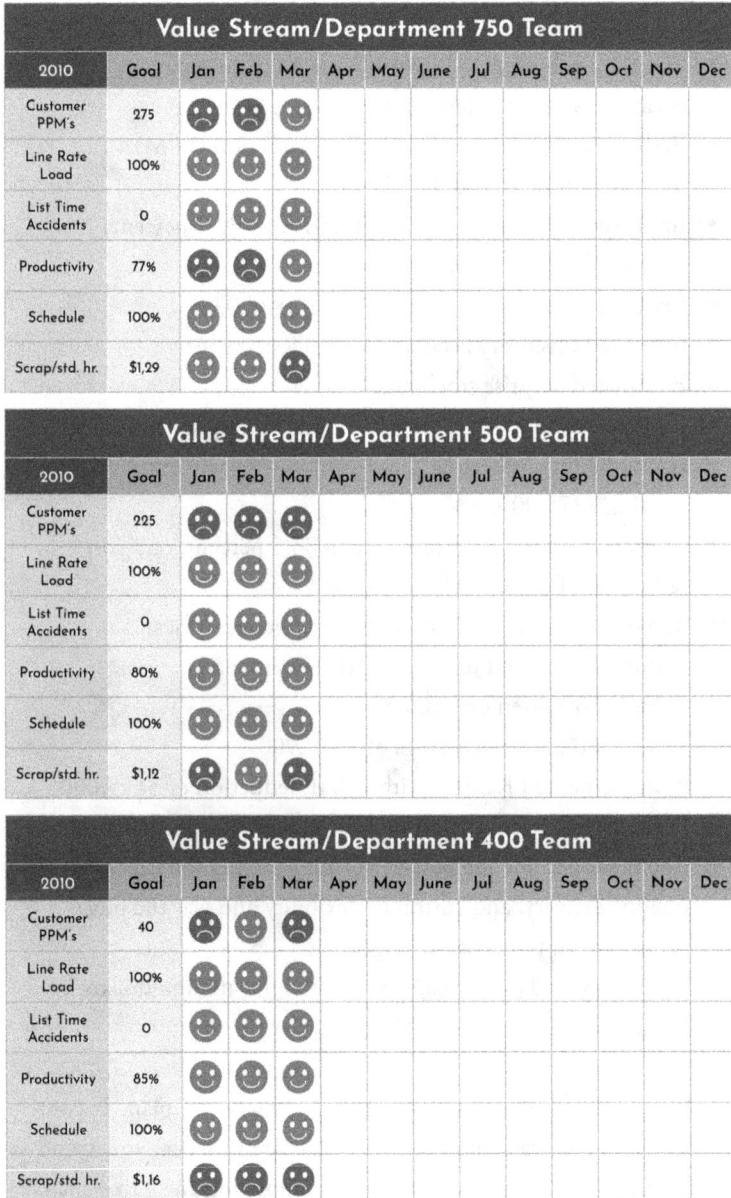

Value Stream/Department 750 Team

2010	Goal	Jan	Feb	Mar	Apr	May	June	Jul	Aug	Sep	Oct	Nov	Dec
Customer PPM's	275	☹	☹	☺									
Line Rate Load	100%	☺	☺	☺									
List Time Accidents	0	☺	☺	☺									
Productivity	77%	☹	☹	☺									
Schedule	100%	☺	☺	☺									
Scrap/std. hr.	$1.29	☺	☺	☹									

Value Stream/Department 500 Team

2010	Goal	Jan	Feb	Mar	Apr	May	June	Jul	Aug	Sep	Oct	Nov	Dec
Customer PPM's	225	☹	☹	☹									
Line Rate Load	100%	☺	☺	☺									
List Time Accidents	0	☺	☺	☺									
Productivity	80%	☺	☺	☺									
Schedule	100%	☺	☺	☺									
Scrap/std. hr.	$1.12	☹	☺	☹									

Value Stream/Department 400 Team

2010	Goal	Jan	Feb	Mar	Apr	May	June	Jul	Aug	Sep	Oct	Nov	Dec
Customer PPM's	40	☹	☺	☹									
Line Rate Load	100%	☺	☺	☺									
List Time Accidents	0	☺	☺	☺									
Productivity	85%	☺	☺	☺									
Schedule	100%	☺	☺	☺									
Scrap/std. hr.	$1.16	☹	☹	☹									

Figure 12.2 Value stream monthly results

Below is an account of the outstanding results the team was able to achieve.

Results

- The team achieved 1,000,000 hours on three separate occasions without a lost-time accident.
- Reduced customer parts per million rejection (PPM) decreased from 249 to 99.
- Improved on-time deliveries from 97.8 to 99.9 percent.
- Reduced lead time from 20 to 3 days.
- Reduced inventory by 30 percent or $1,400,000.
- Improved inventory accuracy to +99.8 percent.
- Eliminated surprise stockouts.
- Empowered four self-directed teams with responsibility and accountability, offsetting the cost of four salary positions totaling $275,000.
- Improved efficiencies from 67.1 to 83.5 percent, or a cost reduction of $2,375,000 annually.
- The organization implemented the principles of lean manufacturing and total preventive maintenance.
  - Held 36 Kaizen events.
  - Generated annual savings of $479,900.
  - Implemented Kanban with a WIP reduction of $175,000.
  - Improved machine uptime from 84 to 99.3 percent.
- The plant became the best-performing facility for safety, quality, delivery, and customer flexibility and was the most improved for total cost management.
- Over three and a half years, we created five million dollars in annualized savings.

Entropy Busters allows you to manage your game plan. If your supply chain management fundamentals are in place, you spend less time firefighting and more time completing the game plan. Envision Entropy Busters as your management's front line to manage your **daily/weekly/monthly game plan(s).**

Dive Log 12 (Art's Commentary)

For the past 30 years, I've been developing and refining entropy busters. It is the amalgamation of several important concepts and philosophies, including the Toyota Manufacturing System (TPS) and Hoshin Kanri (Compass Management), which is a multistep strategic planning process in which the goals are actionable and communicated throughout the business enterprise. It includes Heart Principles from The Atlanta Consulting Group, and all the pieces are combined with my decades of personal experience to create a robust, sustainable three-phase process.

When implementing the entropy busters methodology, the most common errors are trying to run before crawling and not prioritizing team member development and data integrity. Leadership will often see the first signs of process improvement traction, declare success, and return to their offices. Entropy busters is a transformation of how business is conducted. Leadership must be participative, visual, inclusive, rewarding, and fun.

The biggest distractions any organization can have are negative surprises such as parts outages, customer line down, or quality issues. These deficiencies can derail forward progress and throw any organization into great turmoil. It may take several months to recover gains previously realized.

Follow the three phases of entropy busters to the letter. Your organization will be transformed. You will achieve significant operational improvements, sustainability of profits, and a company valuation never realized!

At a high level, I believe operations and supply chain leadership's role is to support their CEO and board of directors. The CEO and board are responsible for two basic directives: risk mitigation and increasing shareholder value. Supply chain process sustainability and teamwork improve significantly by successfully implementing the Entropy busters methodology and creating a force field around the core operating process and systems. Entropy busters reduce the risk associated with systems and process failures. Implementing the entropy busters methodology moves the organization toward the pinnacle of sustainability.

Buddy Check: Questions From Coach Art

- Are the associates a real team? Do they work together toward a common goal?
- Does everyone on the team have a role to play in the business model's success?
- Has an atmosphere of a family been cultivated? Are there friendly rivalries between teams?
- Are you able to quickly and visually identify data integrity issues?
- Does a culture of red being good exist so you can fix root-cause problems, or does the messenger get punished?
- Are the departmental and cross-functional status meetings visual? Could someone outside the organization quickly assess the business's status and the actions required for the next 24 hours of success?
- Do you often have surprises that disrupt the team's priorities and cadence of work?
- If you were to win the lottery and retire, would the business fully embrace entropy busters Phases I, II, and III to sustain long-term success after you rode off into the sunset?

Art's Deep Dive

After implementing the methodology of entropy busters process and data VDM (Figure 12.1), how many of the surprise parts shortages have disappeared?

If it were easy, it would have already been done!

PART 2

Structured Framework

CHAPTER 13

Supply Chain Health Check Advisory

As a diver, if you haven't been diving for an extended period, it is wise to take a refresher course. The design of a scuba refresher course is to reconnect past muscle memory with today's muscle reflexes. It's quite a simple endeavor. The instructor will guide you through all the necessary core skills: equipment setup, mask clearing, equalization, and maintaining proper buoyancy. Once you've completed these skills several times, prior muscle memory kicks in, and you will be well-prepared to dive again.

A refresher course is an example of reactive planning. As stated in earlier chapters, the lack of proper planning causes organizations to become reactionary. Entropy creeps into business processes this way. The real solution to maintaining diving competence is to never stop using those skills and risk losing muscle memory. The best way for businesses to ensure they are not viewing their processes, results, and teams' members with "rose" colored glasses is to have periodic supply chain health checks by an impartial third party.

How do we become proactive and stay ahead of problems or opportunities? If we continue diving, our skills remain sharp. For divers, it is easy to keep active by diving every few months. In our personal lives, we go to the doctor for a physical exam and blood work to ensure that we are healthy and that the body is functioning correctly. Regular visits to the doctor are an example of predictive and preventative maintenance.

What I find to be a common scenario within organizations is that they expend critical resources to solve problems. Once resolving issues, they celebrate success and move on to the next problem. They often don't do the necessary follow-up to fix the root cause of problems.

More importantly, they don't make proactive improvements to their processes. The lack of monitoring of a problem resolution often results in the original issue resurfacing or the solution falling apart entirely. Entropy Busters® I, II, and III methodologies are necessary to prevent entropy creep so you can solve the problem at its root cause permanently.

I recommend the supply chain health check to support the process improvements in the supply chain, which operations have worked hard to resolve. It's like having a trainer or coach within the organization. The purpose of the supply chain health check is to help the team adhere to the fundamentals of new solutions, advise them through the nuances and course corrections of the original resolution, or periodically complete a health check on the supply chain vital signs.

An example of a solution with a high potential for success and failure is vendor managed inventory (VMI) programs. I worked with a client to implement VMI programs. We used the stratification methodology of 80/15/4/1 on purchase orders placed, part shortages, and expedites to set the stage.

Using facts and data, we highlighted to the buying team that 47 percent of the purchase orders, 35 percent of their expedites, and part shortages were associated with the last 1 percent of supplier spend. Or, about 45 percent of their total workload was absorbed, managing the last 1 percent of supplier spend.

We selected a supplier and implemented a pilot 200-part number VMI. Everything went to plan until seven months into the pilot, surplus inventory was consumed, and all 200 bin quantities approached their target levels. By lower inventory levels, we exposed opportunities in the process, and the stockroom order fulfillment team started to have frequent shortages when picking orders. The initial knee-jerk response from the buyers was to bring in all demand for the parts or revert to the prior process.

If I, another supply chain professional, or a third-party adviser to the VMI process improvement weren't engaged with the team at the critical time, all the efforts would be lost. The buying team would have lost their confidence in adopting new solutions. I'm happy to say the buying team and supplier worked through their challenges. The VMI pilot succeeded and resulted in adding several suppliers to similar programs. In total, the team was able to reduce inventory by 75 percent, eliminate surprise outages, reduce expedites by 95 percent, and cut back office tasks by 70 percent.

Supply Chain Health Check Advisory

The supply chain health check advisory is applied to recently implemented projects to improve bottom-line results and sustainability. It's also applied to mature supply chain organizations to ensure they are not letting entropy creep into their processes. The health check focuses on preventing backsliding of the initiatives already in place. The supply chain health check advisory aims for processes to become autonomic and part of the organizational DNA.

The supply chain health check advisory can also have a positive impact on your people. We can achieve high-performance results and improve team confidence through continuing education, mentoring, and follow-up. I recommend having an outside person working with teams in an advisory capacity to follow up on actions taken during assessments or projects, close gaps in processes, track improvements to operational performance, and coach the teams in charge of leadership oversight.

The supply chain health check advisory typically covers a 12-month period, which allows enough time for process variations to occur and for the solutions to become part of the organization's DNA. It is critical to have one person as the sole voice and resource for the health check processes to provide feedback and advice to senior leaders and managers. This person will ensure that the top leadership understands the new methods, that the entire organization sees the buy-in at all levels, and that the change management process is not underestimated.

Implementing the health check processes is most successful when the person leading the effort is part of the original design. They must be available during workdays to advise on questions and team comments. This person must attend on-site, virtual monthly status meetings, and monthly and quarterly on-site follow-ups to provide coaching and mentoring and hold the team accountable for results.

Following the outline of this book, my supply chain health check advisory typically follows (refer to Figure 1.1), Art Koch's Profit Chain® the three Fs of supply chain management.

The 14 categories that make up the people and process foundation, structural framework, and financial focal point all work together to improve supply chain and operational processes. As the project is nearing completion, transition to a regular supply chain health check advisory to prevent backsliding of a new solution's fundamentals and advise the team through the nuances and course corrections of the original resolution.

Dive Master Briefing (Client Example)

Some of the best lessons learned come from failures.

The supply chain health check was born out of a frustrating disappointment. In this case, the project was with a long-term client. The professional relationship with this valued client was, and still is, excellent. The original plan was to design, beta test, and pilot a Kanban process for purchased parts integrated with their legacy ERP system.

More specifically, the plan was to beta test and pilot 4 suppliers and 87 part numbers. After successfully beta testing two suppliers, 18 part numbers, and writing standard work, my client was eager to use my skills to launch a new assembly plant.

At the time, we felt the team was strong enough to continue with the final piloting and rollout of the new Kanban process to suppliers. We underestimated that conflicting priorities and a lack of crucial decision making when nuances arose would disrupt the team's harmony. As with any new system or process, the initial design misses some minor details, just like computer programs have "bugs" that must be corrected.

After I had transitioned to the new assembly plant, the original team lost their compass setting, became disenfranchised, and could never move forward with adding more suppliers and part numbers. By the time we learned of the breakdown, I had become too integrated with the launch of the new factory and could not be spared to return to the prior site to help.

The lesson learned here is that no matter how solid the team is, all teams need a leader to guide them through the early stages of improvement and to help them maneuver the nuances of change management, ensure sustainability, and to coach them through the decision process. From these failures, the supply chain health check was born.

Client Testimonial

Art's vision for implementing a Kanban system was spot on, and we anticipated some of the frustrating challenges we were facing. Art had won over team members. Right after the systems were developed and the beta testing was completed, he was pulled into managing another project, and initial project traction was lost. There are always lessons to make the team better. I'm proud we were able to get the team refocused, implemented the Kanban, and are now using the Health Check to sustain results.

—Kartik R.—Global Vice President of Supply Chain Management
($500 million capital equipment manufacturer)

Dive Log 13 (Art's Commentary)

Overall, the supply chain health check is a practice that all organizations need to follow. It's an example of what "Good" looks like and gives individuals and teams a methodology to emulate. The supply chain health check is an excellent approach to maintaining progress and demonstrates how advisory services can benefit your organization by building team confidence and sustainable results.

- Art's supply chain health check cheat sheet:
  - Have all team members received their annual performance review?
  - Does each team member have development plans?
  - Are planning parameter assessed and updated at least annually?
  - Are parts stratified into ABCD classification, assessed, and updated at least annually?
  - Are blanket purchase orders, long-term agreements, and memorandum of understandings current?
  - Are supply scorecards in place? Are results communicated with suppliers and corrective actions addressed? Are there scheduled supplier visits?

- Is the replenishment planning team following exception-based buying practices?
  - Not buying early or late;
  - Following up on late-order acknowledgments;
  - Expediting;
  - Addressing cancels and defers.
- Is there a formalized cycle counting process? How are root causes addressed?
- What is the process to reduce and compress lead times?
- What processes are in place to reduce dependency on forecast?
- Is inventory velocity improving?
- Is obsolescence being disposed of monthly?
- Is there a supplier development initiative?
- Are supply chain team members actively attending VDM meetings?
- Is there a supplier and part number rationalization initiative?
- How is complexity being addressed?
- Is the team adhering to the relevant few KPIs for their functions?

Buddy Check: Questions From Coach Art

- Does the team tend to be reactive, causing them to respond to surprises after launching a project?
- Are team members disbanded too soon after project implementation, only to learn that additional tweaks are needed?
- When completing projects, is there a process that proactively ensures sustainability by correcting nuances of the original design?

Art's Deep Dive

Material requirements planning (MRP) is a push system; and Kanban's are pull processes.

For additional information and free tools, please scan the code.

CHAPTER 14

Developing a Supply Chain Business Transformation Agenda

My wanderlust started early, and my love of scuba diving and underwater photography only amplified my desire to wander the globe. When I first started diving, my destination bucket list consisted only of the Caribbean islands. As I checked locations off, my list gradually extended to further reaches of the world. Currently, my diving bucket list is down to the Red Sea, Antarctica, and Midway Atoll in the middle of the Pacific Ocean.

To arrive at this point, I've learned a great deal of planning and preparation is needed before you can check off extreme bucket list destinations for scuba diving and underwater photography. On my first couple of trips to extreme locations, I just showed up with my old diving mindset and expected to dive into warm bathtub-like conditions with no currents.

My very first exotic and extreme location trips were to Truk Lagoon and Palau Islands, both in Micronesia. Truk Lagoon was a stress-free, World War II wreck diving similar to diving off the North Carolina coast of the United States. There were no issues with currents or other challenges.

It was a whole different story when I arrived in Palau the following week. Again, I came with my Caribbean diving mindset and was surprised by the fast and swirling currents.

I was unprepared mentally, physically, and from an equipment standpoint for these rough conditions. My mask nearly ripped off my face, and I had too much gear attached to my buoyancy control device (BCD).

My lack of preparation dragged my diving down, got in the way of simple tasks, and negatively impacted my air consumption.

There are important lessons learned from these adventures.

Detailed planning and preparation for extreme dive trips are essential. Mentally, we need to have a vision of where we are going and what conditions lie ahead for diving in a particular location. Start making your plans by reading and talking to others who have had experience in similar settings. Then, apply what you have learned to trip planning so that you have the proper mental, physical, and dive gear preparation for your journey.

Let's bring this into the world of supply chain management. By combining Art Koch's Profit Chain® model, the three "Fs" of supply chain, I created a 101-point assessment called the supply chain framework builder. The assessment is a quantitative and qualitative analysis of the supply chain practices and processes. It analyzes the team's readiness to support the enterprise's vision and strategies for the next three to five years of supply chain transformation.

The assessment process establishes the current state of the supply chain. It then acts as a conduit to the organization with the necessary baseline information so that the team can effectively develop a plan to fulfill the strategy and vision of senior leaders.

Components of a Good Supply Chain Assessment

In most cases within organizations, the only measures of success are past performance, such as profitability, margins, or inventory velocity. Employee and supplier engagement or benchmarking against peer groups is often not done. In leadership roles, we need to know which direction the organization is traveling, and what storms lay ahead (how the competition is performing). Without the information of this type, it's like keeping score against yourself in a foot race of one!

Not only are we only keeping score against ourselves, but when an assessment, benchmarking, or process audit is performed, it's often completed using internal resources, which causes the results to be biased. The bias comes in many forms. The most prevalent is when it's your organization, you tend to rate yourself higher than actual, especially if someone's compensation or a customer scorecard is involved.

There is a profound need to measure organizational performance against other industry peers by conducting an unbiased assessment. Sports teams hold internal practices, then have scrimmage games against opposing teams before the regular season starts to validate their baseline performance. When playing in the regular season, the best teams make the playoffs. Then the season's grand finale ends with the crowning of a champion.

All organizations must have a process to benchmark their actual performance using an unbiased assessment method. This objective evaluation is best achieved by having an external team perform the supply chain assessment of the organization's performance.

There are four major components of any comprehensive supply chain assessment.

The first component is a quantitative rating, the scorekeeping, and the details of how information is used to implement changes and improvements.

The second component is the qualitative rating of management's commitment and involvement in leading the team to transformative operational excellence. If you follow any sport, the analysts predict which team will win the championship at the beginning of each new season based on their height, weight, reach, or speed. However, they cannot predict who will win due to the team's intrinsic attributes: the heart, passion, and leadership components of winning. These intangible factors are what the qualitative rating assesses. There is no exact science to determine the size of a team's desire to win. However, you can evaluate the level of commitment and involvement within the organization that is in place to leverage the potential of winning. This is the intent of the qualitative portion of the assessment.

The final two components of the supply chain assessment are the core competencies and skills the team requires to execute the strategies that transform the organization into management's future vision. In this chapter, we will discuss both topics in detail.

When determining a supply chain assessment to utilize, I recommend, at a minimum, that it consist of the seven areas described below. If these components are not included in an evaluation, then it's challenging to understand the total picture of supply chain management. The eight areas to be evaluated for quantitative, qualitative, core competence, and skills factors are as follows:

1. Supply chain management strategy;
2. Strategic sourcing strategy;
3. Demand planning (forecasting);

4. Supply planning (replenishment);
5. Production and inventory control;
6. Warehousing, distribution, and fulfillment;
7. Logistics and transportation;
8. SCM integration with supplier partners and engineering.

As mentioned earlier, the two components that best measure the performance for each area assessed need to be quantitative and qualitative scores.

Quantitative rating uses KPIs and metrics to understand the current state, the deviation from the standard, and trends over time. Accurate baseline data allows effective metrics usage to achieve operational excellence through continuous improvement driven by facts and a data-driven environment.

It's critical to keep scoring as simple as possible.

Most standard assessments focus on how the organization is performing at a moment in time. I believe this is reactionary. Too often, I've walked into an organization with excellent KPIs and everything accurately measured. However, there was no evidence of improved performance over time. Someone was told to collect the data, but no one used the information for corrective action. As you can imagine, this wastes valuable resources and can create cracks in trust between team members.

The best assessments consider how information and data are used to steer the enterprise toward long-term sustainable improvements.

Below are simple scoring guidelines that apply information and data to steer the organization toward improved performance.

Quantitative scoring guidelines are as follows:

- No KPIs. Score = 0.
- KPIs are only found in some locations (25 percent). Score = 1.
- Corrective action plans are developed for negative deviates. Score = 2.
- KPIs are commonly found, but not in most (50 percent), and are or aren't part of long-range strategic planning. Score = 3.
- KPIs are very typical (75 percent), with some exceptions, actively tracked and part of strategic management for two or more years. Score = 4.

- KPIs are found everywhere (100 percent) and are part of building customer and supplier partnerships. Score = 5.

It can still be tricky, even when attempting to keep the scoring process simple. The prevailing belief of managers is that as the consistency of KPIs improves throughout the enterprise, so should the degree to which information and data are used for corrective actions. Thus, driving strategic initiatives and enhancing the building of partnerships across the supply chain.

The **qualitative rating** is management's commitment and involvement in leading and supporting the team to transformative operational excellence. It determines the level of commitment and participation of senior leadership's involvement in driving the enterprise toward world-class status.

Qualitative scoring guidelines are as follows:

- Level 0:
  - Leadership is unaware and uninvolved in the process design and problem-solving in operations.
  - Leaders judge performance by monthly financial reports.
  - No central planning process exists.
  - Department metrics do not measure the improvement process.
  - Leaders have poor communication with team members.
  - No corporate operational excellence plan exists.
  - There is zero training or on-the-job training.
  - Score = 0.
- Level 1:
  - Most problems are hidden from leadership.
  - Only a team member or supervisor knows the real problems.
  - There is an inconsistent leadership presence on the shop floor.
  - No formal process improvement review is performed.
  - Central planning exists. However, objectives are not related or meaningful to operations.

- Objectives and results are rarely communicated to team members.
- Some lean and operational excellence efforts are implemented with limited effectiveness.
- Score = 1.
- Level 2:
  - Leadership is involved only in high-level problem resolution.
  - Leaders have limited operational presence or experience.
  - Metrics and results are reviewed and kept in the office.
  - Corporate objectives are developed. However, operations and corporate goals or metrics are not tied together.
  - Expected targets and results are not visible at the worksite.
  - Limited verbal feedback is provided to team members.
  - Corporate operational excellence plans are incomplete or not effectively implemented.
  - Score = 2.
- Level 3:
  - Leadership has an interest in and some involvement with system improvements and problem-solving.
  - Inconsistent operational visits are made to check the status.
  - Department managers interpret corporate objectives to establish goals and metrics; senior leadership does not monitor their performance.
  - Daily performance results are reported to team members, often verbally and usually focused on problems.
  - The corporate operational excellence plan is published and used in most areas.
  - Score = 3.
- Level 4:
  - Leadership has an interest in system improvements.
  - Gemba, "Go and see," is practiced regularly.
  - Leadership supports team members' suggestions and problem-solving.
  - Formal scheduled reviews of systems implementation are performed.
  - Objectives are developed cross-functionally.

- Department metrics tie into company objectives.
- Metrics are monitored accurately, and performance feedback is given to team members hourly or daily.
- An effective corporate operational excellence plan is in place.
- Score = 4.

- Level 5:
  - Leadership is highly involved in the design and implementation of systems.
  - Daily operational visits occur to check the status.
  - Monthly and quarterly reviews of corporate operational excellence status are carried out to identify problem areas, trends, and recommended adjustments to any implementation plans.
  - Mentor and coaching style applied to problem-solving versus autocratic management techniques.
  - Objectives cascade to operations, with relevant metrics visible at all times.
  - Corporate operational excellence metrics are used to achieve objectives.
  - Frequently monitored performance with real-time or hourly feedback given to team members.
  - Highly visible interactive corporate operational excellence management process versus information pushed to TV monitors.
  - Active cross-organizational improvements are implemented. Training is budgeted into the operational excellence plan and evaluated for effectiveness.
  - Score = 5.
  - As you can see, this is a detailed assessment process.

The process I use with my clients to optimize performance and create sustainable improvements and profitability is called the supply chain framework builder assessment. It consists of a 101-point deep dive into my three "Fs" of SCM: people and process foundation, structural framework, and financial focal point.

This process analyzes and assesses quantitative and qualitative practices, procedures, and the team's readiness to support the leadership's strategy and vision for the next three to five years of transformation. The supply chain framework builder assessment typically requires four weeks of total commitment, two weeks working remotely with the client's team on data analysis and preparation, two weeks of my on-site interviewing of team members, and physically walking through the processes with the appropriate team members. It is a significant organizational commitment but quickly provides a thorough foundation for future performance improvements.

Once the assessment is complete, the team will have a detailed picture of its current status and the barriers to improved performance. With the new assessment results, the team can develop a comprehensive action plan for the next 12 to 24 months, incorporating an operational excellence strategy and vision as guiding principles.

Dive Master Briefing (Client Example)

Due to the highly confidential nature of the supply chain framework builder assessment data, I've opted to use hypothetical data to illustrate the status of the client's current state, as shown in the red (black) line in Figure 14.1. The purple (dark gray) line is the average of previous clients' assessments used for benchmarking. The blue (light gray) line is the client's future stated goals for action plans once the implementation is completed.

The assessment process provides supply chain organizations with a thorough understanding of their current status and establishes a benchmark to compare their business with other businesses. This knowledge helps the organization build an action plan for a future state that aligns with its strategy and vision.

Most clients use the assessment results as a launchpad to transform and implement their supply chain strategy and vision. The impact of post assessment gains can be substantial. One of my clients used this process and achieved nearly nine million dollars in year-over-year cost reductions, dramatically improving profitability, cash flow, working capital, and company valuation.

Focusing on the basics of SCM can be very profitable.

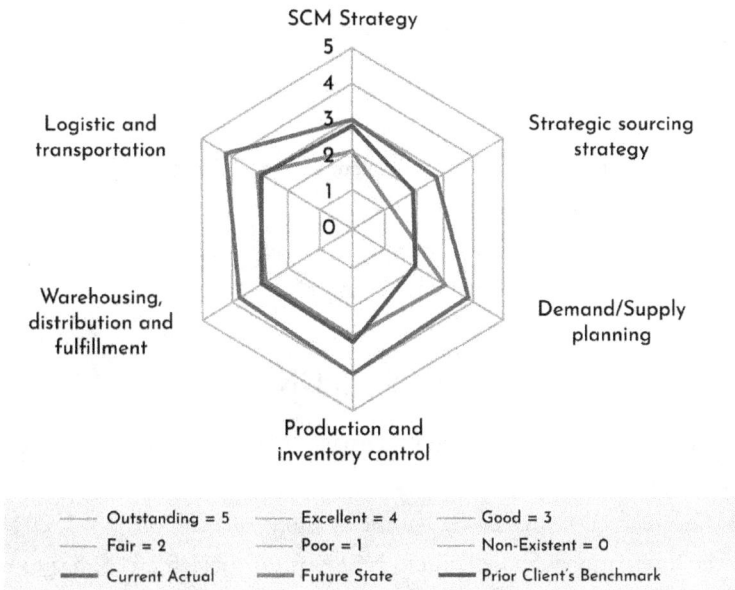

Figure 14.1 Supply chain framework builder assessment

Dive Log 14 (Art's Commentary)

I'm surprised that few companies use an outside, unbiased assessment to benchmark their supply chain organization and processes. Such behaviors highlight a lack of foresight and knowledge by the leadership of where to find skilled supply chain practitioners who can comprehensively assess an organization's supply chain processes.

Whenever I perform a supply chain assessment, the local team starts the process very defensively. Team members have likely become conditioned to be silent, believing that negative or constructive feedback will be used negatively during their next performance review. We must help organizations overcome this shortsightedness and consider constructive feedback a gift.

Lastly, a supply chain assessment cannot be confused with an audit. A supply chain assessment analyzes the results and the processes employed to achieve those results. An audit is a checkup of the final results and their accuracy.

Buddy Check: Questions From Coach Art

- Is there a routine supply chain assessment of your organization's operations?
- Does an unbiased party complete your supply chain assessments?
- Does the supply chain assessment process include both quantitative and qualitative ratings?

Art's Deep Dive

You have heard me recommend internally friendly rivalries. Here is one for the record books.

On the final NASA Space Shuttle mission, Atlantis, on July 8, 2011, to the International Space Station, NASA astronauts left a U.S. flag to be retrieved by the next group of astronauts to arrive from American soil. This friendly competition was between Boeing and SpaceX. On June 1, 2020, nearly nine years later, a team of NASA astronauts captured the flag when they arrived at the International Space Station aboard SpaceX's Dragon spacecraft!

How does your organization cultivate internally friendly rivalries?

CHAPTER 15

Is Your Supply Chain Organization Designed for Sustainable Success?

During my first scuba training class, I learned to calculate safe diving times using dive tables. Dive tables calculate dive times based on the depth of the dive. How many of you remember slide rules? The process when using dive tables is similar to using a slide rule. The task wasn't difficult. It was just a nuisance. But we all learned to use dive tables proficiently because if we did not, we could get the bends, become injured, or might die.

When I purchased my first set of dive gear, dive computers were becoming common. They were highly functional, reliable, small (like the size of a hockey puck), and reasonably inexpensive. Dive computers do an excellent job of calculating in real-time your nitrogen absorption based on dive time and depth, and they determine how long your dive can safely last. Now dive computers have made dive tables obsolete. Having a dive computer has allowed me to explore the undersea world safely with less hassle and improved accuracy.

The transition from slide rule and dive tables to purpose-driven computers has allowed for fast calculations that have improved safety, quality, and efficiency.

Let's apply the same concept of slide rules and dive tables to supply chain management organizational development.

When I was in leadership roles, I found it challenging to find information on how to assess the supply chain team. For example, what skills does a new supply chain manager need? And how do we develop them? There were no guidelines. Also, because supply chain management was not considered a profession like accounting, engineering, or human resources (and my goal is to change that perception), there is a significant knowledge gap on what core competencies and skills are necessary to be successful or even where to find the information. One of the main reasons many leaders struggle to assess a team's performance is the lack of knowledge of essential subject matter.

Imagine if your organization had a methodology determining the depth and breadth of team members' core competencies and skillsets to become subject matter experts.

For this purpose, I've developed the four-step supply chain core competencies and skills assessment that identifies the organizational and individual core competencies and skills required to achieve leadership's supply chain vision. The supply chain core competencies and skills assessment method will help the organization identify the core competencies and skills needed to sustain success and help leaders develop a plan to train and educate the team. Following my 11-point core competencies and 20-point skill sets for supply chain management will give you the framework to build your team for sustainable success and profitability.

Assessing Core Competencies and Skills

There is a good reason the topic of a full assessment is addressed toward the end of this book. Many organizations make the mistake of tackling opportunities on the scale of solving world problems while looking for the silver bullet that will solve all their woes. Leaders need to be cautious, as they can get lured into trying to resolve a problem's symptoms before the root cause is understood.

My experience has shown when the people and process foundation and structural framework fundamentals are addressed. The company is on a path toward ongoing long-term sustainable improvement. There is a better understanding of the fine details of existing problems and less of a tendency to look for silver-bullet solutions.

When the foundation and framework of supply chain and operations management are in place, it is easier to develop the corporate mission, realize leadership's vision, and outline a viable strategy for supply chain management's future success.

By completing a full assessment, teams are more likely to accept the results, are less defensive, and are compelled to act swiftly to complete corrective action plans. Before any organization starts assessing its team members, leaders and associates must instill shared trust and teamwork. As I mentioned earlier, there is a need to get all team members involved during the transformation process. My recommendation is to start by:

- Getting everyone on the bus by making them part of the solution, outlined in Entropy Busters® Phase I.
- Training and educating the team on the fundamentals of problem resolution, outlined in Entropy Busters Phase II.
- Ensure everyone has a task, is part of the solution, and understands the bigger picture vision, outlined in Entropy Busters Phase III.

Mutual trust will develop when a team sees legacy problems resolved by leadership engagement, individual ownership, and coordinated teamwork. If all parties' intentions are well placed and sincere, there will be an acceptance for the next level of assessment, core competencies and skills.

Let me emphasize the importance of building trust and how fragile and delicate it is to maintain trust in the long term. Celebrate success, analyze unexpected results, and eliminate blame. Remember, leadership is a contact sport. As a leader, be participative in the problem-resolution process, take responsibility for setbacks, and never take credit for successes.

Sometimes, I see leaders fall into the trap of thinking that the entire team needs replacing. Individuals and teams desire leadership. They want training and development and need to be part of something bigger. Once they are in motion with initiatives for training and development, it's amazing how engaged and successful those teams and individuals become. Some more successful organizations realize that individuals are not all "A" players. Teams are a blend of A, B, and C team members. The best leaders can coach their team members to "punch through" higher levels than expected.

To achieve and maintain trust within the team, terminate only the individuals with behavioral issues or who refuse to accept new methods without sound reasons (which could be considered behavioral). Both the team and the employee will thank you later. For marginal associates sincerely trying their best with little success, leaders must find them a position to succeed and contribute to the team's effort. Failure to take this action will keep the team from its full potential.

Struggling individuals know who they are, and, in most cases, they are looking for help. Again, the organization and individual will recognize your leadership in making these challenging yet meaningful organizational transitions.

Art's Gold: If a concerted effort is made to get people on the bus, into the correct seat, and involved as part of the solution, then you're moving toward creating a world-class team.

Designing the Supply Chain Management Organization for Sustainable Success

The following are powerful questions for leaders to think about:

- Do you understand the organization's strengths, where competencies are missing, and where skill gaps are hidden?
- Do you have a clear mission, vision, and strategy for the direction to take to achieve world-class success?
- Have you completed the 360-degree feedback to understand the gaps in core competencies and skillsets of your organization?

To help you answer these questions, I've developed a four-part assessment process called supply chain core competencies and skills assessment to determine a team's potential for transforming the supply chain into the corporate vision's future state.

The first step is to outline the ideal organizational design for implementing the corporate strategy.

The second step is to outline the core competencies required to fulfill that strategy. Here are the 11 core competencies I've created to build a high-performance supply chain and operations team. Each of the 11 core competencies is specifically developed to aid in the execution and sustainability of an operational excellence strategy.

11-Point Supply Chain Management Core Competencies

1. **Inventory Management Knowledge and Improvement.** Knowledge of material flow, purchasing, inventory management, schedule, synchronous flow, and lean manufacturing.

2. **Continuous Improvement and Change Agent.** Visionary, innovative, self-motivated. Implements change, believes in the impossible, views change as a journey, thinks outside the box, and remains flexible.

3. **Customer/Partnership Orientation. Effective negotiator.** Exceeds customer expectations, develops partnerships, keeps customers' needs at the forefront, and bases strategies on customers' needs.

4. **Problem-Solving Skills.** Effectively uses data, sees problems as opportunities, uses analytical tools, understands total cost, balances intuitive and analytical thinking, displays implementation skills, and draws practical conclusions from a minimum of data analysis.

5. **Effectively Simplifies Situations.** Achieves results by reducing complexity, increasing the speed of activities, focusing on critical tasks, and believing in the value of simplicity.

6. **Coaching and Leadership Skills.** Effective team manager or leader. Takes risks, learns from mistakes, sets clear expectations, holds people accountable, leads through change, deals effectively with all levels, empowers others, and demonstrates collaborative skills.

7. **Capable of and Values Continuous Learning.** Has a passion for continuous learning, learns from successes and failures, and embraces new ideas.

8. **Action and Results Oriented.** Adds a sense of urgency but not carelessness, values reducing the time it takes to get things done, sets aggressive goals, decisive and persistent.

9. **Demonstrates Integrity.** Honest, trustworthy, fair, shares successes, inspire others, and admits mistakes.

10. **Has a Strategic Focus.** Broad-based thinker, sees the big picture, looks externally, and develops a vision.

11. **Communication Skills.** Effective at all levels, persuasive, authoritative without being abrasive, negotiates effectively, listens actively, and keeps appropriate people informed.

These are the core competencies that I've had the most success with, but they are not just limited to the previous list. I recommend developing your own set of core competencies. My best advice is to keep the list to about 10 core competencies and have specific definitions for each.

The third step is to outline the skills required for each role. To accomplish this, I recommend using a cross-functional team, from senior leaders to the associates in the positions assessed. The cross-functional team accomplishes two essential things. It will increase trust through transparency across functional areas or silos and help to build inclusion by having team members part of the process.

Below is the skill set list I've had the most success with, but this list should not be limited to the skills I have mentioned. As always, I recommend developing your own skill set list:

Art's Gold: Great leaders thrive at the edges—they have a unique ability to interact and achieve buy-in across departments, executives, and team members.

20-Point Supply Chain Management Skill Sets

1. Certified purchasing management—CPM designation (Institute for Supply Management) or BS/MBA in supply chain management
2. Certified professional in supply chain management—CPSM (Institute for Supply Management) or certified production and inventory management CPIM designation (APICS) or BS/MBA in supply chain management
3. Bachelor's degree in business/industrial engineering/supply chain/ operations Mgt—preferred
4. Detail-oriented
5. Negotiation skills
6. Cost analysis skills
7. Knowledge of global markets
8. Mastery of critical component technology
9. Time management skills
10. Problem-solving skills
11. Ability to maintain a lean and 5S-driven work environment

12. Interpersonal skills (ability to work well with team members)
13. Communication skills
14. Computer skills (excel, tableau, etc.)
15. Creativity and innovation (simple solutions to complex problems)
16. Prepares thoroughly for a meeting
17. Organizational development (not only develops themselves but also develops and teaches those around them)
18. Flexibility and adaptability to change
19. Results-oriented (drives to the result)
20. Project management skills

The intent is to identify the core competencies and skill set requirements for the ideal supply chain management candidate. Do not expect the individuals in these roles to have 100 percent of the identified traits. The preceding skill set list aims to enhance understanding of what an ideal candidate "looks" like and then identify the necessary training and development by individual and function to transition the team and the organization toward the perfect state. Construct a matrix matching core competencies and skill sets to organizational roles to track team members' progress in their development. Scan the QR code below for an example.

After completing the upfront work, the fourth step is to complete a 360-degree evaluation of team members' competencies and skills. My preference for individuals taking part in this process is as follows:

- The individual team member conducts a self-review.
- Their manager completes a review of the team member.
- If there are subordinates, they each should complete a review of the team member.
- At least one peer should conduct a review.

I have found that the best evaluation results are achieved when the associate selects their peers for review. Additionally, all results must be kept strictly confidential.

The final step is to create and implement training and development that covers the core competencies and skill gaps that individuals have so they may improve their performance.

Dive Master Briefing (Client Example)

The client was a major wholesale and distribution company with annual sales of $1.3 billion, 2,750 employees, 675,000 specific part numbers, 1,725,000 stock-keeping units, and 7 distribution centers.

Due to aggressive competition and rapidly changing consumer expectations, product offerings had significantly increased. To remain competitive, they needed to continue expanding their product offerings. This increase in offerings caused a considerable strain on the internally designed demand and supply planning software, distribution center capacity, and the planning team. These negative impacts compromised the company's ability to maintain the high standard for customer fill rates the industry demanded.

Working with Alicia, the chief supply chain officer, Jeff, the chief operating officer, and Debbie and Carl, the VPs of merchandising and supply chain, we determined a three-part solution was necessary:

1. Redesign the organization to fit their future state business model.
2. Increase the professionalism and skills of team members.
3. Implement state-of-the-art or best-in-class demand and supply planning solutions.

Their business model had two distinct segments. About 90 percent of the product offerings and 50 percent of sales were based on traditional repetitive forecast-driven demand. The remaining 10 percent of the product offerings and 50 percent of sales had a demand pattern similar to merchandising in the fashion industry. The product would move through the product lifecycle at different rates depending on consumer sentiment. With this knowledge, we redesigned the organization into two parts: supply chain and new product merchandising.

Supply chain planning was highly automated and transaction-intense and typically represented products that were further along through the product lifecycle. New product merchandise planning requires planners to have a detailed knowledge of the product artists and authors and a handle on newsworthy information that would influence demand.

Debbie and Carl assessed the team for their understanding of demand and supply planning fundamentals and their product knowledge to determine training and development requirements and the best fit for each team member from the individual skill sets.

We used this knowledge to select and implement a world-class best-in-class demand and supply planning software solution that could meet the SKU demands and the unique demand and supply planning challenges.

The results were significant.

We shifted paradigms on inventory and customer service (squashing the false belief it takes lots of inventory for excellent customer service). We put accurate planning stratification classes and exception-based planning in place and achieved inventory reductions while simultaneously increasing customer service. Inventory decreased by 30 percent or $80,000,000 ($114,000,000 in today's dollars), and the customer fill rate improved from 84 to 96 percent.

The improvements to inventory and customer fill rates allowed for the closing of two distribution centers. The industry norm was to return unused inventory within 60 days. Improved demand and replenishment planning tools reduced reverse logistics by 75 percent. Additionally, with better planning tools, we were able, through attrition, to reduce full-time equivalents (FTE) in the supply chain organization, saving $975,000 year-over-year.

Even with these excellent results, we learned three significant lessons.

We underestimated the team member's desire to be part of merchandising versus supply chain planning. Alicia and Jeff helped reinforce to the team that supply chain planning was critical to the company's success and that it was a career path they could be proud of. Debbie and Carl did an excellent job of training and certification on the new software solution. However, many individual daily tasks significantly changed. When coupled with learning a new software application, there was a lot of change to absorb. Overall, many struggled more than we anticipated. Finally, in the early phases of replenishment orders, we needed to rebalance inventory positions, and during the first few months, receiving was flooded with part numbers in small quantities.

Dive Log 15 (Art's Commentary)

Before starting the core competencies and skills assessment, team members should already be engaged as part of the solution to improve company performance. My assessments are not designed to blow up the organizational architecture. Instead, the intent is to use the information to find the gaps in core competencies and skills and to create and implement a detailed skills development plan.

Show that you care and demonstrate your commitment to the team by investing in their development, building their professionalism, and setting the stage for the team to exceed expectations. Remember, supply chain team members are professionals, like CPAs, engineers, financial managers, or human resource managers. They deserve the same level of ongoing professional development and respect.

Buddy Check: Questions From Coach Art

- Is there a defined list of core competencies for the organization?
- Do you have a list of the required skill sets by role to make the organization successful?
- Are the core competencies and skill sets aligned with the corporate mission and vision?
- Have competency and skill gaps been identified?
- Is there an individualized training and development plan in place?

Art's Deep Dive

You have zero control over the events that impact you. However, you have 100 percent control over your response to these events. (Figure 15.1)

We have **0% control** over the events that impact us. However, we have **100% control** over our response to those events.

THIS IS THE FORMULA OF SUCCESS!

Figure 15.1 0% and 100% control

Someone once asked me. "What happens if we invest in the training and development of individuals, and they leave the company?" My response was: "What happens if we don't?"

For additional information and free tools, please scan the code.

CHAPTER 16

The Law of 1 Percent = 50 Percent

A big part of diving involves understanding how to calculate how long you can dive without decompression. The premise is that proper and good planning allows for unanticipated events. If your dive ends with an unplanned decompression safety stop, you could run out of air and die or be severely injured. As I've mentioned before, my goal for diving is to explore the underwater environment for as long and as safely as possible while maximizing the fun!

One of the best locations for large sea life encounters is the Cocos Islands of Costa Rica. The only inconvenience factor is a 36-hour boat ride to get there. When you finally arrive to dive with whale sharks, schooling hammerhead sharks, and many other large animals, the goal is to safely maximize dive time without decompression.

Another of my favorite dive sites in the world is Bajo Alcyone. It is a legendary seamount where you can see, swimming in harmony, schooling hammerhead sharks. The major challenge with this dive site is that the depth is between 90 and 120 feet, and often there is a strong current. As I mentioned, the goal is to dive for as long and safely as possible. Using standard air tables to determine no-decompression dive times at various depths are as follows:

- 60 feet for 55 minutes;
- 90 feet for 25 minutes; and
- 120 feet for 13 minutes.

As we dive deeper, there is increased pressure on our bodies from the water and atmosphere above, and for every 30 feet of depth, dive times are reduced by half. As you can imagine, 13 minutes is not much time, and it goes by fast with lots of large animal action happening all around you. Considering the travel time just to get to this location, this creates significant motivation to make the most of the experience.

In business, we have a similar relationship with complexity.

As businesses organically grow or by acquisition, their complexity typically grows exponentially. The deeper we dive, the cost per minute of dive time increases dramatically.

In business, we need to tame complexity to control costs. In diving, we must be sure each minute of diving is maximized to the fun-to-cost ratio.

As introduced in Chapter 7, I stratify part numbers, demand, purchase orders, and purchases by 80 percent, 15 percent, 4 percent, and 1 percent of supplier spend or customer demand in units' multiplied cost per unit.

When reviewing any stratification of the law of 1 to 50 percent, the last 1 percent of demand typically represents 50 percent of suppliers, customers, part numbers, and purchase orders. Figure 16.1 is the typical inventory segmentation by part number multiplied by cost or purchase orders issued.

In diving, the diminishing returns of dive times past 100 feet do not correlate with having more fun. In business, the last 1 percent of demand often creates 50 percent of a business's complexity. This 1 percent increases many factors such as part numbers, stock-keeping locations, and management costs. This complexity significantly diminishes profitability.

Imagine if you can eliminate the last 1 percent of complexity, you can also eliminate 50 percent of business complexity, which will substantially positively impact the overall profitability.

Art's Law:
1% = 50% as an aid to PFEP—Typical Segmentation

Classification	% Demand	% Total Items	Demand Variability
"A" Items	80%	5-15%	Low
"B" Items	15%	10-20%	Low-Moderate
"C" Items	4%	10-20%	Moderate-High
"D" Items	1%	35-55%	High

Figure 16.1 Art's law 1% = 50%

I often ask my clients, "Do you want to deploy resources this foolishly?" They always answer emphatically "NO." My point is organizations forget about the last 1 percent of demand and supplier spend or assume that nothing can be done, stating the excuse, "It's the cost of doing business." I disagree.

The Elegance of Simplicity

In August 2020, Apple Computers passed the market value of two trillion dollars! How did it become the first company with a trillion-plus-dollar valuation? In my opinion, the reason for Apple's incomparable success was Steve Jobs' and Tim Cook's fierce focus on simplicity. They both understood that the simplest things are the most difficult, and they had the determination to achieve their vision.

> *Simple can be harder than complex: You have to work hard to get your thinking clean to make it simple. But it's worth it in the end because once you get there, you can move mountains.*
>
> —Steve Jobs

How does this philosophy translate to supply chain and operations? No companies go from 0 to $100 million or $1 billion in revenues overnight. Most companies start with a $50,000 or $100,000 purchase order, followed by a $200,000 or $500,000 purchase order, or they take a completely different track and acquire a competitor. If you're lucky, you eventually reach $100 million in sales.

As the business grows organically or with acquisitions, complexity also increases. At $500,000 of sales, supply chain and operations can run on index cards and Microsoft Excel spreadsheets. The processes business founders like friends Vicente and Sonia used in the early years of their business to manage and maintain inventories and production operations are no longer viable with higher sales, more complex bill of materials, sophisticated production planning, and the addition of international suppliers and customers.

Throughout my career, I often hear from senior leaders, "We need to upgrade our ERP. It will fix the issues we're having with inventory accuracy and customer service. Once the new ERP is in place, all problems

will be resolved." If this were true, every company would rush to implement a new ERP to improve their profits substantially. The truth isn't in
a new ERP; it's in preventing entropy.

What actually occurs is that management allows entropy to creep into
the organizations by failing to keep pressure on constant improvement
and quality standards—see more examples below.

Entropy creep starts with:

- A few wrong lead times grow into many that cause expedites
  and part shortages.
- A few part numbers with unplanned demand that aren't
  corrected become part shortages.
- By tolerating a few late deliveries from suppliers, late
  deliveries become a new normal.
- Planning parameters are not updated and are inaccurate.
- A few suppliers grow into thousands, and the organization
  cannot manage effectively.
- A few customers grow into hundreds or thousands without an
  effective method to determine which is profitable.
- Finished goods part numbers increase exponentially without a
  methodology to cull unprofitable part numbers.
- The requirement to support service parts for 10 to 20 years
  after the end of the product life cycle without end-of-life
  procedures expands dramatically with the growth in parts,
  sales, and customers.

Once entropy creep sets in, it's not long before the team gets caught
up in a failure spiral of just trying to keep up with daily tasks, and they
never get to solve the root causes of problems.

Let's review the combined probability of error. The calculation is
the same for inventory accuracy, bill of materials accuracy, or a data
element:

- Per attribute estimate a 99.0 percent accuracy.
- Number of discrete attributes 25.
- Combined Probability of Error = 0.99^{25} = 77.8 percent.

Pause for a moment to let this sink in. If we are not managing the data integrity processes, a few errors become many, and it becomes a substantial undertaking to address the issues. Incidentally, I see this happening so often that I developed the Entropy Busters® methodology. The best solution to maintain data accuracy in supply chain and operations is to employ entropy busters techniques such as daily visual management and safety quality delivery inventory production (SQDIP) processes.

Due to entropy, I can't overemphasize the difficulty of sustaining processes such as data and inventory accuracy, replenishment planning, or supplier order acknowledgment, to name a few. Making certain data stays accurate doesn't have the same sexiness as a shiny new ERP. However, the financial rewards are much higher.

Suppose you follow the entropy busters methodology to keep entropy creep from taking charge of your life. Then, one day, you will stop and notice the surprise part expedites and unexpected shortages nearly disappear. The team develops a better understanding of how systems and processes work. Profitability and customer service will improve. Finally, the team is no longer requesting a new ERP. Instead, they will focus on simple, elegant solutions to previously complex problems.

Rationalizing the Enterprise

Many articles have been written about the advantages of complexity reduction and, after the fact, implementation of corrective actions while outlining steps to reduce complexity and symptoms. There is little focus on the root cause of entropy creeping into any enterprise or how to eliminate the disease from starting. We are not doing a good enough job of asking, "Do we need so many exceptions?" or commenting, "That's an idiotic rule." We should ask, "What is the driving force of complexity creation?"

Would you believe me if I told you I had the following results from my 80/15/4/1 analysis for every business I have worked with?

- The last 1 percent of purchases:
  - Represents 50 percent of the part numbers, suppliers, and purchase orders.

- Or the last 1 percent of customer demand:
  - Represents 50 percent of finished goods part numbers, and customers.

Many managers believe the myth that "If you focus on the top 80 percent of the 80-20 rule, the results will come." In the short term, you can argue that this is correct. But long-term results are not sustainable because the last 1 percent of demand depletes the team's resources, consumes their time, and distracts them from caring for your best and most profitable customers.

Art's Gold: We must shift the paradigm and focus on eliminating the root causes of the last 1 percent of demand and 50 percent of the complexity.

We must reframe the focus and ask, "How would the business look after reducing complexity by 50 percent?" Would there still be a need for a complex ERP or MRP? My emphatic belief is that you would not.

There are such complex processes because of the sheer scope of product offerings and the parts required to be "everything to every customer," creating exception after exception to requirements.

Hence, entropy creep occurs.

During the past 30 years, much has been written about how businesses keep increasing complexity to satisfy customer expectations. Companies continue adding more product differentiation with greater functionality and increasing size. In many cases, these changes and additions occur without adequate processes to support such a large variety of options.

We need to take a hard look and consider that there is a tipping point where the existing systems and processes cannot handle more variation.

Has a radical, disruptive event created a need to increase profitable product offerings? Look at Southwest Airlines and Apple, for example. Southwest is a discount air carrier, and Apple is a high-end consumer electronics manufacturer.

Ninety-eight percent of Southwest aircraft are Boeing 737, using only one jet engine type. The strategy of a narrow aircraft fleet is brilliant because when Southwest trains its maintenance staff, one topic covers 98 percent of the aircraft in service, and the depth and breadth of service parts required to maintain their fleet properly are substantially smaller. The overall strategy reduces cost and improves customer service by having fewer maintenance delays due to service part availability.

Apple revolutionized cell phone technology with the application-based smartphone.

Both are brilliant examples of companies operating complex business models with simple designs.

How can your business be designed to succeed without the last 1 percent of demand, which creates 50 percent of the complexity?

Suppose your business model consists of a complex product line, that is, the service parts industry. Your business model must support and supply customers for decades after the final product has rolled off the assembly line. How can you build a business model with radically reduced complexity without sacrificing product line complexity?

Let's make the business case for 3D printing, additive manufacturing, and deploying the technology to disrupt the competition.

The Elegance of 3D Printing or Additive Manufacturing

The ultimate in postponement strategy, how does 3D printing transform your supply chain and operations to reduce the total cost of ownership?

- **Reducing Inventory.** Service parts inventory is expensive, with obsolescence, damage, spoilage, and shrinkage, all at high costs. When printing on demand, warehouse and storage space is not required, there will be 60 to 100 percent long-term savings for every dollar of inventory reduction.
- **Supply Base Changes.** There will no longer be the need to keep hundreds or thousands of suppliers to support the last 1 or 2 percent of demand and niche items. Consider the complexity reduction in supplier negotiations, supplier data management, logistic management, accounts payable, and so on.
- **Lead-Time Reduction.** If printing is on demand, there will no longer be a supplier and raw material lead times. Just print time!
- **No More Minimum Order Quantities**. Once the part is designed and the computer aided design (CAD) drawing is

saved, the component can be printed on demand for material cost and machine operator time.

- **No More Tooling Costs**. With 3D printing, the fixtures and jigs of traditional manufacturing are no longer required.
- **Print at Demand Source.** Reframe traditional thoughts on manufacturing. Have 3D printers at the source of demand, eliminating costly and lengthy transportation and customs clearance processing.
- **Machine Complexity Reduction.** Eliminate the complex machine shops used to produce a vast array of parts. Successful 3D technology adoptees use a printer for multiple purposes. It should satisfy most of your needs if procured to the proper specifications.
- **CAD Design, Customization, and Accuracy.** With CAD, the engineering team will have greater design freedom, customization, and the ability to meet the most demanding tolerance requirements.

3D Printers were first available in 1986. We now have 30-plus years of improvements to use to our advantage. I'm confident the industry is at the inflection point for adopting additive manufacturing of service and inter-mittent and lumpy demand parts. The implications for transforming the TCO and disrupting the competitive supply chain stage are enormous.

This moment presents an unprecedented opportunity for early adopt-ers to disrupt the market with shorter lead times, extraordinary product offerings, and lower costs. I believe the 3D printing revolution is similar to the Industrial Revolution, such as the first industrial use of the transis-tor and semiconductor.

Are you ready to print money?

Don't think narrow or small of a process, committee, or new initiative for complexity reduction. Expand your thought horizon and explain to the team and customers that you're eliminating the once-stocked parts to support the last 1 percent of sales and that you will create the product on demand with additive manufacturing.

Throw away the current model, become disruptive, and become entropy busters!

What would reducing parts by 50 percent, changing to print-on-demand, or both mean for your business model, supply chain, customer base, or profitability?

Dive Master Briefing (Client Example)

A former client requested my assistance in selecting a new ERP. Juan Antonio, the president, had already budgeted $15 million for software purchase, design, training, and implementation. Additionally, Juan Antonio had mentally picked the new system. Juan Antonio had heard about how many peers had implemented the new ABC Enterprise System, and he felt left behind. Representatives of ABC had met with my client, Juan Antonio, and assured him that all their financial struggles would be a distant memory: "Once their new ERP System was in place, all cost variances would jump off the ledger sheet and resolve swiftly."

During the due diligence process, I asked, "Why is such a complex and expensive system required?" Maria Pilar, the VP of Marketing, stated that they had the industry's most extensive product offering and its competitive advantage by being a "one-stop" shop for most customers.

"If it was such a significant competitive advantage, why were margins so thin and EBITDA significantly less than their industry peer groups?" I asked. Without hesitation, Maria Pilar responded, "Well, it's all because operations can't make the product efficiently."

In response to Maria Pilar's statement, I analyzed their sales for the past 24 months by using sales per part number and created a Pareto chart in the following way (Figure 16.2).

Class	% of demand	Part Number Count	Typical % Distribution	Client Actual
A	80%	521	5 to 15%	6.7%
B	15%	1,058	10 to 20%	13.6%
C	4%	1,424	10 to 25%	18.3%
D	1%	4,778	40 to 55%	61.4%
Total	100%	7,781	100%	100%

Figure 16.2 Client analysis

The last 1 percent of sales represented 61.4 percent of the product offering complexity and 4,778 active part numbers. After discussions with Juan Antonio, we hit the pause button on the ERP discussions and focused on the last 1 percent of sales. Juan Antonio challenged the sales and marketing team, that is, gave the ultimatum to eliminate 100 percent of the 4,778-part numbers within 90 days. In the worst-case scenario, sales would decrease by 1 percent or $3MM. We found that 50 percent of the part numbers had direct replacements in the ABC categories, and customers were never required to take the new product. For approximately 30 percent of the part numbers, there was a suitable substitute that customers would have no issue taking, and the remaining 20 percent was split between an opportunity for a one-time end-of-life buy or ~450-part numbers we needed to keep the product in the portfolio.

Sometimes, people say, "This is a simple or stupid question...." If not for my stupid question of "Why was such a complex ERP required?" we would not have addressed and eliminated the last 1 percent of sales that significantly increased their profits and valuation by $12 and $60 million respectively (Figure 16.3)!

Getting back to the new ERP, after the significant complexity reduction, we were able to rethink the size of expenditures. We found a mid-tier ERP solution that met the client's company requirements at a fraction of the price and required fewer implementation resources.

Improvements to Business and Valuation Increase

Net Changes to Business:	EBITDA
Negligible impact on sales: **Less than $300,000 year-over-year**	
Reduced Part Number Complexity by **56%**	
Improved on-time deliveries, flexibility, and responsiveness	$2MM
Canceled all open positions and let attrition eliminate 60 FTEs	$5MM
Total enterprise effectiveness gains not including FTE reduction	$5MM
Total saving and benefits	$12MM
Valuation Increase using a 5x multiple	$60MM

Figure 16.3 Improvements to business

Reframing our focus can transform our understanding of problems. In this instance, complexity and how incremental entropy creep erodes profits and EBITDA.

Client Testimonial

What is different here is the step of adding the "D" designation to strip out the most overlooked secret of what is driving Supply Chain costs. New technologies such as component printers enable solutions not previously available. But Art has highlighted that the fundamental solution is to eliminate the need for much of this one percent of demand, driving 50 percent of the complexity and, thus, costs. When you get this message to the ears of the C-level leaders, you have the chance of driving real systemic change in your supply chain!

—Bob Ratay—Former—Director of Supply Chain and Logistics Consulting Services—Avery Dennison.

—Retired—Senior Business Architect for Business Transformation—SAP

Dive Log 16 (Art's Commentary)

Going back to the Southwest Airlines example of the elegance of simplicity:

- Of their 706 aircrafts, 98 percent are Boeing 737-300 and 737-800, and both use one engine type, the CFM56, which significantly reduced the maintenance training, maintenance part inventory, and TCO by, thus, in turn, increasing customer service by having more on-time flights.
- They eliminated complex and costly ticketing systems by having open seating.

Southwest has addressed complexity head-on. We must remember rooting complexity out of our businesses requires tenacity and a long-range game plan. Few leaders have the needed perseverance to accomplish this goal.

From my experience, I believe leaders are not successful in rooting out complexity for three reasons:

1. Not understanding the "size of the prize" and the impact on the TCO.
2. The sheer magnitude of the problems and not knowing how to start.
3. Not having the board of directors' support and understanding that this is often a long-term initiative and the pressure to meet short-term quarterly numbers.

This journey takes commitment and a "thick skin" against the cynics. If you're up to the challenge, the rewards are transformational in a leaner operation, less complex processes and operating systems, improved EBITDA, and increased corporate valuation.

The law of 1 percent = 50 percent brings awareness and corrective action to organizations.

Having a plan to reduce and manage the parts necessary to succeed in business is critical. Earlier, we discussed 3D printing on demand as an alternative to stocking the potential of thousands of service parts.

Many suppliers specialize in managing inexpensive parts at their customer locations for the items required daily, using vendor-managed inventory (VMI) programs. Therefore, the supply chain team should have a strategy addressing these low-cost parts, such as hardware, fasteners, safety supplies, electrical components, and maintenance repair and operations (MRO) parts, to name a few.

Another client had 47 percent of their annual purchase orders for the last 1 percent of dollars spent. The client is achieving significant workload reductions within the procurement team by implementing VMI programs. The client is redirecting the time saved by buyers not buying the last 1 percent weekly to more valuable tasks, such as developing supplier partners and working with engineering to rationalize and reduce the cost of existing part numbers.

There will always be low-volume items essential to success. Amateurs do nothing about these items. Profession teams that thrive develop and implement solutions to reduce the TCO for the law of 1 percent = 50 percent.

Buddy Check: Questions From Coach Art

○ Does the last 1 percent of sales represent 50 percent of suppliers, finished goods part numbers, or customers?
○ Is there a process to avoid product proliferation?
○ How is a product's end-of-life inventory managed?
○ Does the last 1 percent of inventory use 50 percent of obsolescence reserves?

Art's Deep Dive

Nothing stifles creativity as swiftly as the silent, passive-aggressive voice of "not invented here."

Art's Gold: It's critical to set aside prior beliefs to achieve greatness.

CHAPTER 17

How to Create the Perfect Supplier Partner

If you're like me, you likely started your dive certification process at the first dive store you unintentionally wandered into one day. Selecting supplier partners for your supply chain is like searching for the perfect dive store.

When selecting the perfect dive store, I've discovered four key elements to consider:

1. Store personality. Some dive stores are similar to clothing boutiques. They have excellent lighting, play lots of tropical music, and have comfortable sitting areas. Some are utilitarian. They have fins, regulators, wet suits, and a place to sit for trying on equipment. Others treat dive gear like an afterthought; they're just another sporting goods store.
2. What are the brands stocked? Purchasing dive equipment is like buying jeans or shoes, though more expensive. We all have different body types and personalities. Finding a store with the equipment that fits you well is essential to enjoy the underwater environment safely.
3. The type of diving interest. There are hunters, techies, and recreational divers, with each store catering to their customer's needs.
4. Location, location, location. How far are you willing to travel to fulfill your diving passion?

As my skills and number of dives increased, my needs as a customer changed. Initially, all I needed was a vendor to provide me with a mask, fins, and a wet suit, and due to my basic needs and lack of knowledge, the purchase price was essentially the only deciding factor.

After about 30 to 40 dives, I needed a dive store that could fit me with a higher quality mask that would not leak and with a softer and more comfortable silicone seal, fins that improved my speed and agility, and a wet suit that fit me better than a burlap bag. My purchasing decision was no longer about price. It was about improving the quality and fit of the gear to enhance the total diving experience.

Today, I have what I feel are good partnerships with three dive stores. Since each one knows who I am as a diver, they can recommend gear that fits my body type and specific diving interests. Additionally, they can safely service my equipment and recommend dive boats and travel partners to optimize my total spending dollars.

This analogy translates to your business, as well. Do you have vendors that sell on cost, suppliers that have different levels of quality, or supplier partners that understand your unique needs and can make proactive and specific recommendations?

How Is Your Supply Chain Management at Building Long-Term Partnerships With the Supply Base?

Throughout Art Koch's Profit Chain® and the three Fs of supply chain management, the critical theme has been improving the total cost of ownership. This chapter discusses the relationship with suppliers and how they can be part of a sustainable solution.

Before starting, let's discuss whether procurement's only play is negotiating better pricing and terms with suppliers.

Many companies are still in the dark ages when dealing with their suppliers by only shopping for the lowest price and not reviewing the supplier's financial soundness or manufacturing capabilities. This dated approach of only negotiating purchase price is 100 percent adversarial. From the time of the quote or purchase order, the thought process is "Let the flogging begin." We will beat the best price out of them.

My rule is if you want to get treated well, treat others with the same respect. Why make the relationship adversarial? If they're good enough to supply your business, shouldn't they know significantly more about their products than you? From product design to the best-performing material and the most cost-effective manufacturing processes, why wouldn't you want to tap into their knowledge to reduce your total cost of ownership?

The first question to ask yourself should be: Do I have vendors, suppliers, or partners?

- **Vendor:** Vendors sell you hot dogs, peanuts, and cotton candy at ball games. Nothing more.
- **Suppliers:** Suppliers provide goods or services to recognized customers or consumers.
- **Supplier Partnerships:** Your company and the supplier are linked strategically. Partnerships have mutually agreed upon performance results, full disclosure, openly shared information, and joint problem resolution that improves communication, speed of delivery, and TCO. The best partnerships include several factors, such as:
  - Early design development with engineering teams from the supplier, your internal engineering team, and the customer's engineering design team.
  - Working together to eliminate non-value-added processes, attributes, and materials while improving manufacturability and quality, all while reducing the total cost of ownership.
  - Supplier partnership relationships typically result in the acquisition of multiyear purchase agreements.

The strategy of supplier partnerships is to:

- Integrate supply chain management into collaborative relationships with suppliers and internal and external customers.
- Focus on processes that improve process velocity and reduce the total cost of ownership.
- Generate improvements throughout the program life cycle.

The longer a product remains in the manufacturing cycle, the greater its cost.

—Henry Ford

Implementing Supplier Development and Partnerships

Step One

Implementing supplier scorecards is the first phase of changing your frame of reference from a vendor to a supplier mentality. Scorecards build a grading system that establishes a framework and ground rules so that procurement and suppliers can manage their expectations for key deliverables.

When kicking off the process, it is critical that procurement report the scores to suppliers promptly and hold them accountable for their results.

Supplier quality engineers are pivotal in educating and training suppliers on everything from quality and engineering requirements to labeling, packaging, transportation, and electronic data interchange (EDI). They also work with the supplier to correct deficiencies and coordinate the total cost of ownership (TCO) improvement initiatives. Figure 17.1 outlines my three-step plan-do-check-act (PDCA) process for implementing supplier score cards.

> **Electronic Data Interchange (EDI):** Intercompany, the computer-to-computer transmission of business information in a standard format. An EDI transmission consists of business data, not accompanying verbiage or free-form messages.
>
> **Total Cost of Ownership (TCO):** TCO includes all the direct and indirect costs associated with an asset or acquisition over the product or service's entire life cycle. TCO consists of the purchase price and the cost of transportation, handling and storage, damage and shrinkage, taxes and insurance, redistribution, cost of quality, interest, and engineering cost.

Step Two

The second step toward a supplier mindset is rationalizing the supply base and eliminating the worst-performing suppliers.

It's essential to rationalize the supply base. Rationalization or culling is eliminating suppliers that do not fit your business model. Some traits to look for are financial soundness, poor quality and delivery, redundant (another supplier does the same work better), or challenging to work with. However, you don't want to eliminate the wrong suppliers. Remember, we shifted our focus to the TCO, not solely the lowest purchase price. When working with some of the best suppliers, you must utilize their design teams and logistic channels to reduce TCO and not exclusively make the buying decision based on the purchase price.

When starting, you will discover that many suppliers have the necessary skills and core competencies but are not required to meet scorecard requirements. Throughout this process, you will find out who the players are versus pretenders. Weed out the pretenders and grow and nurture the players.

Don't be concerned about trying to turn all supplier relationships into partnerships. Start with the suppliers that make up the top 50 percent of the spend. It will be approximately 10 suppliers, and you should develop three partnerships from this group. Look for suppliers who make you a better partner to your customers. They might have a niche technology and the ability to go deep or very broad within specific expertise. Potential partners would be suppliers who have made intellectual capital and property investments in their particular expertise channel. Of the few chosen for partnership, you must work on developing the relationship.

Supplier partnerships are a two-way street.

You each have something the other one needs, and the process of forming and developing a partnership relationship is a behavior you both will learn together. The goals are improving the TCO and partnering with suppliers who make you a better customer partner. Scan the QR Code at the end of this chapter for a supplier scorecard example.

Why are supplier development scorecards and partnerships so important?

- To extend your mission, vision, and values into the supply base.
- Allows progress tracking and course corrections to meet long-term goals.
- It is no longer a price game. We must understand the supply chain's TCO.
- It will allow us to change processes to improve programs and product velocity.

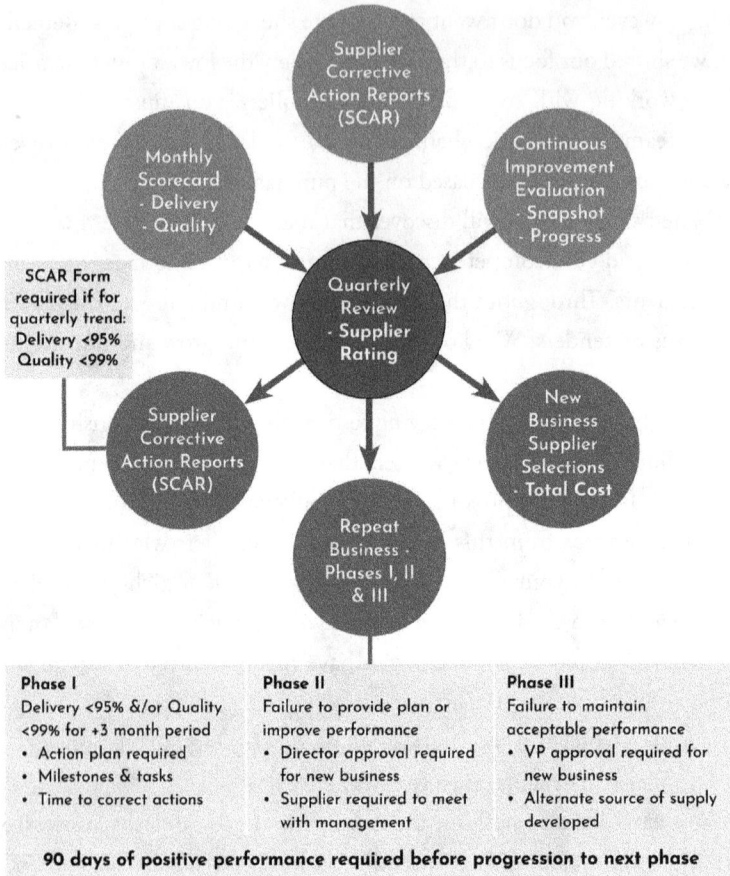

Figure 17.1 Plan-do-check-act of scorecards

- To gain competitive advantages through intellectual property, you don't have or can't develop.

  The eighties were about quality, and the nineties about re-engineering, the 2000s will be about the velocity of business to consumer.
  —Bill Gates, Microsoft

The goal of supplier partnerships is to reduce TCO. I have found that the best method to accomplish this is to evaluate suppliers through continuous improvement performance. (Figure 17.2) Suppliers must develop

Today and the Future
–Getting more from Continuous Improvement

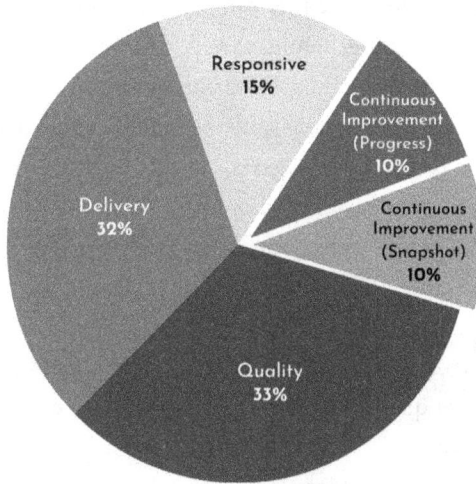

Figure 17.2 Getting more from continuous improvement

core manufacturing performance to achieve and sustain quality and delivery targets. The next priority is to increase design and program velocity to reduce the time from concept to delivery to the consumer. Within the design and development of new and existing products, suppliers need to be zealots for TCO improvements.

Additionally, they must become the bridge for future business development back into the supply base with their key suppliers. The concept is that partnerships don't stop with your supplier. They need to be driven back to the supplier's suppliers.

The Vision of Partnership Initiatives

- Establish the *total* cost of suppliers. This is the cost to set up, expedite, de-expedite, triage quality issues, manage design changes, and overall supplier maintenance.
- Achieve a reduction on TCO; 5 percent year-over-year reduction.

- ° Long-term agreements change the relationship dynamic. There is the elimination of the "Spot-Buy" tax with multiyear contracts in place. Suppliers are inclined to give better costing since they can plan capacity and labor and invest in long-term initiatives.
- ° With a partnership, both parties can invest in electronic data exchanges, significantly reducing manual non-value-added back-office processes.
- Data-driven rationalization of supply base; 20 to 30 percent reduction within three years.
  - ° Identify suppliers that fit in with your mission, vision, and values.
  - ° Strengthen relationships with "key" suppliers—assist with supplier quality engineers and joint Kaizen events when necessary.
  - ° Learn about problems before they become a crisis.
  - ° Eliminate poor performers.
- Deliver quality improvements to greater than 99.5 percent conformance.
- Improve delivery performance to greater than 99.5 percent compliance.
- Improve inventory velocity by greater than 20 percent within one year.

Dive Master Briefing (Client Example)

We initiated supplier partnerships when I worked with a client who was the supplier to a significant ABC Power Solutions, a global manufacturer of HVAC solutions. When Joshua, my client's regional sales manager, won the contract for a new compressor motor supplied to ABC Power Solutions, it was a solid win for the sales team. However, the first year did not go as planned, and ABC Power Solutions ended up having three significant issues with the client:

1. An inside diameter that connected the part my client machined to the customer part had an ongoing defect.

2. Lack of schedule flexibility and responsiveness.

3. Schedule adherence.

To add insult to injury, my client's facility was their sole source of supply, and they were part of a new product line's significant expansion of the U.S. market. To lose the contract would result in nearly $50 million in lost sales and would give my client a major black eye within the industry.

Cheryl, the purchasing manager from ABC, and I implemented the following three corrective actions that solved the underlying issues:

Phase One

The first thing we did was to work on lead-time reduction. Because schedules were continually changing, Pina, the manufacturing manager, and Angie, the materials manager, believed that the customer's order service department or ABC themselves had no idea what they were doing. The changes caused the assembly line to be in constant turmoil. My client's standard lead time to customers was 12 weeks. But ABC Power Solutions was different from most of their other customers. They shipped primarily to end contractors, and a 12-week lead time would not be sufficient. Joshua from sales and customer service tried to compensate by adding more safety stock. The more they increased safety stock, the worse the quality and service became.

- Joshua, Angie, and I analyzed the raw material for our final assembly and determined that two-part number families were of concern. We worked with the suppliers to get them to hold a safety stock of their base materials. If the customer provided us with a 52-week forecast, we could translate it into component base material forecast for the supplier, and the lead time would be two weeks. During the analysis, all but a few parts were common. For the few exceptions, we increased our safety stock.
- We developed a planning bill of materials (BOM) to forecast raw materials, labor, and capacity. The planning bill represented the blended mix of the parts used.

- ○ Summarizing: We implemented a 52-week planning horizon using the new planning BOM, linked it with suppliers, and added safety stock for low-volume lumpy demand items.

Phase Two

Joshua, Cheryl, and customer engineering worked together to rationalize several designs and tolerance characteristics that made raw material purchases less complicated. Doing so addressed several of the ongoing quality concerns. During this process, the engineering teams discovered there were no matching sets of gauges for critical characteristics, and packing allowed critical dimensions to become damaged. They implemented a gauging program, and reinforcement of more robust packaging plans nearly eliminated defects.

Phase Three

Angie and I created a Kanban pull process from the client's finished goods, reducing the lead time to transit time. The new production schedules were now 100 percent aligned with customer Kanban pulls. Over the next two months, we systematically reduced finished goods inventories to reflect Kanban sizing. We worked with suppliers to help them understand the new forecast process and to balance their raw materials.

Results

- We reduced lead time from 12 weeks to 3 days.
- Total pipeline inventory for suppliers, clients, and ABC Power Solutions was reduced by 70 percent for the specific product family. They freed up a manufacturing bay with the internal inventory reduction, allowing the addition of a new product line.
- Manufacturing efficiencies increased by 20 percent due to the 100 percent reduction of schedule break-ins.
- On-time to customer Kanban increased to +98 percent.

- Eliminated premium freight to the customer and nearly removed it from suppliers.
- My client and ABC Power Solutions freed up critical resources for other long-term initiatives.
- Cheryl, ABC's purchasing manager, and their team were ecstatic and used the relationship as a model with other suppliers.
- The TCO reduced by nearly 15 percent in the first year.

Dive Log 17 (Art's Commentary)

In today's competitive environment, we need to win on every front. Neglecting to build supplier partners is one of the most significant business mistakes of the past two decades. Often companies think these relationships are reserved for larger enterprises. No matter the size of your business, there must be an investment in professionals that can deliver year-over-year reductions to the TCO.

Suppose there are no processes to support critical thinking and deep work, or the team is staffed with nonprofessionals. In that case, the supply base becomes narrow, stagnant, and populated with vendors because this is the path of least resistance.

The larger picture of supplier partnerships must be front and center. Companies of all sizes need supplier partnerships that streamline business communications, have the resources to improve designs, support today's rigorous quality standards, and have the depth and bandwidth to support customer needs fully.

Lastly, partner with suppliers that make you more competitive by adding intellectual property you don't have and supporting your business mission and strategy.

Buddy Check: Questions From Coach Art

- Do you have vendors or suppliers or supplier partnerships?
- Are the procurement team just placing orders or enhancing supplier relationships and knowledge?
- Is the supplier's performance measured with scorecards?

- Do you rationalize the supply base each year using scorecard results?
- Are your supplier partnerships reducing TCO by at least 5 percent annually?

Art's Deep Dive

The current decade is about compressing lead time by in-sourcing, reshoring, and near-shoring by partnering with suppliers that can add mission-critical expertise while reducing the TCO. This requires process integrity, developing the supply chain team, organizational alignment, commitment, and effective supplier integration.

I "cut my teeth" in supply chain at a tier one manufacturer supplying Ford, GM, and Chrysler. I felt the pressure firsthand at the plant manager's meetings at the Ford Wixom plant. We took our beatings and went home to fix our opportunities. From these early days, I've always believed within the supply chain, the further we move away from the final customer, the performance expectation placed on each supplier reduces significantly because tier two and three suppliers might crumble under pressure. There is no need for public humiliation. However, don't be guilty of reducing performance expectations of suppliers the further they are from the customer.

For additional information and free tools, please scan the code.

CHAPTER 18

The Inventory Doctor®

Both oxygen and inventory are critical for the survival of humans and businesses, respectively. We take a breath in, and we exhale. We issue purchase orders, receive raw materials, and ship products to customers.

The process of materials flowing through organizations has become autonomic, just like our breathing.

There are significant benefits to autonomic processes. Breathing keeps us alive without thinking. An autonomic materials process flow keeps our operations humming along smoothly while keeping customers satisfied without giving it any thought.

However, with anything good, there are often adverse side effects. Oxygen toxicity is the harmful effect of breathing molecular oxygen (O_2) at increased partial pressures. Oxygen toxicity symptoms are tunnel vision, ringing in the ears (tinnitus), nausea, twitching, anxiety, dizziness, and even death. It impacts the:

- Central nervous system
- Pulmonary (lungs)
- Ocular (eyes)

Inventory also has adverse side effects. I say "Inventory is Evil" because it delays problem resolution, and the autonomic nature of today's material replenishment processes can tend to hold inventory above optimal levels without a trained buyer or inventory specialist doing periodic reviews for reasonableness. It is common for managers and associates to just forget about inventory until there is a problem.

Here are common symptoms of having too much stock: poor customer service, low flexibility and responsiveness, obsolescence, and inventory inaccuracy.

As divers, we need to monitor our depths and cumulative dive times because oxygen becomes toxic at 200 feet, and toxicity increases with dive times. As supply chain professionals, we need to monitor inventory levels and not become complacent about allowing levels to creep up and damage profitability.

Why Inventory Is Evil

Many people are surprised when I say, "Inventory is Evil." There are three reasons I like to use this phrase. It gets leadership's attention, reminds everyone not to take inventory for granted, and to become aware of trade-offs.

Inventory's primary function is to cover variability and is necessary to supply items for sale to customers. However, excessive inventory delays problem resolution, costing enterprises valuable profits. (Figure 18.1)

What many leaders forget is that inventory is a depreciating asset. The longer it is on the shelf, the lesser its value is due to spoilage, obsolescence, or lack of freshness. For example, losing freshness requires cleaning or

Figure 18.1 Inventory is evil

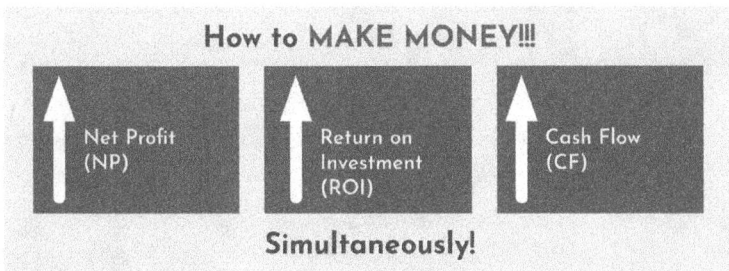

Figure 18.2 Top level performances measures—KPIs

repackaging. Adding resources to refurbish or to find and remove obsolete inventory erodes profits.

My initial education on inventory's impact occurred at Michigan State University's supply chain management program, where I completed an independent study program in South Korea and Japan. We studied Edward Deming's teachings on quality operating systems and how Japan and South Korea's industries embraced his practices and material pull processes such as Kanban.

After graduate school, a colleague introduced me to Eli Goldratt's books, *The Goal* and *Theory of Constraints*. Goldratt does an excellent job of reminding us that any business aims to make money. Making money is accomplished by increasing net profits, return on investment, or cash flow (see Figure 18.2).

The operational key performance indicators (KPIs) for improving net profits are increasing throughput, decreasing inventory, and reducing operating expenses (see Figure 18.3).

- **Throughput:** The rate at which the system generates money through *sales*.
- **Inventory:** The money invested in procuring items to sell.
- **Operational Expense:** The money spent to turn inventory into throughput.

However, for over two decades, from the mid-1990s to the late 2010s, our nation lost its compass heading regarding inventory velocity

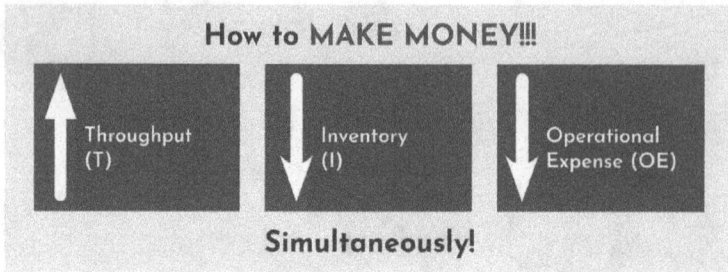

Figure 18.3 Operational performance measures—KPIs

fundamentals. Many in corporate leadership were misinformed and did not understand the total cost of ownership, which led to a herd mentality of chasing low-cost labor halfway around the world. Countries like China enticed western corporations to relocate their operations with low-cost labor and by using currency manipulation, raw material subsidies, and tax incentives that, in the short-term, artificially reduced costs. During this same period, the average inventories of American industries increased by 31 percent. Swelled inventory was in the form of everything from beverage (70 percent), automotive parts (43 percent), aerospace (14 percent), and broadline retail (11 percent).

During the late 2010s, international pressure ended China's currency manipulation and raw material incentives. However, the damage had been done. Leaders saw their inventories increase, cash flows decrease, profits tighten, and they lost critical flexibility and responsiveness to customers' needs.

In 2019 and 2020, when the COVID-19 pandemic hit, straining most and breaking many global supply chains, it was the final tipping point that pushed industries to start reshoring, nearshoring, and insourcing local and increasing regional manufacturing.

What is the main goal of any enterprise to ensure its survival? What's the purpose of any company? To make money! (see Figure 18.4).

From these frameworks, I've learned and developed methodologies that help corporations improve their inventory performance, customer service, and profitability, as represented by Art Koch's Profit Chain® model—the three Fs of supply chain management.

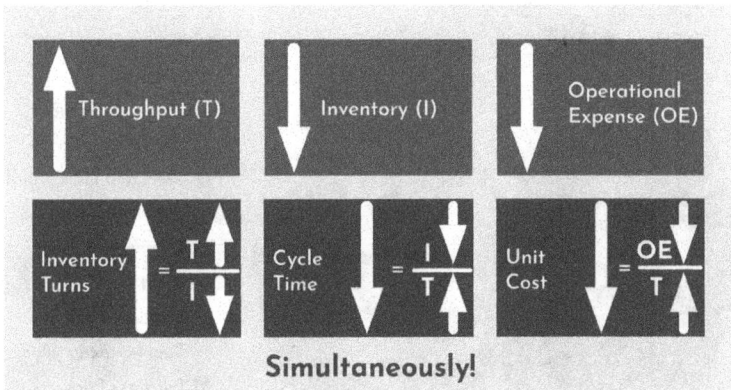

Figure 18.4 Operational performance measures—KPIs

Art Koch's Profit Chain

> Dramatic improvements to inventory velocity, increased customer
> service, and enhanced corporate profits.

What is meant by Art Koch's profit chain? Consider the costs associated with all supply chain transactions, from supplier selection through customer receipt of a good product. In general, the total cost of ownership begins with identifying and setting up a supplier and ends with getting an excellent product to the customer. Why is this important? When done efficiently and effectively, it can represent approximately 70 percent of the total cost of goods sold. Inefficiencies and poor processes will drain your profits dry.

Figure 18.5 illustrates how the enterprise is impacted when poor decisions are made by sourcing products with inferior processes to support supply chains. As you can see, sourcing from a supplier further away from operations and customers increases lead times and "soft" costs that ultimately drive down profits.

Figure 18.6 illustrates when sourcing locally and regionally, "soft" costs reduce. By developing supplier partnerships, the total cost of ownership decreases, and profits increase.

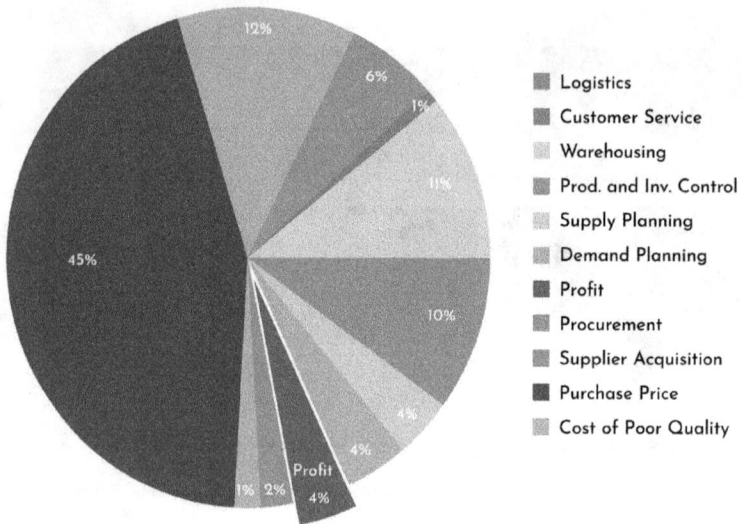

Figure 18.5 Poor sourcing and SCM processes

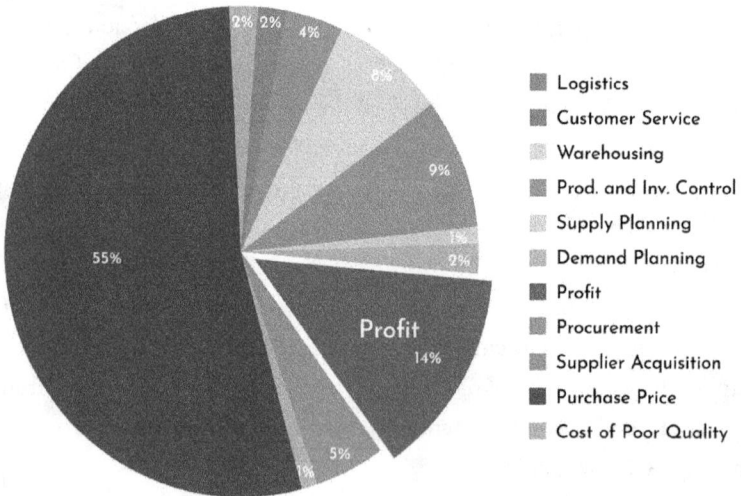

Figure 18.6 Excellent sourcing and SCM processes

Short-Term Thinking and Underestimating the "Size of the Prize"

The short-sightedness of not acknowledging the total cost of inventory ownership keeps organizations from underestimating the "Size of the Prize" by using a short-term and incremental cost-center mindset that diminishes profits. I've worked with some of the best organizations worldwide and have been highly influential in guiding them to shift their perspective to the long-term total cost of ownership. Because I have executed this winning mindset during my career, I've directly impacted the process of improving inventory velocity by greater than 250 million dollars, or an average of a 23 percent reduction, improved customer service by an average of 18.5 percentage points, and improved corporate valuations by over one billion dollars.

After reading this book, you can dive deep into the root causes of underperforming inventory by utilizing my proven trademarked methodologies and developing a strategy for improving inventory velocity and customer service. Then, you will become an Inventory Doctor.

My methodology follows a three-phase top-level process to achieve sustainable inventory velocity and customer service improvements:

1. Process improvements to supply chain management.
2. Application of systems-based tools.
3. Applying operational excellence (Toyota Production Systems) and systematic improvements.

As supply chain professionals, we must understand that inventory flowing through the industry is like the air we breathe. If we can't breathe, we suffocate and die. If we don't have manufacturing and customer inventory, the business will suffocate and die.

The Inventory Doctor—Step I—Inspection

Achieving sustainable improvements to inventory performance requires the organization to understand that it is not only the SCM's responsibility.

It's the entire organization's responsibility, including senior management, sales, marketing, finance, engineering, operations, and quality assurance.

Start by using a visual daily management process to get the team on the same page and ensure that daily priorities are addressed to make the next 24 to 48 hours of business successful. Once the team has "jelled," the following steps will help improve inventory velocity, customer service, and corporate valuation:

- Establish the relevant few KPIs that will drive success for the next 24 to 48 hours.
- Daily review of purchase orders placed.
- Establish daily spending budgets defined down to individual buyers.
- Determine the actual quantity and dates needed for aged purchase and work orders. Then cancel and defer accordingly.
- Address early and late deliveries with suppliers. Reduce the supply-side variability of delivery. High supply variability negativity impacts safety stock level requirements.
- Track supplier invoices without receipts and correct root causes. An often-missed KPI of receiving errors is of purchase parts physically delivered to a facility and never entered into the computer systems as a receipt, hence the missing receipt.
- When first starting the process of increasing inventory velocity, it's common for slow-moving and obsolete inventory to be 40 to 50 percent of the total on-hand balances. It's crucial to address ownership, responsibility, and accountability by having all functions of the organization become part of the solution to eliminate obsolete inventory and be sure the root causes are corrected to keep the inventory from returning.
  - Obsolete items: Make sure sales, marketing, and customers assume timely responsibility for disposition. Be sure you are adhering to a product's end-of-life schedule. Scrap at appropriate reserve timing.
  - Slow-moving inventory: Again, ensure that sales, marketing, and customers assume timely responsibility.

Hold a fire sale. And be vigilant that quality rejection and hold locations are processed timely.

  ○ Overall, there must be a mindset change on how to deal with obsolete and slow-moving inventory. It's *not* OK for it to linger, and there *must* be an urgency for timely disposition.

Inventory accuracy must be of the highest priority. Without world-class inventory accuracy, you will never be able to sustain a high-velocity level.

After observing the team in action, you, as a leader, will understand some of the professionalism gaps within the group. Learn how team professionalism can be developed with training and education and recognize when an injection of outside talent is necessary.

Next, work with suppliers to compress lead times and reduce the minimum and multiple order quantities. Remember, this is not shifting inventory to suppliers but reducing total pipeline inventory.

Postponement Strategy

Implementing Long-Term Agreements and Improved Inventory Velocity

I've had significant success working with suppliers by implementing two to three years of strategic long-term agreements (LTA) that compress lead times and postpone the product's final definition on repetitive parts. These agreements assure the supplier that you're there for the long term. Once an LTA is in place, make a 52-week top-level forecast available to suppliers. It's a simple implementation once the forecast is in place. Then divide the planning horizon into raw materials, work-in-process, and finished goods authorizations. The typical authorization horizons are:

- Finished goods—one to two weeks.
- Work-in-process—two weeks.
- Raw materials—six weeks.

As you can see, this gives the supplier 10 weeks of lead time to procure raw materials, manufacture the product, and stock finished goods to support customers' needs. The model's significance is that the supplier is authorized to hold material at differing stages, which postpones product definition and additionally reduces the lead time to one or two weeks for repetitive supply planning parts. Next, set minimum and multiple order quantities to bin box levels. Stop making spot buys on repetitive items.

As part of the LTA, it is essential to include and enforce packaging, labeling, and EDI standards. Including these items in the LTA will improve receiving velocity, inventory accuracy, and reduce the frequency of supplier invoices without receipts.

After successful LTA implementation for raw materials, work-in-process, and finished goods authorizations, implement physical Kanban pull processes over system-based methods for repetitive supply planning. Remember, in the short term, MRPs are push systems. Actual events in operations occur faster than the speed an MRP can respond, causing information lag. The lag time of information flow creates inventory excesses and shortages.

Use improved supplier relationships and partnerships to streamline new product introduction speed to market.

The Inventory Doctor—Step II—Tactical Exploration

How good is the application of your current system-based MRP and ERP tools? What percent of the capabilities are used if you looked inside the current device your company uses to forecast, replenishment plan, and manage inventory? With any tool, you are only as good as the individual's level of expertise. Many businesses desire system-based solutions to adopt standardized processes and demand and supply-side exception-based planning. It's critical to follow the process. Inventory velocity, customer service, and corporate valuation will improve when following these fundamental principles:

- Make sure supply chain professionalism matches the requirements of any systems-based solution.
- Ensure exception-based demand and supply-side planning are adhered to for early, late, and accurate order quantities. Use visual daily management and Entropy Busters® methodologies to address conformity.

- When available, use system-based stratification classification methodologies: ABCD classification, order frequency, minimums, and multiple parameters.
- Additionally, use system-based analysis for safety stock and service-level optimization.
- Most world-class ERP and inventory planning solutions are highly configurable to match business needs to improve flexibility and responsiveness to customers.
- Don't accept commentary from team members that the new tool does not complete any steps correctly. There cannot be any work outside the new system.
- Often, new demand planning solutions are purchased to improve forecast accuracy. Nothing is incorrect with this methodology. However, forecasts are always wrong. Therefore, we need to reduce our dependency on forecasts by reducing lead times.

The Inventory Doctor—Step III—Differential Diagnosis

Before any organization decides to make systematic improvements, such as selecting and implementing a new ERP system, leaders must spend the time needed to ensure the three Fs of SCM: people and process foundation, structural framework, and financial focal point are on solid footing. When fundamentals are in place, the organization is less likely to try solving large-scale supply chain or inventory problems incorrectly with a new system. Instead, they will focus more on the exact causes of low-level issues that must be solved.

Before selecting a new system, one of the first questions is, "What competitive advantage" does the new system provide?

There are three critical elements when considering a new system. The first is to move the organization to one platform, *"one system, one process."* The second is to *build automation of routine processes.*

The third is to *standardize exception-based processes* for demand and supply planning.

Critical reasons for a new system are:

- The legacy system is no longer supported.
- To establish a competitive advantage.

- Creating a process for "one platform, one process."
- To develop a strategy of exception-based supply and demand planning.
- To improve long-range forecast accuracy.
- To optimize inventory, networks, and utilize multiechelon inventory optimization.

The Inventory Doctor—The Goal

Specific goals must be established to measure progress with any new initiative, process, or system. Below are typical improvements that organizations should target for achievement:

- Improving inventory velocity by 20 to 40 percent.
- Improving long-range forecast accuracy by 5 to 10 percent.
- Eliminating the need for short-range forecasting.
- Decreasing part outage duration by 50 percent.
- Increasing customer service and fill rates by 5 to 20 percentage points.
- Increasing process standardization to 100 percent.

This book and the above outline illustrate the steps and methodology I've used to build a successful supply chain management career. Following this methodology, we've reduced inventories by over $250 million, an average of 23 percent, while simultaneously increasing customer service by an average of 18.5 percent and increasing corporate valuations by an estimated one billion dollars. (Figure 18.7)

Dive Log 18 (Art's Commentary)

Are you using your supply chain as a competitive advantage and differentiator? The previous 17 chapters outlined the areas of supply chain excellence. By adopting these philosophies and methodologies of the three Fs of SCM: people and process foundation, structural framework, and financial focal point, you can use SCM as a profit chain and competitive advantage.

Art Koch's Profit Chain® Model
The Three F's of Supply Chain Management
Fundamentals for Sustainable Success

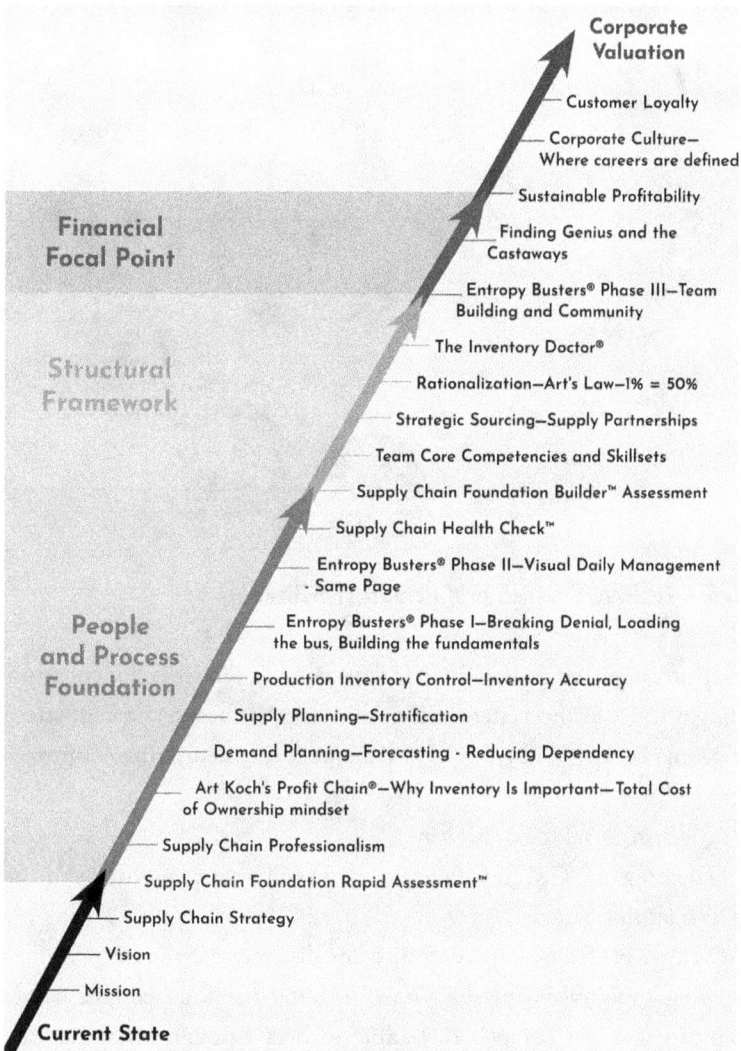

Figure 18.7 Art Koch's profit chain model

Take a moment to visualize how different your team, processes, and results would be if you transformed the supply chain into Art Koch's profit chain and used an inventory carry cost reflective of the total cost of ownership! (Figure 18.8).

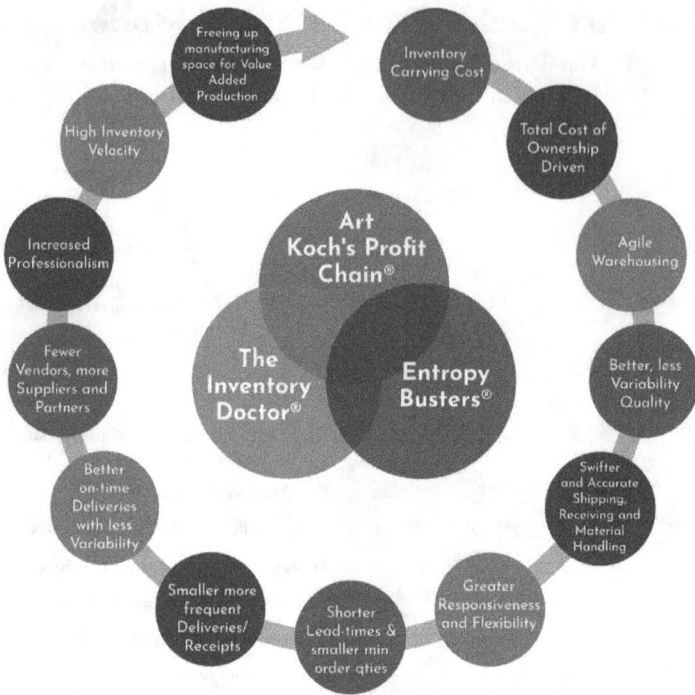

Figure 18.8 Art's Koch profit chain visualization

Think about your shop floor. Is the paging system or radios constantly going off? Or in the materials control offices, is there a constant stream of people coming and going? How frequent are there surprise shortages or expedites?

It doesn't need to be this way.

Focusing on SCM fundamentals, there will be less noise and surprises to distract the team.

With new focus and freedom from distractions, the deep work of building supplier partnerships and reducing the total cost of ownership can now get completed, leading to breakthrough innovation and accomplishments.

Envision the entire organization working toward common goals, becoming zealots for improving inventory velocity and reducing the total cost of ownership. Siloed cost center management will vanish. Entropy busters is your enabler for deep work and long-term operational and profit sustainability.

World-Class Hack to Standard Deviations

Inventory is a resource of any company and must be used wisely. My preferred methodology for applying safety inventory is to use safety time as defined in Chapter 7.

As discussed in Chapter 7, safety time inventory quantities will automatically adjust based on demand changes. This model works perfectly for parts with a less lumpy and more repetitive demand pattern. We often need to set fixed safety stock quantities for parts with lumpy and sporadic demand patterns often observed in service parts.

One of the challenges in calculating fixed safety stocks is understanding if the standard deviation is a large or small statistical variation. To overcome this issue, consider using the coefficient of variation (CoV) to normalize and then stratify standard deviations. The CoV is the ratio of the standard deviation to the mean.

CoV = Standard Deviation/Mean

The CoV is beneficial since the standard deviation must be understood in perspective to the mean of data. Adding CoV to your analysis tool kit allows for the contrast between data sets with different units or widely different means.

Using CoV, you can stratify parts based on low, medium, and high variation. Using the CoV calculation results gives you the knowledge to apply service level Z-Factors to the appropriate part number with a better understanding of the impacts on safety stock quantities, service levels, and the TCO. Working with clients, we have successfully created tiers for low, medium, and high CoVs and assigned service level Z-Factor to the appropriate tier. This methodology gives the client a guideline to manage the trade-off of safety stock quantity, dollars of inventory, and the cost of expediting.

Defining Z-Factors: Z-factor of 1 is equal to one standard deviation of demand or a service level of 84 percent. A Z-factor of 1.64 and 2.33 equate to service levels of 95 percent and 99 percent, respectively. Take note that as we increase the desired service level, the Z-factor multiple in the calculation exponentially increases safety stock inventory. By using CoV stratification in harmony with Z-factor service levels helps to make a more informed decision to manage the cost trade-off or expediting versus safety stock.

Entropy Busters

Stop letting the process manage you. Become the champion of your game plan and manage your processes to achieve sustainable profits.

Art Koch's Profit Chain

Leap forward to become an industry leader with dramatic improvements to inventory velocity, increased customer service, and corporate profits (Figure 18.9).

Industry Leading

Figure 18.9 Pinnacle of sustainability

Buddy Check: Questions From Coach Art

- Is your organization complacent about inventory?
- Are you addicted to your inventory? I know I once was....
- Does your organization let short-term thinking underestimate the "size of the prize" of improving the TCO?
- What are your inventory postponement strategies?
- Can the application of your current systems-based tools work better? For example, do you apply the methodology of exception-based planning? Are you attending to the system-based alerts for order acknowledgments, expedites, de-expedites, and cancels?
- Can you consider your supply chain a competitive strategic advantage?

Art's Deep Dive

Third Law of Thermodynamics: As the temperature approaches zero kelvin, absolute zero, an organism's entropy approaches a constant minimum. *Enterprises with high growth have more entropy, but the growth usually hides the entropy and problems. Process controls must be established and proven sustainable to prevent entropy during rapid growth.*

You might remember the phrase, "Measure me, and I'll tell you how I'll perform." If you only measure and reward incremental carrying cost of inventory at prime plus one results, you get *just* that, to the detriment of the TCO.

Think about how you define your company: leaders, followers, or amateurs. If you're not a leader already, I'm sure you would like to be an industry leader and not be considered a follower or an amateur. Following is a theoretical case study to help prime the brain's gray matter pump. Let's not wait. Start the process now. Mobilize the team, utilize the lessons, and get immediate results (Figure 18.10).

Thinking Big: Size of the Prize

Scenario: AKMC, INC is a manufacturer of widgets.
Annual revenue of $1 billion. Worldwide supply and customer base.
Key markets: automotive, capital equipment, heavy industry and
consumer white goods. Total inventory is $250 million
or three inventory turns/year.

Steps:

1. **Assemble:** President and Controller, the Head of Operations, Supply Chain, Marketing/Sales, Engineering, and HR.

2. **Set Goals:** Set the goal of reducing inventory by 50%, or $125 million.
   a. Don't try to eat the elephant.
   b. Start with the target of $35 million in 90 days.

3. **Divide and Conquer:** There are seven department heads, each will have the objective of reducing inventory by $5 million in 90 days.

4. **Reporting Cadence:** Daily, this actually means every day. They must shift the corporate culture to create urgency. Make it the first priority every day.

5. **Create a "million Room":** Don't hide in an office or cover the windows. Remember we are changing culture.

6. **Who Reports out:** The Department Head, not their subordinate, no delegation of duties. Yes, their team can and will be doing most of the work, however, in this meeting, the Department head needs to feel the heat.

7. **Track:** Task completion to action plan, actual working capital to objectives.

8. **Celebrate:** the accomplishments every 30, 60, and 90 days.

9. **Outline four to six lessons learned, setbacks and accomplishments.**

10. **Replicate:** Keep replicating until the culture transforms leadership's thought process to the fact that high inventory velocity is good.

Figure 18.10 Thinking big: size of the prize

Client Testimonial

Art and I have worked as supply chain professionals in Fortune 500 environments. He contributes his atypical career experience to the group … an invaluable insight you cannot find in any textbook. There is no substitute for hands-on experience, and that's one of Art's most valuable assets.

—Khalil Jada, owner of JMS supply chain solutions.

PART 3

Financial Focal Point

CHAPTER 19

Are You Finding the Genius and the Castaways?

When I first started diving, all my dive buddies and I talked about was 150 feet of visibility! Let me explain. One hundred and fifty feet of visibility is nearly unheard of; it's like diving in "Gin" clear waters. A typical lake might have 3 to 10 feet of visibility, while a swimming pool is likely to have 30 to 40 feet of visibility. You get the picture. We would swim continuously, just taking in the sights. It's such an alien world we dreamt of having 150 feet of visibility to soak it all up!

As the number of logged dives and total dive time increases, so do your skills. Your buoyancy and air consumption improve. High visibility isn't as important as before. It's more about seeing everything there is to see, even the little things.

After diving for a couple of years, I started hearing the phrase "Muck Diving." What the heck is "Muck Diving?"

When slowing down during a dive, you discover the coral reef where the shrimp, crabs, and small reef fish reside. Muck diving is about slowing down even more and hovering over a 20- by 20-ft. area for the entire dive. Even smaller sea life has an entirely different type of beauty. I like to say, "A face only a mother could love."

The lesson to learn is that we first start by seeing the larger picture before the intricate nuances are visible. This translates well to us as business leaders. Early in our careers, many managers fly past the reef 40 feet below, searching for 150 feet of visibility. It's not until we learn the business, slow down, and dive into the muck that we can see the details that lead us to find the hidden talent, the lost geniuses, and the castaways.

Finding Genius and the Castaways

What if I were to tell you that you have an untapped resource within your organization and that it's free to you if you know how to slow down and dive into the muck to find it? It is how leaders discover, cultivate, and sustain the hidden genius in their organization.

The more time I spend working with team members, the more I realize the importance of leadership. Anyone can have excellent individual achievements. Good leaders can rally a team and get good results. However, exceptional leaders have honed their skills to find and nurture the genius and the castaways within organizations, unlocking their true potential and mobilizing them into the team to achieve extraordinary results.

All organizations employ such individuals. They may be lost, pigeonholed, or just castaways. These individuals have been told to check their brains at the door upon arrival to work. They may be the person with their head down, working hard, and not heard. Or the wisecracking stock-car racer with multiple regional championships, the troop master who has graduated the most Eagle Scouts in the nation, or someone with a disability.

They may never have had family support. Perhaps they were never told they were great at something, leading to a complete lack of self-confidence. They can be individuals who matured late in life. They are often intelligent but never had the opportunity or the right timing to blossom in their careers. Their true potential was locked away because they might have said something wrong or not been polished enough to address a critical issue.

Because these individuals don't fit the mold with either traditional education or fit into the corporate setting, they get sidelined, and their talents and skills go untapped. Often, they find other avenues to achieve success and challenge their minds.

Dive Master Briefing (Client Example)

Once, I had an opportunity to work at the same company twice, a "re-tread," so to speak. The first engagement was as a materials manager, and the second was as an operations manager. It was a great workplace, focused on safety, quality, delivery, and costs, with a healthy family culture.

The facility's equipment had been relocated and repositioned multiple times due to site consolidations and attempts to be closer to customers. Some machines were new, and some had seen better days. However, the team maintained everything to the best of our ability.

Like most companies, we had a work cell that always seemed to have a unique set of problems or distinctive personality. The work cell was made up of large-capacity precision machining equipment. It consisted of a hodge-podge of machines, some new, some +30 years old, and all very temperamental. If one broke, the others weren't far behind. They were expensive to maintain, replacement parts were costly, and all had long lead times. To make matters even worse, they were always covered in nasty oily coolant.

These machines were a thorn in my side.

When they broke down, it was a big deal. Sonia, the maintenance manager; Jorge, the engineering manager; and Leyre, the area facilitator, were always there by my side. And no one was happy.

Every time we showed up, the operators would clean up, look busy, and move on to a different job. I kid you not. This process went on for years. We even held a few maintenance Kaizen events in the area. Things would get better temporarily, but only for a few months. Then they would start all over again. It felt like I was the star in Bill Murray's *Groundhog Day* movie.

As part of the effort to improve employee engagement, we held monthly birthday lunches. The events were very low-key, with no set agenda. It was a way to take time to celebrate and recognize employees' birthdays, nothing more. I would always try to sit with a different group of people each time to get to know them and to avoid the appearance of favoritism.

This particular month, I decided to sit with a gentleman named Vicente and his table of co-workers. As usual, we talked about the factory, including what schedules looked like for the rest of the month and year, and discussed safety and key customer visits. I took pride in knowing the team members' names and learning something about them. I did not know Vicente very well. He worked at our problem cell. So, to get to know him better, I started asking questions.

I wanted to know how long he had worked at the plant, "30 years," and what areas he worked in, "fractional and hermetic rotors." Was he married? "Yes." Children? "Yes." I asked what they do? "Well," he said," two are medical doctors, and one is an attorney." Vicente's other child was a teacher, policeman, or fire person. I kid you not; here was this guy who had been working his blue-collar job all his career, and he and his wife had nurtured a very successful family of professionals!

I was in mild shock. Here was a man who was as quiet as a mouse, never spoke up, did his job, and was always there. Vicente came from a time and place where factory workers did what they were told and were discouraged from asking questions. Sad but true!

At this point, I felt foolish. This man must be smart as a whip and I missed it! I thought he probably had some great ideas about the issues in his work cell.

Within a few days, I was the lead character in *Groundhog Day* again.

The broaching machine broke down. Our crack team of managers arrived and started to diagnose the situation. The typical scenario began to play out.... The guys started to clean up, but I stopped them from disappearing this time. I asked Vicente if he had any ideas as to what the problem might be. He kind of said "yes," but mostly "no."

Vicente gave us a few nuggets of wisdom and clues as to what the problems could be. We got to work on these ideas over the next few months and held a couple of Kaizen events later, all with Vicente in attendance. With Vicente's guidance, we accomplished many breakthroughs. His knowledge of machine cycle times, speeds and feeds, coolant life cycles, and cleaning opened the door to our understanding of many problems and their actual root causes.

Once we gained Vicente's trust, he opened up, felt more comfortable sharing his ideas, and led us to several root causes and long-term solutions. Without Vicente's knowledge and insight, we would have never been able to get ahead of the curve in improving customer performance and cost reductions within the rotor department.

Client Testimonial

Art leadership helped our team focus by using proven systems, methodology, and experience to achieve positive results that profoundly influenced bottom-line performance and organizational culture.

His processes combining using facts, data, and Lean techniques with visual management while communicating at all levels of an organization to create change and drive results made us a better team. He is truly one of the best I've seen in developing a shared vision, executing a plan, and achieving excellent results through stretch goals. There is no doubt, Art's methodologies helped our team become A+ players.

—Carl Steinbicker—Plant Manager, Regal Beloit, Hermetic Electric Motors

It's All About the Core Skills

What does it take to unlock one's greatness and find the castaways? As with diving, to see the small sea life, you need to move slowly across the reef, and this can't be done without fine-tuned skills.

Leadership requires essentially the same type of expertise. The ability to slow down, listen, watch, and establish an inclusive environment for team members to flourish. This section will discuss the team's ability to unlock greatness and find individual castaways within the organization.

It's critical to remember that each person has a vital role on any team. It starts on the shop floor by learning the value of being thoughtful and respectful to everyone, including the janitor. We are taught not to judge a person by their appearance. You don't know their story or journey in life. I've met many people with great wealth or education, and you would never know it by their humble appearance.

It's often said, "If it were easy, it would have already been done, or it's not worthwhile." From this, I've learned that success follows when we combine willpower, humility, and tenacity.

Don't underestimate the power of family. With a family-like culture, teamwork, and trust, you can build the foundation for sustainable success. Throughout life, we see how teams can come together to achieve remarkable results—each time attributed to family-like bonds and values of respect and caring.

Life has taught me to slow down and learn the details of any situation. Initially, I trained as a machinist, then worked as a motorcycle racing mechanic, and was educated in biochemistry and supply chain. My training and education's common thread is: **the best lessons are often learned**

from those around you. Listen and then ask for clarification. Watch and emulate the best behaviors and characteristics of leaders you respect and build your knowledge of the fine details.

Team members deserve consistency. People excel when they know what to expect. They don't want a manager who, at one moment, is hot and the next one cold. They need to know your temperament for all situations. Early in my career, one of my supervisors, Lanny, mood changed with the weather. When we arrived at work, we would check with each other on his temperament. If it was not so good, we knew to keep silent and not disrupt the day. Lanny's unknown dispositions kept us from freely discussing issues, and on several occasions, the lack of communication allowed smallish issues to fester and become more significant problems.

Inclusive teams thrive. As a leader, if you create an environment where team members are treated fairly and consistently, they will feel comfortable voicing their ideas and opinions. The team will flourish as a result.

The exact opposite of Lanny was Barb.

She was my supervisor at another company. Barb fostered a culture of inclusion. Her temperament was nearly always predictable. Please understand she was human, with good and bad days. However, we could always approach her with issues; she would listen to our ideas and help us find the best solution. Sometimes we agreed to disagree. We always walked away with a solution to try.

Barb's disposition was very even-keeled, allowing us to not be on eggshells and be ourselves. It allowed us to have fun while working hard!

Lost at Sea—Nine Warning Flares

When transforming the organization with the three Fs of supply chain management: people and process foundation, structural framework, and financial focal point, ponder a simple question: "How do you determine if your organizational environment is conducive to building a thriving and inclusive culture?"

The following Figure 19.1, shows nine warning flares that indicate that the organization is not ready to find hidden geniuses or castaways. If any of these conditions exist within the organization, work must be done to move the company culture in the right direction. Don't expect

#1. High employee turnover	#2. Culture of gossip	#3. High absenteeism and tardiness
#4. Lack of team participation	#5. Team members not recommending family and friends for job openings	#6. Lack of urgency
#7. Sabotage	#8. Disgruntled workforce	#9. Us vs them mentality

Figure 19.1 Nine warning flares in organizations

perfection from yourself, other leaders, or the team. Rate the organization using a score of 1 to 10 in each area, with 10 being the best. Focus on improving the weakest areas first.

Lastly, how do you rate personally? Can you name at least one or two people per year throughout your career who were once thought to be damaged goods or pigeonholed that you helped by creating the environment for their greatness to shine and now are valuable contributors to the team?

Navigating Your True North

No matter the organization, there will always be areas that need improvement. It is similar to improving your buoyancy skills while diving. I've outlined my top nine rules for establishing behaviors to nurture finding genius and the castaways.

Top 10 Rules to Finding Genius and the Castaways

1. The absolute first rule is to learn and remember. Leadership is a contact sport. Leaders led by getting out of their offices, out from behind computer monitors, and physically leading the team. Estab-

lish Gemba: senior executives need to spend up to 30 percent of their time on the frontlines and managers up to 60 percent of their time. Gemba defined (*source*: Lean.org):

> The Japanese term for "actual place," is often used for the shop floor or any place where value-creating work actually occurs.

> The term often is used to stress that real improvement requires a shop-floor focus based on direct observation of current conditions where work is done. For example, standardized work for a machine operator cannot be written at a desk in the engineering office but must be defined and revised on the Gemba.

2. Lead from the HEART. I was lucky enough to be part of an organizational development initiative earlier in my career. I had the opportunity to work with Jack Rosenblum, Aubrey Sanford, and Hyler J. Bracey, the authors of *Managing From the Heart*.[1] It was transformative and gave me the foundation to sharpen my skills as a manager and grow into a leader's role.

> Lead from the HEART
> **H**ear and understand me
> **E**ven if you disagree, don't make me wrong
> **A**cknowledge the greatness within me
> **R**emember to look for my loving intentions
> **T**ell me the truth with compassion

3. Eliminate these "dirty" words: me, my, and I. We all have heard the phrase "There is no 'I' in team." Listen during discussions and hear how often "dirty" words of me, my, and I are used. How do managers refer to their teams? Do they say, my employee or my team? Managers need to lead and manage. I've seen some managers who believe they own departments or the people in them. They think they were given the responsibility, rather than the opportunity, to lead the teams in these departments. Great leaders know how to let go of ownership and lead the team. True leaders refer to our team.

It is a subtle yet significant distinction between leadership and managerial mindset. Create a culture of OUR, WE, and THE team.

4. Ensure the team knows and understands the product you make, who it's manufactured for, and how it makes the world a better place. Teach and educate your company's value to society.

5. Be sure the team members know the "why" of key performance indicators (KPIs), measures, and goals. Ensure they understand how KPIs roll up to the bigger picture to make the enterprise more competitive, world-class, and "The Place" to work. Develop a safe environment to share ideas, where bad results are no longer "red" with messengers punished. Instead, "red" KPIs are seen as opportunities for improvement and growth.

6. Establish visual daily management with KPIs to drive communication, daily workflow, rapid problem resolution, and critical long-term initiatives improvement.

7. Develop a culture of inclusion for all associates to build a team. Sponsor a buddy system for new and newly transferred team members. Establish a community, and have face-to-face communication meetings, monthly informal birthday lunches, and quarterly performance meetings. Have team members present their team's quarterly KPIs and have the entire team accept the award for the best-performing quarter.

8. Establish transparency, both individual and shared accountability, and ensure a "no-blame" culture.

9. Make operational excellence part of the culture. Have everyone involved in continuous improvement and Kaizen events and prioritize on-the-job training for continuous improvement (CI) and lean manufacturing principles. Ensure everyone **has a role** in the operational excellence model. All team members need an area to shine. Get the team to actively volunteer for Kaizen events. "Voluntold" doesn't count.

> **Kaizens** are the systematic, organized improvement of processes by those who manage them using straightforward analysis methods. It is a "do-it-now" approach to continuous improvement.

10. Look, listen, and hear all the team members for the extraordinary achievements in their private lives. The regional stock-car racer and

boy scout leader mentioned earlier are real people that we were lucky enough to tap into their skills and talents for greatness at work.

As you build team participation and inclusion, the journey will be successful if you remember and apply the aforementioned essential principles. Here are a few personal lessons I've learned.

You get by giving. The more you teach, share, and serve your team, the more they return.

Leadership isn't from behind a computer screen or sitting in an office all day. Leadership is a contact sport.

We must go to where the work is done, learn the challenges from the team firsthand, and become the "sounding board" for ideas and problem resolution. We truly want to shift mindsets and behaviors, from red results being perceived as bad, and to stop shooting the messenger.

We need to be willing to admit when we're wrong. When our teams see their leader realizing that they interpreted the data or delivered a message incorrectly, then acknowledge their error and circle back to solve the opportunity differently, they will speak more freely and be willing to take the first step based on their situational analysis.

Dive Log 19 (Art's Commentary)

I pride myself on working well with and getting the most out of the team members' strengths. I hold myself to a higher standard in getting to know the team and the individual members professionally and personally. I'm embarrassed that I nearly missed engaging a key team member by not getting to know their personal story. I asked myself, what could have been done differently to close the gap so that the same mistake isn't repeated?

Remember, leadership is a contact sport. I can't emphasize this enough. You must get involved and take personal responsibility to learn about the people and processes.

If it wasn't for the environment we created with the informal birthday lunches, we might never have known Vicente's true potential and may have overlooked the opportunity to build a climate of trust. We would still be reliving *Groundhog Day* repeatedly. Leadership isn't a science.

If you continually manage from your heart, you'll win more often than you lose.

Buddy Check: Questions From Coach Art

- Do you and your team manage too much from behind a computer?
- Are you guilty of not slowing down to connect personally with your team?
- Does your team routinely apply the HEART principles?
- Is there trust and inclusion built into your organization?
- Does the team know "what you make" and "why it makes the world better?"
- Is there an understanding of the "why" and "how" of KPIs?
- Are lost geniuses and castaways regularly found in the organization?
- Are you aware of at least three of your team members' unique accomplishments?

Art's Deep Dive

Anyone can be a manager. Few people are natural leaders. Even natural-born leaders need to refine their skills continuously. I rely on the HEART principles. What do you use?

For additional information and free tools, please scan the code.

CHAPTER 20

Leadership Advisory

The "giant stride" is a scuba diving technique for safely entering the water. Simply put, it's a matter of standing at the edge of the boat and stepping feet first into the water. That big first step can be a bit overwhelming, but once you have taken that critical step, you have entered the magnificent world of the ocean.

After reading this book, there is no better time to make a giant stride entry into the journey of making your supply chain world-class.

Before making that giant stride entry, take some time to review Art Koch's Profit Chain® model, the three Fs of supply chain management, and evaluate how well your enterprise is performing in each area (see Figure 1.1).

There is an important sequence to these models. It's essential to start with stabilizing the people and process foundation and then construct the structural framework before the financial focal point can catapult your organization into an industry-leading corporate culture with exceptional customer loyalty and sustainable profitability.

Client Testimonial

I have taken the "Giant Stride" with Art numerous times, having brought him in to support our teams' multiple times across different industrial businesses. We focused on every aspect of Art's "3 Fs" at one point or another. Each time the team achieved success. One thing that really stands out about Art is that he takes a strong "operator-centric" approach—by that I mean he builds strong relationships and really invests the time to coach individual team members through the change process.

—Joel Stanwood, MBA
Founder and Partner
StoneTree Investment Partners LLC

Getting Started With a Giant Stride

I recommend starting the evaluation of your supply chain's performance with a rapid assessment of your supply chain, as discussed in Chapter 4. From this assessment, identify and focus on two to four priorities.

Remember, when there are too many priorities, nothing is a priority.

Next, use the growth chart I've developed (see Figure 20.1); the chart correlates with the three Fs of SCM and the respective chapters within this book; spend a few minutes to place the rapid assessment scores into this chart for excellent visualization of your enterprise's current state.

Please note, the order of priority is to work from the bottom up on both sides of the growth chart, reaching the pinnacle of sustainability, culture, customer loyalty, and profits.

After objectively completing the rapid assessment processes and, therefore, the entire spider chart, select the lowest-ranking areas on the chart. From these, determine your short-term priorities by identifying two to four goals that need improvement.

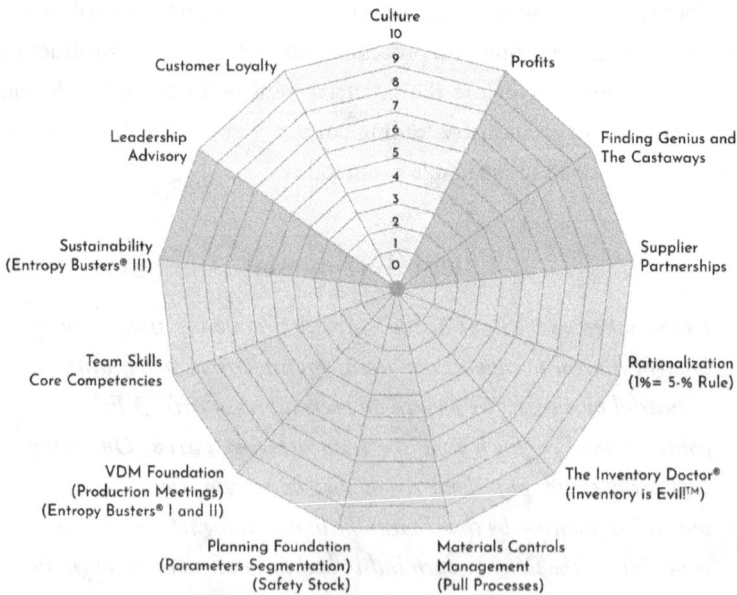

Figure 20.1 Art Koch's Profit Chain growth chart

Quantify the desired outcome for each selected goal on the chart.

Next, outline a value statement that is the monetized outcome multiplied by the total time, which can be one month or several years, of the benefit. Add benefits in perpetuity (e.g., customer retention) and emotional impact (e.g., better work-life balance, easier to recruit, and retain talent) Figure 20.2.

Then add other variables (e.g., decrease annual obsolescence accrual expense). Subtract, the cost to make change equals the return on investment (ROI) for the individual goal.

This process will help you focus on the highest and most critical areas with the most significant profit potential.

Inventory Reduction of $2.5 Million—An Illustration

Goal: Reduce inventory by 25 percent or $2.5 million. The target reduction will not only reduce inventory but will free up two bays, 20 by 100 feet, for value-added manufacturing.

Follow this process to pinpoint the areas with the most impactful opportunities for improvement. For example, create a pilot cell to demonstrate what excellence looks like.

Another example of enhancement is part number rationalization, consolidating wiring harnesses, and using this method to capture the total cost of all improvements to exhibit what the opportunities are for the business.

Apply the supply chain health check from Chapter 13 to improve bottom-line results and sustainability.

With each set of improvements, update the growth chart with your new scores. Then focus on areas with the lowest score to keep expanding the current state. Then rinse and repeat all the steps above and with each change iteration, improving the three Fs of supply chain management: people and process foundation, structural framework, and financial focal point (Figure 20.3).

Next, complete the deep dive into the supply chain and core competencies and skills assessments. This action will help you find blind spots within processes and the corporate vision.

If appropriately used, unbiased feedback supported by facts and data will catapult the team to the next performance level. They subsequently

Calculating a Value Statement

Inventory Reduction goal of: $2,500,000	Incremental cost of inventory	Annual Dollar Savings per line item	Five Year Savings
Incremental Cost of Inventory			
Interest (Prime +1%)	7.5%	$187,500	
Opportunity (What could you do with the cash?)	12.0%	$300,000	
Handling (How many people, full time equivalents?)	3.0%	$75,000	
Space (Square footage)	1.0%	$25,000	
Damage (Scrap)	1.5%	$37,500	
Shrinkage (Reserves, write-off, and obsolete product)	1.0%	$25,000	
Taxes (Personal property)	1.5%	$37,500	
Insurance	1.0%	$25,000	
Transactioins (Counting, moving, retrieving, issuing, reconciling)	6.0%	$150,000	
General and Admin. Staff (Managers, planning physical management)	6.5%	$162,500	
Total Incremental Cost of Inventory	41%	$1,025,000	$5,125,000
Incremental Cost of Implementation			
Hiring Outside Expert (One time cost)		($200,000)	
Short term help to supplement team members on project (One time cost)		($50,000)	
Health Check and Advisory Services (One time cost)		($100,000)	
Total Incremental Cost of Implementation		($350,000)	($350,000)
Total Saving over a five year time period:			$4,775,000
Increase to Corporation Valuation: (6x Increase)			$6,150,000

Figure 20.2 Value statement

will develop the road map to process sustainability that becomes part of the business's DNA.

To highlight the driving point of sustainable change that comes from within, I have started to use the phrase, "Your Supply Chain, Your Supply Change, Your Supply Leadership." As always, encourage clients to leverage their team members' skills and abilities to change their behaviors, create sustainable improvements, and use an external expert to help guide change management.

This chapter, Leadership Advisory, intends to create a paradigm shift and to acknowledge that all great championship teams and organizations have outside mentors, coaches, and advisers that they utilize as sources of unbiased feedback, expert advice, and accountability partners. It's equally important to select an expert who can help leaders achieve personal and professional growth.

While working on your continuous improvement processes, follow the strategies outlined in The Inventory Doctor® for step-functional improvements to inventory velocity. The pinnacle of sustainability: customer loyalty, corporate culture, and profitability will emerge to propel you toward world-class performance.

You don't need to do this alone.

Most organizations use external consultants and experts as impartial eyes to help navigate transformative process improvements. And so should your organization.

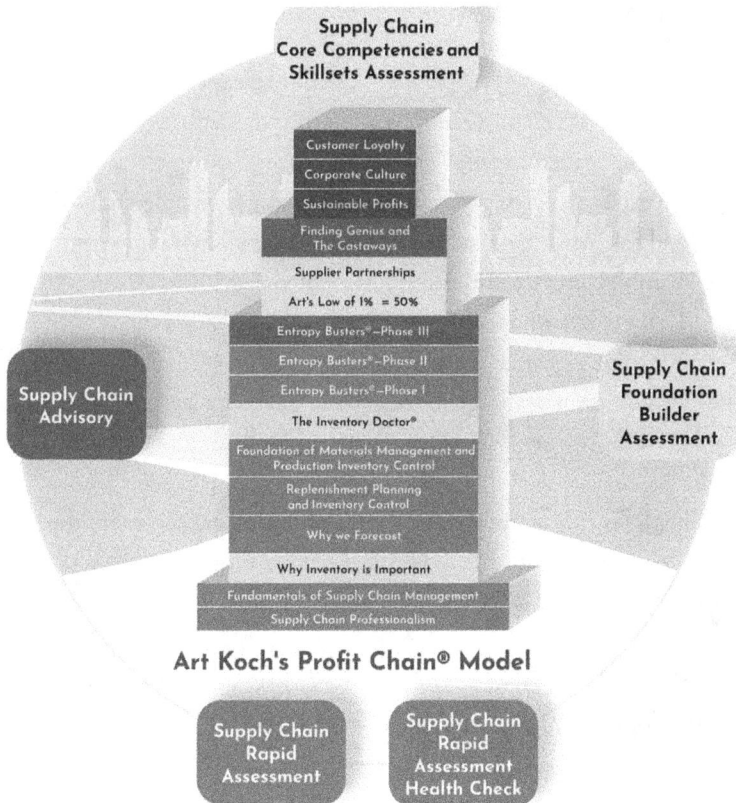

Figure 20.3 Art Koch's Profit Chain model

How do you select and work with the right expert? Of course, I want you to pick up the phone and call me. However, you need to ensure you're selecting the right expert. Outlined below are several attributes to consider when making this critical decision. The expert must be:

- A professional you can learn from and emulate to make your organization better.
- Exhibits the traits and behaviors your corporation wants to emulate.
- A good fit for your corporate culture.
- An individual with similar philosophies to those of leadership.
- They need to be a good teacher and a good listener.
- Someone who understands that disagreements don't end with "burning bridges." Constructively uses the debate process to gain understanding, challenge the status quo, and foster knowledge growth.
- Don't look for a "yes" person. Seek out an expert who can tell the truth with compassion, give unfiltered feedback, and call out the team on complacency.
- An expert who brings a wealth of experience from other industries and has "been there and done that" for where you want to go.
- Exhibits urgency and is results-oriented.
- Real experts who are not looking for their next job or a consulting project between jobs.
- A professional who genuinely wants to leave a legacy after working at your company.

When selecting an outside expert to help your organization improve, the above boxes don't all need to be checked off. However, the vast majority should be checked off to have an excellent ROI.

Art's Gold: Leadership starts with change, and change begins with leadership.

A leader must understand that a system is composed of people, not mere machinery, activities, or organization charts.

—Dr. W. Edwards Deming

As you have read, I firmly believe that a supply chain organization cannot be an industry leader without the development of supporting team members. An organization's leaders are responsible for enrolling and engaging all the organization's stakeholders in every initiative, no matter how large or small the organization or project.

Your Supply Chain, Your Supply Change, Your Supply Leadership

Throughout my career, this has been the approach I've used for my personal development, and I believe it's the winning trait for world-class businesses—such as the potential for your organization!

At the same time, my experience has shown that the transformation of systems, processes, and machines must break the status quo. However, these processes are not, in and of themselves, comprehensive elements of success.

The difficulty arises when the human component is absent or even ignored.

I believe in integrating organization and leadership development in supply chain change management. Organizations must take ownership and ongoing responsibility for sustainable change, own their success, and not leave it to an outside resource.

The outside resources must facilitate, coach, and motivate the change management process and not do the change. I believe this is what separates consultants from advisers.

Consultants will outline the needed improvement, often do the "heavy lifting" analysis, and attempt to implement the improvement. I think all of us will agree this is not the desired outcome because you want your people to own the process and gain the skills from the changes.

But why does this occur?

Too frequently, leadership claims that the organization cannot free up an internal subject matter expert to support the new initiative because they are too valuable to daily business operations.

This is precisely why they should be on the team!

Once the consultants step away, stakeholders don't have enough project knowledge and understanding to successfully make process modifications for sustainability.

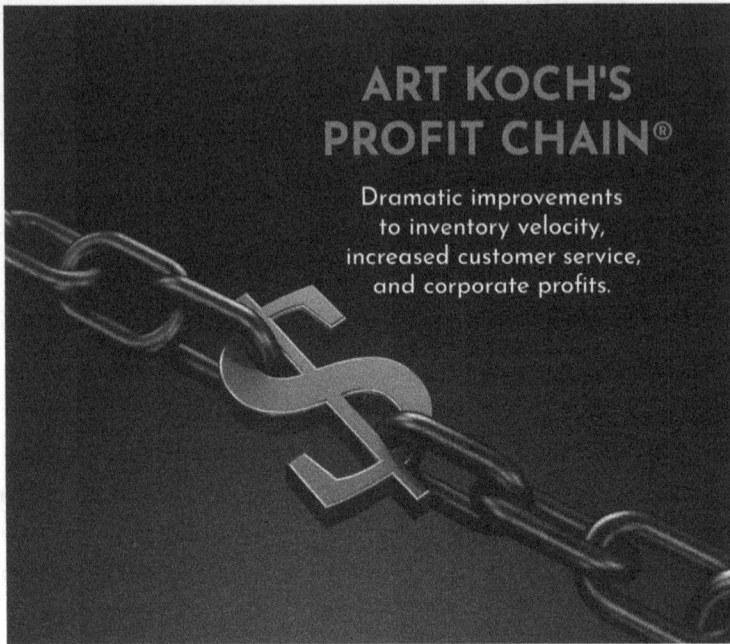

Figure 20.4 Dramatic improvements

Advisers help the team see their opportunities, teach and educate the organization on multiple solutions, facilitate change, and become the team accountability partner.

This is the long game. However, the rewards are tremendous: team member growth, pride of ownership, and sustainable improvement.

It's vital that whoever you choose as an adviser applies research-based, industry-leading knowledge and expertise to your supply chain. They must collaborate with your team members to *help you* transform your supply chain process and leadership through assessment, development, application follow-up, and ongoing advisory services.

Choose advisers wisely. EBIDTA and corporate valuation depend on it.

Buddy Check: Questions From Coach Art

- Has the enterprise's supply chain been assessed and benchmarked versus peer groups?

- Is there a detailed road map for supply chain improvements?
- When forming teams for critical projects, does the organization free up the most talented team members for participation?
- Are you using an unbiased outside adviser to facilitate supply chain improvements?

Art's Deep Dive

Since the COVID-19 pandemic, three out of four CEOs are rethinking their supply chain strategy. What are your plans? (Figure 20.4)

CHAPTER 21

Turning Operational Problems Into Profits

Case Study: International Distributor. The generation of 50 million dollars in cost reduction and increased valuation of 160 million dollars.

With corporate offices in North America and a global operational footprint, the client generated one billion dollars in revenue. The company is a supply chain solutions provider of custom hardware and engineering support in the distribution sector. They are dedicated to helping businesses increase the effectiveness of their operations with minimal supply chain management interaction.

To achieve success, the client has a suite of internally developed custom systems and processes that ensure customers' parts are delivered and stocked while the processes are invisible to their client. In addition, the client provides engineering support for their clients' change management and design functions and provides feedback to improve effectiveness and service levels.

The client has professional teams in North America, the United Kingdom, Europe, and Asia Pacific. Most teams have over a decade of working in the industry, as well as exceptional customer service experience. With such a strong foundation, they seemed ready to become the premier total cost supply chain solutions provider.

However, legacy mainframe computer hardware, homegrown software programs, and outdated software solutions were designed for a different industry of substantially lesser size.

This combination of outdated hardware and software greatly hindered their ability to achieve and sustain target profits.

The Search for a Solution

The client launched a search for a demand planning, inventory optimization, and replenishment planning solution provider that would support their past and projected growth targets.

The new solution needed to have capabilities that embodied six criteria:

1. Customer-facing collaboration demand planning
2. Extensive part number offering
3. Exception-based planning
4. Part number inventory and service level optimization
5. Best-of-class performance for "lumpy" and long-tail demand
6. And one solution: one process across worldwide operations

Concluding an extensive search, the selection team narrowed the field to two contenders. After completing a robust "bake-off," supply chain leadership selected ToolsGroup SO99+.

Barriers on the Road to Success

There often are barriers to great success stories, and this story isn't any different.

Though the client has strong team members, the new software solution, SO99+, sat on the shelf unimplemented after two years.

Initial Barriers

- The project was the initial part of the private equity's (PE) business transformation agenda. However, once the PE better understood all operational processes, more pressing issues of commercial demands, geopolitical issues with sourcing, and employee bandwidth took precedence.
- Changes in the CEO and several to the supply chain organization leadership positions caused false starts and clouded visibility to the project.

- Many of the current executive team members originally created several of the homegrown legacy systems. In a few cases, their careers were built upon the system's past success. When it came to "killing their babies," too often, their egos got in the way.
- Internal politics of individuals publicly saying yes to the project but passively not supporting it blocked progress.
- It was not the right time for this level of change with the existing team.

The new ownership and the existing executive realized that a different approach was required to tackle the amount of work necessary to implement the new solution.

The client knew their team members' work would suffer if stretched thin or forced to rush implementation. Critical design elements and milestones would likely be missed. Additionally, the current client's customer requirements could not be missed. They still needed to provide quality service as promised—especially if the business continued to grow.

Furthermore, they knew that they needed supply chain and operations subject matter expertise to guide them through barriers and help define and refine future state vision. Not doing so would only lead to increased overhead and additional future problems.

The client realized they had a problem and had some good initial ideas of how to resolve it. However, it took a little more digging for them to find a solution that worked best for the organization.

The Next Steps

Internal leadership recommended bringing on a known outside expert, and I immediately took the reins for implementing ToolsGroup SO99+. The following critical elements were maintained:

- Installing SO99+ software with no added resources.
- Managed the project on time and within budget.
- No impact to current inventory levels.
- No effect to existing service levels.
- Invisible to customers.

In addition to implementing ToolsGroup SO99+ for the client, we also applied several of the methodologies described in this book to clean up and optimize data and process integrity and address supplier lead times. It was slow and steady progress as we built on many small successes.

Despite our successes, there were significant challenges.

A key executive had their own set of priorities and sent in their B-team to support this project. Few team members were 100 percent dedicated to the project, even with executive and boardroom support. In contrast, the others on the team were overworked with their existing responsibilities, let alone implementing a new software solution.

Barriers Turned Into Bridges Over Oceans

There was a needed changing of the guard. Past "Blockers" moved on to different roles outside the company, and the new CEO, COO, and CTO became significant project champions.

We added several new team members to the project, bringing fresh perspectives and skillsets that elevated the existing team. Additionally, we emphasized getting current team members into roles matching their strengths and core competencies.

Business results	Financial impact of results
• Current State Inventory of $180 million, with target reduction of 15%–20%, was achieved at an estimated inventory carry cost of 32%. • Increased customer service. Reduced stock outs by 49%. • Worldwide FTE attrition and reassignment.	• $55 million inventory reduction. • 23% inventory reduction. • Enabled $17.6 million long-term cost reduction. • Customer retention value of approximately two million dollars annually. • Five million dollars annually (included in inventory carry cost).

Shareholder Value or Return on Investment

- 55-million-dollar annual cost reduction.
- 55-million-dollar immediate shareholder value (inventory reduction).
- 143 million dollars of incremental long-term value creation through cost reductions and customer retention.

- Increased customer loyalty by having better customer service and less expediting noise.
- Increased supply chain management professionalism as demonstrated in highly trained in demand planning and inventory optimization.
- Project success set the stage for ongoing inventory and cost reductions to further improve financial performance and increase EBITDA, a key driver of shareholder value.

Stakeholder's Value

- Created a path to eliminate outdated mainframe computer and software support with an annual cost of seven million dollars.
- Created and built more professionalism in supply chain management by hiring key outside professionals that raised expectations of the current team and building a more inclusive team.
- For private equity, made the portfolio more attractive to future acquirers or investors.
- Resulted in a more professional leadership team and information systems that were ERP-ready.

For additional information and free tools, please scan the code.

Appendix

Aligning KPIs for Sustainability and Connecting With the Author

Ever wonder what supply chain KPIs to implement? Below is a good framework to start with.

First Level

- Inventory accuracy
- Quote to cash cycle time
- Inventory turns or days on hand
- On-time delivery to external and internal customers
- Obsolete inventory: 3, 4, and >5 years without usage
- Supplier and part number lead-time; high to low and mean
- Open purchase order book and open purchase orders greater than customer demand

Second Level

- Safety stock total and by part number
- For planned stocked parts, zero on hand balances
- Supplier scorecard: incoming part PPM, on-time delivery to required and promise, and responsiveness
- List of no quote suppliers
- Supplier early and late deliveries
- Exception-based planning:
  - Replenishment planning KPIs:
    - Are part being bought early, on-time, or late to MRP
    - Supplier order acknowledgment
    - Cancels and de-expedites
    - Expedites

- ° Demand planning:
  - • Action messages for abnormally high and low demand to forecast
- • Forecast accuracy (MAPE):
  - ° How is the team reducing their dependency on forecasting?

The Art Koch Methodology and Philosophy: How Art Can Help Your Business to Improve Operational and Financial Performance?

Attuned to your organization's operational and financial goals and constraints in leveraging your supply chain solutions, our consulting projects are customized for your unique situation and company parameters.

Our approach may include Art's trademarked methodologies:
Art Koch's Profit Chain®—Supply Chain and Leadership Assessment

- • A top-to-bottom assessment of your supply chain system, processes, people, and results. We will compare your supply chain's performance to industry competitors and other benchmark standards. We will develop solutions that support your organization's financial and operational requirements and ensure sustainable performance excellence. We drive toward dramatic improvements in inventory velocity, increased customer service, and corporate profits.

The Inventory Doctor®—Inventory Velocity Improvement

- • Inventory delays problem resolution. Delays cost money. Your leadership team will learn and apply proven, time-tested leadership capabilities to drive change and lead your supply chain team to new levels of achievement. Coaching and mentoring over time ensure that these leadership behaviors become part of your organization's culture and "just the way we do things around here."

Entropy Busters®—Supply Chain Team Success

- Stop letting the process manage you. Become the champion of your game plan and achieve sustainable profits. We will provide your supply chain staff with the skills required for outstanding individual and team performance. Highly effective "just-in-time" research-based and real-world-focused training gives your team members the practical, applicable tools necessary for success.

Art Koch will personally lead and oversee relevant client initiatives. He brings decades of hands-on experience and insight from implemented solutions across a broad range of industries and geographies. As you can see, there are significant benefits from Art's background with real-world applications in your professional interactions.

Connecting With the Author

- **Arthur Koch Management Consulting LLC:**
  - E-mail: **info@arthurkochmgt.com**
  - The Web: https://arthurkochmgt.com/
  - LinkedIn: www.linkedin.com/in/kocharthur/
  - The Book Web: https://thesupplychainrevolution.com

Chapters Description

Chapter 1

How this book can benefit your team to build a supply chain organization that stands above the competition.

Chapter 2

Supply chain management is a profession like that of CPAs and professional engineers. Your SCM team deserves the same professionalism and respect found in other disciplines.

Chapter 3

The introduction to Art Koch's Profit Chain® and the three Fs of supply chain management incorporate closed-loop problem resolution and sustainability countermeasures.

Chapter 4

A swift and thorough assessment of operational supply chain practices, processes, and team readiness to support business transformation initiatives and lean manufacturing principles.

Chapter 5

We care about inventory because excess inventory costs money and hides problems. Hopefully, everyone will agree with this fact. However, that's not the case, especially after pandemic-caused shortages.

Chapter 6

The methodology of Art Koch's Profit Chain® highlights the significance of the total cost of ownership and educates how to use the supply chain as a competitive differentiator.

Chapter 7

How to reduce the dependency on forecasts. Use "plan for every part" planning and parameters to maximize inventory performance and improve profits.

Chapter 8

What supply chain management is and isn't; it's an important distinction. How the layperson and executives oversimplify SCM. The intricacies of materials management and control that are relevant to profits.

Chapter 9

Introduction to the three phases of Entropy Busters® and the entropy force field of sustainability.

Chapter 10

Breaking denial, loading the team bus with the right people, and engaging them.

Chapter 11

Visual daily management is about knowing your numbers and your priorities and getting everyone on the same page.

Chapter 12

Team building, establishing community, and having fun. *Note: Entropy Busters® Phase III is part of the financial focal point. I've included the chapter here not to lose the cadence of this important discussion.*

Chapter 13

Leading the organization through a supply chain health check. Be an internal adviser and change agent to the team on follow-up of corrective actions taken due to health check findings. Close gaps, lead metrics review, and recommend course corrections to improve operational performance.

Chapter 14

Understanding the components of a supply chain assessment and the supply chain foundation builder assessment. An assessment of qualitative and quantitative supply chain practices, processes, key metrics, and the team's readiness to support the next one to five years of business transformation.

Chapter 15

What are the supply chain team's skills, core competencies, and strengths? Where are hidden gaps? What is the vision of the steps to achieve world-class success?

Chapter 16

Rationalization of part numbers, suppliers, and best supplier strategies: What is your plan for the last 1 percent of demand or purchases?

Chapter 17

You buy hot dogs, cotton candy, and cracker jacks from vendors. Steps to progress from vendors to suppliers, then to supplier partnerships.

Chapter 18

Applying Art's methodologies to become The Inventory Doctor® and simultaneously increase inventory velocity, customer service, and profitability.

Chapter 19

You have an untapped resource within your organization, and it's free to you if you know how to find it. How to discover, cultivate, and sustain your organization's hidden geniuses and castaways.

Chapter 20

The steps in working with outside experts. How to use your supply chain as a competitive advantage and differentiator.

Chapter 21

Generated $50 million in cost reductions and increased valuation by $150 million for an international distributor.

Appendix

Aligning KPIs for Sustainability and Connecting With the Author.

Notes

Chapter 2

1. Deloitte Development LLC (2014).
2. U.S. News & World Report. Best Colleges Rankings (2023).

Chapter 3

1. Marchwinski (2014).
2. Ibid.
3. Ibid.
4. Ibid.
5. Ibid.

Chapter 4

1. Professional Association of Dive Instructors (2023).
2. Goodson (2002).

Chapter 5

1. Council of Supply Chain Management Professionals (2023).

Chapter 7

1. Council of Supply Chain Management Professionals (2023).

Chapter 11

1. Marchwinski (2014).
2. Tuckman (1965).

Chapter 19

1. Bracey, Rosenblum, Sanford, and TrueBlood (1993).

References

Bracey, H., J. Rosenblum, A. Sanford, and R. TrueBlood. 1993. *Managing From the Heart*. New York, NY: Dell.

Council of Supply Chain Management Professionals. 2023. *CSCMP Supply Chain Management Definitions and Glossary*. https://cscmp.org/CSCMP/ Educate/SCM_Definitions_and_Glossary_of_Terms/CSCMP/Educate/ SCM_Definitions_and_Glossary_of_Terms.aspx?hkey=60879588-f65f-4ab5-8c4b-6878815ef921 (accessed August 2013).

Deloitte Development LLC. 2014. *Supply Chain Leadership. Distinctive Approaches to Innovation, Collaboration, and Talent Alignment*. www2.deloitte. com/content/dam/Deloitte/de/Documents/strategy/supplychain-leadership-report.pdf.

Goodson, E.R. 2002. "Read a Plant—Fast." *Harvard Business Review*.

Marchwinski, C. 2014. *Lean Lexicon*. 5th ed. Cambridge: Lean Enterprise Institute.

Professional Association of Dive Instructors (PADI). August 2023. *Peak Performance Buoyancy*. www.padi.com/courses/peak-performance-buoyancy.

Tuckman, B. 1965. *Developmental Sequence in Small Groups*. Bethesda, Maryland, MD: Naval Medical Research Institute.

US News & World Report. 2023. *Supply Chain Management and Logistics Programs*. Best Colleges Rankings. www.usnews.com/best-colleges/rankings/ business-supply-chain-management-logistics.

About the Author

Art Koch is a globally recognized supply chain transformation expert. With over three decades of transforming business performance at mid-market and Fortune 500 companies, Art's insights into supply chain innovation and profitability improvement make him a sought-after consultant worldwide.

During his career, Art has increased corporate valuations by over a billion dollars, utilizing his proprietary methodologies to improve customer loyalty, reduce inventory by over $250 million, and increase EBITDA by $100 million-plus annually. *The Supply Chain Revolution* distills Art's extensive knowledge to inspire the next generation of leaders to dramatically improve business performance.

About the Author—Fun Facts About Art

Warning: I'm not your everyday operations and supply chain strategist.

I'm scrappy.

My experiences come from surviving several economic recessions while growing up in Flint, Michigan. The overpowering lessons are:

- No challenge is too significant.
- Anything worthwhile is worth fighting to achieve.
- Tenacity and perseverance trump all situations.

During my high school years, I was not college-bound-minded. Instead, I became a journeyman machinist and raced and wrenched on motocross bikes from the mid-1970s until the late 1980s. I worked at a racer-friendly machine shop.

During the late 1980s, I helped machine the turbochargers for 8 of the top 10 Indy 500 finishers, including Al Unser Sr., Michael Andretti, Bobby Rahal, and Arie Luyendyk. During that time, I was part of a pit crew, and my role was to hand tires over the wall to the pit box on race day of the Indy 500.

Today, my number one hobby is scuba diving and underwater photography. However, I'm still a loyal F1 and IndyCar fan.

While witnessing the automotive manufacturing collapse of the late 1970s and early 1980s firsthand in Michigan, I knew that a career refocusing was necessary. So, I went back to school and earned a BS in Biochemistry and an MBA in operations and supply chain management.

My "on the tools" trade experience and formal education gave me the skills and core competencies to guide companies toward sustainable operations and supply chain management processes. From my roots as a machinist, I have enhanced my skills through roles as a mid-level manager, supply chain executive, consultant, strategic adviser, and now as a private equity investor of manufacturing companies.

Throughout my career, I have developed a unique ability and expertise to combine the details, methods, and theories to get the organization's fuel to burn at maximum efficiency with the least amount of resistance, thereby generating superb business and financial results.

My successes come from a passion for people and processes that enhance manufacturing performance and business profitability. For companies I've worked with, we've reduced inventory by over $200 million during my career, increased EBITDA by $100 million-plus annually, and increased corporate valuations by over a billion dollars.

The financial premise for supply chain improvements: Reducing inventory levels and improving manufacturing processes positively impact earnings and valuations.

THE END.

Index

Note: Page numbers followed by "f" refer to figures.

OTHER TITLES IN THE SUPPLY AND OPERATIONS MANAGEMENT COLLECTION

Joy M. Field, Boston College, Editor

- *An Introduction to Global Supply Chain Management* by Edmund Prater and Kim Whitehead
- *Transforming Quality Organizations* by Matthew P. Wictome and Ian Wells
- *Process Improvement to Company Enrichment* by Daniel Plung and Connie Krull
- *Organizational Velocity* by Alan Amling
- *C-O-S-T* by Craig Theisen
- *RFID for the Supply Chain and Operations Professional, Third Edition* by Pamela J. Zelbst and Victor Sower
- *Operations Management in China, Second Edition* by Craig Seidelson
- *Futureproofing Procurement* by Katie Jarvis-Grove
- *How Efficiency Changes the Game* by Ray Hodge
- *Supply Chain Planning, Second Edition* by Matthew J. Liberatore and Tan Miller
- *Sustainable Quality* by Joseph Diele
- *Why Quality is Important and How It Applies in Diverse Business and Social Environments, Volume II* by Paul Hayes

Concise and Applied Business Books

The Collection listed above is one of 30 business subject collections that Business Expert Press has grown to make BEP a premiere publisher of print and digital books. Our concise and applied books are for...

- Professionals and Practitioners
- Faculty who adopt our books for courses
- Librarians who know that BEP's Digital Libraries are a unique way to offer students ebooks to download, not restricted with any digital rights management
- Executive Training Course Leaders
- Business Seminar Organizers

Business Expert Press books are for anyone who needs to dig deeper on business ideas, goals, and solutions to everyday problems. Whether one print book, one ebook, or buying a digital library of 110 ebooks, we remain the affordable and smart way to be business smart. For more information, please visit www.businessexpertpress.com, or contact sales@businessexpertpress.com.

www.ingramcontent.com/pod-product-compliance
Lightning Source LLC
Chambersburg PA
CBHW052107230326
41599CB00054B/4282